CRACKNELL'S
LAW STUDENTS' COMPANION

No. 13. CONVEYANCING

CRACKNELL'S
LAW STUDENTS' COMPANION
GENERAL EDITOR D. G. CRACKNELL, LL.B.
of the Middle Temple, Barrister-at-Law

Cracknell's
Law Students' Companion

No. 13. CONVEYANCING

BY

PHYLLIS E. NEWMAN, LL.B. (Lond).

Solicitor of the Supreme Court

LONDON
BUTTERWORTHS
1970

ENGLAND:	BUTTERWORTH & CO. (PUBLISHERS) LTD. LONDON: 88 Kingsway, WC2B 6AB
AUSTRALIA:	BUTTERWORTH & CO: (AUSTRALIA) LTD. SYDNEY: 20 Loftus Street MELBOURNE: 343 Little Collins Street BRISBANE: 240 Queen Street
CANADA:	BUTTERWORTH & CO. (CANADA) LTD. TORONTO: 14 Curity Avenue, 374
NEW ZEALAND:	BUTTERWORTH & CO. (NEW ZEALAND) LTD. WELLINGTON: 49/51 Ballance Street AUCKLAND: 35 High Street
SOUTH AFRICA:	BUTTERWORTH & CO. (SOUTH AFRICA) (PTY.) LTD. DURBAN: 33/35 Beach Grove

Printed in Great Britain by
Cox & Wyman Ltd., London
Fakenham and Reading

". . . our conclusion must be that you will get the best conveyancing from a good solicitor."—"Which?" Report, Consumers' Association March 1970.

PREFACE

The very nature of land and the number and complexity of interests which can exist simultaneously therein make conveyancing a highly sophisticated field of law. The purpose of this book is to provide the student with a comprehensive selection of cases and statutory provisions for use in conjunction with textbooks and lecture notes.

The statutory material has been taken from a large number of Acts but the formidable quantity of relevant enacted law has made a rigorous selection inevitable. It is assumed that every serious student would already have copies of the Law of Property Act and Land Registration Act 1925. Exclusion of these has enabled the size of the book to be kept within reasonable bounds while allowing the inclusion of useful extracts from the rest of the 1925 property legislation and from a number of other important Acts including the Rent Act 1968 and the Town and Country Planning Acts 1962 and 1968. The latter and a number of cases on planning law have been included because of the practical importance to the conveyancer.

I am grateful to include the glossary prepared by Mr. M. L. S. Passey, M.A.(Cantab.), Solicitor, and I would like to thank the publishers and Mr. Cracknell for their patience.

July 1970   PHYLLIS E. NEWMAN

CONTENTS

vii

CASES

Abbeyfield (Harpenden) Society, Ltd. v. Woods, [1968] 1 All E.R. 352   **[1]**
   (Court of Appeal)

The plaintiff company was a charitable organisation providing for the elderly accommodation, two main meals per day, services of a resident housekeeper and heating, lighting, fire insurance and repairs. The defendant paid £9 per week for a room which he furnished himself under a contract which gave the Society the right to terminate the agreement on one month's notice. *Held,* the contract created a licence, not a lease, which the Society had a discretion to terminate provided it acted in good faith. Although the defendant enjoyed exclusive possession the arrangement was so personal in nature that the defendant was not a tenant but a licensee.

Aberfoyle Plantations, Ltd. v. Khaw Bian Cheng, [1959] 3 All E. R. 910   **[2]**
   (Privy Council)

A contract for the sale of rubber estates was subject to a condition that the vendor would obtain renewal of certain leases, the actual transfer of the leases if renewed to take place "as soon as possible" after the date fixed for completion. The question arose as to whether the agreement could be rescinded on the ground that the vendor had not obtained renewal within due time. Subject to the provisions of particular contracts, the following general propositions concerning the time for fulfilment of conditional contracts for the sale of land were adopted as warranted by authority: (i) Where the contract fixes a date for completion of a sale, the condition must be fulfilled by that date; (ii) where the contract fixes no date for completion, the condition must be fulfilled within a reasonable date; (iii) where the contract fixes a date by which the condition is to be fulfilled, that date must be strictly adhered to and time is not to be extended on equitable principles. *Held,* in the contract in question the renewal of the leases was a condition which must be fulfilled at the latest by the time fixed by the contract for completion of the sale and the words "as soon as possible" in the contract allowed reasonable time in which the transfer of leases renewed could take place but did not provide further time for obtaining renewal of the leases. The vendor, not having obtained renewal by the date fixed for completion of the sale, the purchaser was entitled to the return of his deposits. (See also *Re Longlands Farm.*)

Allen & Co., Ltd. v. Whiteman [1920], 123 L.T. 773   **[3]**

Estate agents agreed to sell land on behalf of one of two mortgagees. The vendor was not named and was referred to by the agents as "our client" but included in the correspondence was a reference to the vendor's husband as "Mr. Whiteman" and the auction particulars stated that the sale was "by order of the mortgagees". *Held,* the Court could consider all these factors and thus find that the vendor had been sufficiently identified to satisfy s. 4 of the Statute of Frauds (now replaced by s. 40 Law of Property Act 1925). (See also *F. Goldsmith (Sicklesmere), Ltd. v. Baxter*; but see *Lovesy v. Palmer.*)

Alliance Building Society v. Yap, [1962] 3 All E.R. 6   **[4]**

By a legal charge the defendants jointly charged leasehold property to the building society. The charge contained an attornment clause but provided that the plaintiffs could determine the tenancy arising thereunder without previous notice. The charge also provided that if payments were in arrear for more than

1

two months the statutory power of sale should arise and be exercisable free from the provisions of s. 103 Law of Property Act 1925. Payments being in arrear the plaintiffs took out a summons for possession. The summons was served on the first defendant who was in occupation, it being impossible to ascertain the whereabouts of the second defendant. It was said for the plaintiffs that in ejectment the person in possession must be served but no-one else need be. *Held*, the plaintiffs were entitled to an order for possession.

Armstrong v. Sheppard and Short, Ltd., [1959] 2 All E.R. 651.   [5]
(Court of Appeal)

The plaintiff owned a house at the back of which was a private pathway leading from the highway to premises owned by the defendants. The strip of the pathway at the rear of the plaintiff's house was part of his property but he was unaware of this as his title deeds were held by mortgagees. In 1957 the defendants asked the plaintiff's consent (among others) to their constructing a sewer under the pathway to join the public sewer in the highway. The plaintiff gave oral consent. In 1958 the plaintiff discovered he owned part of the pathway and required the defendants to remove the sewer on the ground that it had been laid on his property without his permission. The defendants did not comply and the plaintiff brought an action for trespass and an injunction to prevent flow of effluent through the sewer. *Held*, the plaintiff was not prevented by acquiescence from enforcing his legal rights as he had not known he owned the land when he gave consent but he had suffered only trivial damage and 20s. was an adequate award of damages. The plaintiff's oral consent to the construction of the sewer, even though given in ignorance of his title, was sufficient answer to the claim in trespass. It was not a sufficient answer to a claim in respect of the discharge of effluent through the plaintiff's land because such a right could not be granted by parol. If the plaintiff had given licence for the discharge of effluent such licence could be revoked as it was gratuitous and it had been revoked. However, an injunction would not be granted.

Atkinson and Horsell's Contract, Re, [1912] 2 Ch. 1. (Court of Appeal)   [6]

A contract for the sale of land in 1911 provided that title should commence with a general devise in the will of a testator who died in 1842 and whose seisin was to be assumed. The vendor derived title from a disseisor who, in 1874 as a result of a mutual mistake as to the effect of a will, was allowed by the true owner to take possession of the land and the title deeds. There was uninterrupted possession from the disseisor to the date of contract. The mistake was not realised at the time of the contract so that the contract did not mention that the title was partly possessory. The vendor claimed to have shown a good title up to 1874 and a good possessory title since then. *Held*, the vendor had shown good title and it could be forced on the purchaser. But see *Wimpey (George) & Co. Ltd.* v. *Sohn*.

A.-G. v. Beynon, [1969] 2 All E.R. 263   [7]

The mere fact that a road runs between fences, which include hedges, does not *per se* give rise to any presumption that the right of way extends to the whole space between the fences. It is necessary to decide whether the fences were erected to separate the adjoining closes from the highway or for some other reason and that question is to be decided in the sense that the fences do mark the limit of the highway unless there are circumstances to the contrary. When that is decided a rebuttable presumption of law arises that the highway extends to the whole space between the fences and is not confined to only that part of the road which is made up. Where the boundary is a hedge and a ditch the presumption is that the ditch is not part of the highway but this does not prevent the fence to fence presumption applying up to the ditch.

A.-G. v. Parsons, [1956] 1 All E.R. 65 (House of Lords)   **[8]**

Where land was forfeit to the Crown under the Mortmain and Charitable Uses Act 1888, the Crown's entry was not automatic. "Forfeit" in the Act meant "liable to be forfeited" and the land would not vest in the Crown unless and until the Crown took steps to enforce the forfeiture. (*Morelle, Ltd.* v. *Wakeling* overruled on this point.)

Auerbach v. Nelson, [1919] 2 Ch. 383   **[9]**

A receipt for the deposit which evidenced the contract between the parties for the sale and purchase of land read: "21.11.1918 Received of Mr. Auerbach, 197 High Street, Shoreditch, £10 on account of House being sold for £500 from Mr. M. Nelson, 143 Victoria Park Road. Possession to be taken in six weeks after date. (Signed) Morris Nelson." *Held*, there was a sufficient memorandum of the verbal contract, date, parties and price being shown and sufficient description of the property being sold and therefore parol evidence could be given to show to what the description referred. Section 4 of the Statute of Frauds did not require the property to be described in such a way that it would be unnecessary to resort to parol evidence.

Austerberry v. Oldham Corporation, [1885], 29 Ch. D. 750   **[10]**

A conveyed for value to trustees a piece of land as part of the site of a road intended to be made and maintained by the trustees and in the conveyance the trustees covenanted with A, his heirs and assigns that the trustees, their heirs and assigns would make and keep in repair the road and allow its use by the public subject to tolls. The road was bounded by other lands belonging to A. The trustees made the road which afforded necessary access to A's lands. A sold his adjoining lands to the plaintiff and the trustees sold the road to the defendants. *Held*, the plaintiff could not enforce the covenant to repair against the defendants as he had failed to show he took the benefit of the covenant and it was unnecessary to decide whether or not the burden of a positive covenant runs with the land although LINDLEY and FRY L. JJ. gave it as their opinion that, except between landlord and tenant, the burden would not run at law. The doctrine of *Tulk* v. *Moxhay* is limited to restrictive covenants and will not be extended to positive obligations. It was also held there had not been a dedication of the road to the public and the road was not repairable by the inhabitants at large under the Public Health Act 1875, s. 150. *Semble* an individual cannot, without legislative authority, dedicate a road to the public if he reserves the right to charge tolls. (See also *E. and G. C.* v. *Bate*.)

Bain v. Fothergill, [1874–80] All E.R. Rep. 83   **[11]**

Held, the rule in *Flureau* v. *Thornhill* (1776), 2 Wm. & Bl. 1078 applied in the absence of fraud or bad faith. Where a vendor of land cannot complete the contract owing to an irremovable defect in title the purchaser will not be entitled to damages for loss of bargain but only to; (i) his costs of investigating title; (ii) return of his deposit (with interest unless otherwise agreed); and (iii) interest on the balance of the purchase money if, to the vendor's knowledge, it has been lying idle awaiting completion. (See also *J. W. Cafés* v. *Brownlow Trust*; but see *Day* v. *Singleton* and *Re Daniel, Daniel* v. *Vassall*.)

Baines v. Tweddle, [1959] 2 All E.R. 724 (Court of Appeal)   **[12]**

A vendor contracted to sell the unincumbered fee simple of land. The contract contained a clause that if the purchaser "takes or makes any objection or requisition as to title, conveyance or otherwise which the vendor is unable, or, on the ground of unreasonable expense, unwilling to remove or comply with and does not withdraw the same . . . the vendor may rescind . . . the contract." At the time the vendor signed the contract the property was subject to two mortgages, the amount owing in respect of which exceeded the price for which the land was being sold. The vendor thought his solicitor would be able to obtain the concurrence of the mortgagees to the sale but the mortgagees refused to join in the conveyance and the purchaser refused to purchase the equity of redemption. *Held*, the vendor could not rescind under the terms of the contract as, although he had acted honestly, he had acted recklessly in signing the contract without ascertaining that the mortgagees would concur. He was therefore in breach of contract and the purchaser was entitled to damages.

Baker and Selmon's Contract, Re, [1907] 1 Ch. 238   [13]

A contract for the sale of a freehold house provided that the vendor "who is the trustee under the will of James Baker deceased is selling . . . under the trusts and powers vested in him thereunder . . . " It also provided that the tenant for life would join in the conveyance to the purchaser to release her life interest in the property. In fact, the vendor had the legal estate as trustee of the will but had no power or trust for sale thereunder. He had, however, entered into the contract on the request of the tenant for life and all the other beneficiaries, including himself, so that he could compel them to join. *Held*, the vendor had shown good title in accordance with the contract. As the beneficiaries could be compelled to join in the conveyance the purchaser must accept a conveyance made with their concurrence. The trustee-beneficiary relationship had become substantially that of principal and agent. (See also *Elliot* v. *Pierson* and *Re Spencer and Hauser's Contract*.)

Ballard's Conveyance, Re, [1937] 2 All E.R. 691   [14]

In 1906 about 18 acres of land was sold and the purchaser covenanted with the vendor, her heirs and assigns and successors that he, his heirs and assigns would perform and observe certain conditions and stipulations for the benefit of the 1,700 acre Childwickbury Estate retained by the vendor. Could the successors in title of the vendor obtain relief in respect of a breach, or threatened breach, of this covenant by the purchaser? *Held*, they could not as, although a breach of the stipulations might affect part of the Childwickbury Estate, far the largest part could not possibly be affected by any such breach. "I asked in vain for any authority which would justify me in severing the covenant, and treating it as annexed to or running with such part of the land as is touched by or concerned with it, though, as regards the remainder of the land, namely, such part as is not touched by or concerned with the covenant, the covenant is not, and cannot be, annexed to it, and accordingly does not, and cannot, run with it. Nor have I been able, through my own researches, to find anything in the books which seems to justify any such course" (*per* CLAUSON, J.). (See also *Zetland* v. *Driver*.)

Bandar Property Holdings, Ltd. v. J. S. Darwen (Successors), Ltd., [15] [1968] 2 All E.R. 305

A lease contained a covenant by the landlords to insure at Lloyd's or a reputable insurance office and a covenant by the tenants to reimburse the premium. The landlords insured through a firm of Lloyd's brokers at an annual premium of £1,100. The tenants obtained a quotation through Lloyd's at a much lower premium. *Held*, there was no implied term in the lease that the landlords should insure at the lowest premium reasonably obtainable. The court will not imply a term which has not been expressed merely because, had the parties thought of including that term, it would have been reasonable so to do; it must also be shown that it is necessary to imply the term in order to make the contract work.

Bannister v. Bannister, [1948] 2 All E.R. 133 (Court of Appeal)   [16]

The defendant sold two cottages to the plaintiff on his giving an oral undertaking (not included in the conveyance) that she would be entitled to live in one cottage rent free so long as she wished. Subsequently she occupied one room and the defendant occupied the rest of the cottage. The plaintiff brought an action for possession and claimed that the defendant had occupied as a tenant at will and the tenancy had been determined by notice to quit. The defendant counter-claimed that the plaintiff held the cottage in trust for her. *Held*, (i) the oral undertaking by the plaintiff created a life interest in the cottage for the defendant, determinable on her ceasing to live there; (ii) the conveyance could not be set up to defeat the beneficial interest; a constructive trust had arisen and s. 40(1) of the Law of Property Act 1925 could not be called in aid to assist a fraud, nor was it necessary that the bargain on which the conveyance was made should include any express stipulation that the grantee is to hold as trustee; it was sufficient that the bargain included a stipulation under which some sufficiently defined beneficial interest in the property arose; (iii) the defendant was entitled to a declaration that the plaintiff held the property on trust during her life to permit her to occupy for as long as she wished and, subject thereto, in trust for himself and the plaintiff was not entitled to an order for possession. (See also *Dillwyn* v. *Llewellyn*.)

Barclays Bank, Ltd. v. Beck, [1952] 1 All E.R. 549 (Court of Appeal)   **[17]**
In 1949 the defendants, who were farmers, had an overdraft at the bank which they secured by a charge under seal on their property. In 1950 part of the property was sold and the charge discharged by agreement on payment of £4,000. The bank claimed for payment of an amount of the overdraft in excess of the £4,000 paid. *Held*, the merger of a simple contract in a speciality operated only if that were the intention of the parties. On construction, the charge did not show that the simple contract should be merged in the charge and therefore the discharge of the charge did not discharge the debt in full. (See also *Jameson* v. *Kinmell Bay Land Co., Ltd.*)

Barker v. Addiscott, [1969] 3 All E.R. 685   **[18]**
Two sisters were joint tenants for life of property under the Settled Land Act 1925. One wished to sell the property but the other refused as she was residing there and wished to remain. The sister who wished to sell issued a summons seeking an order that the other should concur in selling the property with vacant possession. *Held*, the application would fail. The court would not interfere where powers were not being exercised unless *mala fides* was found. There was no improper motive in opposing the sale of the house on the ground that one tenant for life wished to live there herself.

Barr's Contract, Re, Moorwell Holdings, Ltd. v. Barr,   **[19]**
     [1956] 2 All E.R. 853
Purchasers contracted to buy two properties, one at £50,000 and the other at £30,000. The contract (incorporating the National Conditions of Sale, 16th Edn.) provided for service of a notice to complete, after the completion date in the contract had passed, requiring completion within 28 days and making time of the essence of the notice. The vendors, as agents of the purchasers, at the time of the contract were negotiating a sub-sale but the proposed sub-sale fell through. The contractual date for completion was January 31st and on February 1st the vendors served notice to complete within 28 days. *Held*, the notice to complete must be for such time as was reasonable in the circumstances, being not less than 28 days, and in view of the large price and the failure of the proposed sub-sale, known to the vendors, 28 days was insufficient time and the vendors' notice of recission was ineffective. (But see *Cumberland Court (Brighton), Ltd.* v. *Taylor*.)

Basma (Abdul Karim) v. Weekes, [1950] 2 All E.R. 146   **[20]**
     (Privy Council)
Where an agent contracts in his own name to purchase land, he does not cease to be contractually bound because it can be proved that the other party knew, at the time of the contract, that he was acting as agent and the agreement, made in

his name, does not cease to satisfy the Statute of Frauds, s. 4. If the agent could have sued upon the contract, so can the principal. (See also *Davies* v. *Sweet*.)

Baynham v. Baynham, [1969] 1 All E.R. 305 (Court of Appeal)   **[21]**

A husband appealed from an order under s. 1(1)(b) of the Matrimonial Homes Act 1967, that the husband had a right to occupy the matrimonial home until noon on August 12th, 1968 and thereafter his right should be terminated and the wife should have the right to enter and occupy the house until further order. *Held*, the appeal would be dismissed. Although the wife was not in occupation she had a right, with an order of the court, to re-enter and occupy. As to whether a wife not in occupation can register a Land Charge Class F under the 1967 Act, before leave to re-enter has been given by the court, was left open.

Becker v. Partridge, [1966] 2 All E.R. 266 (Court of Appeal)   **[22]**

A contract provided that the title to land should commence with an under-lease and that the purchaser should raise no objection or requisition thereon. The vendor's interest, which had been described as an underlease, was a sub-underlease and the underlease out of which the sub-underlease was derived contained a covenant against assignment without consent. No application had been made for consent. There had been breaches of covenant which could have entailed forfeiture. *Held*, the purchaser was entitled to rescind despite the special condition in the contract as the vendor had a duty to disclose all defects of which he knew. Although he did not know of the breaches of covenant, he ought to have known such breaches might exist. The court doubted whether the alleged mis-description of the sub-underlease as an "underlease" would in itself give rise to a right of rescission. (See also *Re Haedicke and Lipski's Contract*.)

Beesly v. Hallwood Estates, Ltd., [1961] 1 All E.R. 90   **[23]**
(Court of Appeal)

A lease for twenty-one years was granted by the predecessors in title of the company to the predecessors in title of Mrs. B. It contained an option for a further twenty-one years' lease on the lessee giving six months' notice in writing on certain conditions. Mrs. B. duly gave notice to exercise the option and the company set out the terms of the new lease, subject to the lessee giving an undertaking to redecorate the property. The undertaking was not given but the company executed the lease and the counterpart was sent to Mrs. B. for execution. It was then realised that the option was not binding on the company owing to lack of registration under the Land Charges Act 1925. The company contended that the counterpart not having been returned and the undertaking not having been given, they were entitled to withdraw the offer. *Held*, the execution of the counterpart was the condition which turned the lease from an escrow into a deed. Mrs. B. having executed the counterpart, the document had become a deed and the company could not resile; it made no difference that the lease and counterpart had not been exchanged. (See also *Foundling Hospital* v. *Crane* and *Windsor Refrigerator Co., Ltd.* v. *Branch Nominees, Ltd.*)

Bell v. Balls, [1897] 1 Ch, 663   **[24]**

An auctioneer has authority to sign a memorandum for the purpose of s. 4 of the Statute of Frauds (now s. 40 of the Law of Property Act 1925) in a contract for the sale of land on behalf of the vendor and, at the time of the auction, also on behalf of the purchaser. Where an auctioneer has signed a memorandum as agent for the purchaser a week after the sale, the purchaser having repudiated the purchase at the time of the sale, it was held that the auctioneer's authority had ceased. The auctioneer's authority does not extend to his clerk unless the purchaser has authorised the clerk to sign as his agent. (But see *Chaney* v. *Maclow*.)

Belmont Farm Ltd. v. Minister of Housing and Local [25]
Government, [1962], 13 P. & C.R. 417

The owners of a farm erected an aircraft hangar, partly for use in farming and partly in connection with horse breeding and show-jumping. They applied to the local planning authority under s. 17 Town and Country Planning Act 1947 for a determination as to whether activities in breeding and training horses amounted to a change of use of the farm. The planning authority held that these activities did amount to a change of use and served an enforcement notice under s. 23 of the 1947 Act requiring removal of the hangar. The owners appealed to the Minister who dismissed the appeal. The owners appealed against the dismissal, contending that breeding and training horses was use of land for the purpose of agriculture within s. 12(2), and that erection of the hangar was development for which permission was granted by the Town and Country Planning General Development Order, 1950, being carrying out on agricultural land of a building operation for the use of that land for the purposes of agriculture. *Held*, (i) "breeding and keeping of livestock" within s. 119(1) did not extend to breeding and keeping of horses except for their use in farming and therefore there was material change of use; (ii) the hangar was not "designed" for the purposes of agriculture within the Order, since "designed" in that context meant so designed in the sense of physical appearance and layout. By that test the hangar could not be described as a farm building so that no permission was granted by the Order.

Betts & Sons, Ltd. v. Price [1924], 40 T.L.R. 589 [26]

The defendant, by an agreement in writing but not under seal, leased premises from the plaintiffs as tenant from year to year. The agreement contained a term to pay rent at certain specific times. Later the defendant was given permission in writing by the plaintiffs to assign the lease to a company he had formed, on condition that the assignment should not affect the stipulations in the original agreement. There was no written assignment but the company went into occupation. The company defaulted in payment of rent. The plaintiffs claimed against the defendant as the original tenant for recovery of the rent. *Held*, the mere fact that the original lease was not under seal did not prevent the plaintiffs from bringing an action for the rent. There was a personal agreement between the parties to pay rent which could be sued upon and also the special reservation made by the plaintiffs in granting leave to assign.

Bilkus v. London Borough of Redbridge (1968), [27]
207 Estates Gazette 803

The first two plaintiffs were freeholders of Nos. 73, 75 and 77 High Road, Ilford and their father was the leaseholder. The corporation intended to develop an area which included the plaintiffs' land and proposed to obtain a compulsory purchase order. The plaintiffs opposed this but agreed on January 20th, 1960 to sell parts of the land. The conveyance was to include exceptions and reservations in favour of the plaintiffs and the leaseholder and their successors in title, including a right to car parking facilities. In 1961 the leaseholder surrendered his lease and, on the part of the land they were to retain, the plaintiffs erected new shop premises. In 1962 they incorporated a company, Maison Riche Ltd. (the third plaintiff), and granted to the company a lease of the premises. The agreement of January 20th, 1960 was implemented on August 24th, 1962 by a conveyance between the first two plaintiffs, the company and the corporation, which included a right for the vendors for "themselves and their successors in title, owners, lessees or occupiers for the time being . . . in common with the corporation and all others having a like right . . . to use the land coloured green as a park for the temporary parking of vehicles . . . " By clause 4 the corporation covenanted to permit "general car parking facilities for the vehicles of persons using the brown land (the plaintiffs' property) and any building from time to time erected thereon upon the land owned by the corporation at the rear of the land coloured green".

The corporation erected properties and allocated car parking spaces to the occupiers of these premises. Three spaces were allocated as a common parking area. No space was allocated specifically to the plaintiffs and they were only able to use, in common with others, the three-space common parking area. The plaintiffs claimed for breach of covenant. *Held*, the effect of the covenant was to grant the plaintiffs an unrestricted easement giving them a better right then anyone else to park on any appropriate part of the land.

**Birmingham Corporation v. Minister of Housing and Local   [28]
Government**, [1963] 3 All E.R. 668

Each of three dwellinghouses, formerly in the occupation of a single family, was let in parts to a number of occupiers who paid weekly rent. The local planning authority served on the owners an enforcement notice in respect of each house, reciting that development had been carried out without planning permission by material change of use from a single house to a house-let-in-lodgings and requiring discontinuance. The owners appealed to the Minister who allowed the appeals on the ground that the houses remained residential and therefore there had been no material change of use. The local authority appealed. *Held*, the question of whether there had been a material change of use in any case was a matter of fact and degree for the Minister and therefore the Minister had erred in law in concluding that because the houses remained residential there could not be a material change of use. The appeals were allowed and the cases remitted to the Minister to determine whether what had occurred in each case amounted in fact to a material change of use.

**Birmingham Corporation v. West Midland Baptist (Trust)   [29]
Association**, [1969] 3 All E.R. 172 (House of Lords)

The corporation made a compulsory purchase order in respect of the respondents' chapel. Notice to treat was deemed to be served in August, 1947 but the respondents were allowed to remain in possession. The cost of equivalent reinstatement in 1947 would have been £50,025. In 1958 the corporation allocated a site for a new chapel and it was agreed that the earliest possible date for rebuilding to commence would be April, 1961. At that date the cost of reinstatement was £89,575. *Held*, compensation for equivalent reinstatement must be based on costs prevailing at the time when rebuilding becomes possible, *i.e.*, April, 1961. The House of Lords stated that the so-called rule of the 19th century that compensation should be assessed at the date of service of the notice to treat would work injustice in the 20th century in an economy of rising prices and unstable values and frequent delay between the notice to treat and the expropriation. The right date was the earliest date at which a reasonable owner could have begun reinstatement.

Birmingham, Re, Savage v. Stannard, [1958] 2 All E.R. 397   **[30]**

On January 2nd, 1953, the testatrix bequeathed £10,000 to her daughter Kathleen and on March 31st, 1953, contracted to buy a house for £3,500. On April 10th the testatrix told her solicitors that she would like to leave the house to Kathleen as well as the £10,000. By a codicil dated April 17th the testatrix stated: "Whereas I have entered into a contract for the purchase of [the house], I hereby give the said property free of all duties to my daughter Kathleen." Under the terms of the contract the purchase was to be completed on or before April 27th, but the testatrix died on April 21st and before completion took place. Who should pay the balance of the purchase money? *Held*, Kathleen should as she took the house subject to a charge for the unpaid balance of the purchase money (the vendor's lien for unpaid purchase-money arose at the moment the contract was signed), s. 35 of the Administration of Estates Act 1925, applied and a contrary intention had not been signified either by the testatrix's letter or the codicil to her will.

Blackburn v. Walker, [1920] W.N. 291   [31]

The plaintiff brought an action for specific performance of an oral agreement to purchase leasehold property (a cinema), together with fixtures and fittings and certain chattels and the goodwill of the business. The defendant contended that there had been negotiations only, conditional on the execution of a formal agreement which had been prepared but not executed and the terms of which were never fully agreed. He also pleaded lack of a memorandum in writing sufficient to comply with the Statute of Frauds. The plaintiff relied on two letters between the respective solicitors and a receipt for the deposit, as supplying the necessary written memorandum. The receipt stated: "Received of Mr. J. F. Blackburn the sum of £275 being a deposit on account of the purchase of Mr. Kennedy Walker's lease of the Grand Theatre, Forest Gate, together with all seating fixtures and fittings which belong to me therein, and the business and goodwill thereof, purchase money £3,025. Dated October 20th, 1919. (Signed) Kennedy Walker." *Held*, the two letters did not constitute a concluded agreement and the receipt did not satisfy the statute. A sufficient note or memorandum of the contract meant it must contain all the material terms of the contract. The receipt omitted any mention of agreement as to the value of the chattels, the date for completion, payment of the purchase money by instalments, or that the instalments were to be secured by mortgage. Hence the receipt was not a sufficient memorandum within the Statute and the plaintiff's action must be dismissed.

Blake v. Gale (1886), 32 Ch. D. 571   [32]

The right of mortgagees of real property, whose security proves insufficient, to come against the residuary legatees of the deceased mortgagor, amongst whom his personal estate has been distributed, is a purely equitable right and the court will not enforce it if there are circumstances which would make it inequitable to do so. *Held*, where in 1859 the plaintiff had assented to the distribution of the personal estate and the carrying on of the farming of the mortgaged property by the beneficiaries, he could not, in 1882, when the mortgaged property proved insufficient to satisfy the mortgage debt, after such a lapse of time claim for the balance out of the personal estate of the mortgagor in the hands of the residuary legatees.

Blake & Co. v. Sohn, [1969] 3 All E.R. 123   [33]

The owners of property instructed estate agents to find a purchaser. The agents introduced a purchaser and contracts were exchanged. The vendors could not make the title contracted for and it was held the purchasers were entitled to rescind (*Wimpey* (*George*) *& Co. Ltd.* v. *Sohn*). *Held*, the estate agents were not entitled to commission. In the absence of any agreement to the contrary, estate agents are not entitled to commission until a sale is completed unless failure to complete is due to the default of the vendors; nor was there any implied promise by the vendors to the estate agents that they could make good title.

Blankney v. Minister of Housing & Local Government   [34]
   (1968), 205 Estates Gazette 109

An application for planning permission for change of use of premises from residential to commercial was granted by a local authority, with a condition attached limiting the permission to five years because of the possibility of a new road. The owners appealed against the condition and a public inquiry was held. After the inquiry the Minister's inspector formed the view that commercial user might generate more traffic which would give rise to traffic hazards. This issue had not been raised at the inquiry but the Minister was not so informed. The Minister treated the application as if it were an application to him in the first instance and totally refused the application, basing his decision solely on the traffic hazard aspect. The Minister's order (by consent) was quashed on the grounds that the appellants had not been heard on the traffic aspect.

Bligh v. Martin, [1968] 1 All E.R. 1157   **[35]**

The plaintiff claimed to have acquired ownership of agricultural land by adverse possession from February, 1949 to February, 1961. The defendant contended that adverse possession was terminated in September, 1954 as from that date until March, 1960 he had been employed by the plaintiff as a contractor to cultivate the land and by going on the land had regained possession; also that he had put his cattle on the land in winter when the plaintiff could not cultivate the land. Alternatively, the defendant contended the plaintiff's adverse possession was terminated in March, 1960 when the plaintiff granted the defendant six months' grazing tenancy under which the defendant went into possession. Section 10(3) of the Limitation Act 1939 provides that receipt of rent under a lease by a person wrongfully claiming possession of the reversion is deemed to be adverse possession of the reversion. *Held*, the true owner's occupation of the land had not interrupted the squatter's adverse possession for the purpose of the Limitation Act. *Cooper v. Phibbs* was distinguished on the ground that the lease included land other than that owned by the tenant.

Bolton Corporation v. Owen, [1962] 1 All E.R. 101   **[36]**
     (Court of Appeal)

The defendants, a local planning authority, had prepared a development plan showing some 250 acres in a built-up area as "residential". In the written statement, accompanying the plan, it was stated: "It is proposed to clear the following areas and to redevelop them for residential purposes in accordance with modern standards." The plaintiff's house was in one of such areas and, having failed to obtain a purchaser, he served a purchase notice on the defendants under s. 39 of the Town and Country Planning Act 1959 requiring its purchase on the ground that it fell within paragraph (b) of sub-s. (1) of s. 39 as "land allocated by a development plan for the purposes of any functions of a . . . local authority." The defendants served a counter notice under s. 40 on the ground that the land did not fall within any of the specified descriptions in s. 39(1). The Lands Tribunal held the plaintiff's notice was valid. *Held*, the onus under s. 41(2) of the 1959 Act was on the plaintiff to establish that his house was within s. 39(1)(b) and he had not discharged it. Merely because an area was listed as an area to be cleared and developed, it could not be said to be allocated "for the purposes of any functions of" a local authority within s. 39(1)(b). In the absence of specific reference in the development plan to development by the defendants under their powers under the Housing Act 1957, it was not for the Lands Tribunal to speculate on the probability of the area being cleared and redeveloped by the defendants in the exercise of their functions as a housing authority rather than by private enterprise. The Lands Tribunal's decision was reversed.

Bonnewell v. Jenkins (1878), 8 Ch.D. 70 (Court of Appeal)   **[37]**

The defendant instructed an agent to sell his leasehold property. The plaintiff wrote to the agent: "This offer is made subject to the conditions of the lease being modified to my solicitor's satisfaction." The agent replied: "We are instructed to accept your offer of £800 for these premises and have asked Mr Jenkins' solicitors to prepare a contract." The required modification to the lease was obtained. *Held*, that notwithstanding the reference to a future contract the two letters constituted a completed contract. (But see *Chillingworth* v. *Esche*.)

Bottomley v. Bannister, [1932] 1 K.B. 458 (Court of Appeal)   **[38]**

At common law, in the absence of express contract, a landlord of an unfurnished house is not liable to his tenant, nor is the vendor of real property liable to his purchaser, for defects in the house or land rendering it dangerous or unfit for occupation, even if the defects are due to his construction or within his knowledge. Builders sold a house on an estate, agreeing to make it fit for habitation. The purchasers went into occupation before completion, as tenants at will. The house contained a boiler in the kitchen connected to a linen chute in the bathroom. The boiler and the chute were part of the realty. The purchasers were found dead in the bathroom as a result of carbon monoxide gas poisoning. *Held*, there being no evidence of a breach of any duty which the law cast on the builders as vendors or lessors, a claim by the administrators of the deceased couple under the Fatal Accidents Act 1846 must fail.

Boyle's Claim, Re, [1961] 1 All E.R. 620 [39]

A claim in the county court for damages for trespass and an injunction against further trespass led to the judge holding that there had been an error in the Land Registry as to the boundary and in order to clarify the position and avoid further disputes, the judge ordered, under s. 82(1) of the Land Registration Act 1925, rectification of the register. The registered proprietor claimed compensation for loss caused by the rectification and this was referred to a judge of the Chancery Division in accordance with r. 298(2) of the Land Registration Rules 1925, with the Attorney-General representing the trustees of the insurance fund maintained under s. 85 of the Act. The claimant had purchased a plot of land in 1952 by registered transfer and was registered as proprietor with absolute title. On one side of the plot there was a hedge and on the plan on the transfer this was marked with the words appearing "centre of hedge". The Land Registry filed plan did not mention the hedge and gave no dimensions but showed the plot as wider at one end than the other. On the adjoining land there was a house and garage and this was purchased by D. in January, 1953. Between May and September, 1953 the claimant erected a bungalow close to the boundary and D.'s garage. A dispute arose as to the position of the boundary leading to the action for trespass. Rectification of the register resulted in cutting off a triangle of the claimant's land at the end where the Land Registry's plan had showed that end of the plot to be wider. The result was the footings of the claimant's bungalow were now on D.'s land and the corner of D.'s garage was on the triangular piece of land removed from the claimant's title. In the result, when the claimant had registered his title in 1952, D.'s garage had occupied part of the registered land but D. was not occupying the rest of the triangular piece which was subsequently removed from the claimant's title. *Held*, the claimant was not entitled to compensation for rectification of that part of the land which was being occupied at the time of his purchase by the corner of D.'s garage, as this occupation was an overriding interest to which the claimant took subject and therefore the claimant had suffered no loss; the claimant was entitled to compensation for loss suffered as a result of rectification in respect of the remainder of the land removed from the title as this had not been in the occupation of D. (See also *Re Chowood's Registered Land*.)

Braithwaite v. Winwood [1960] 3 All E.R. 642 [40]

In 1955 the plaintiff sold to the defendant a cottage for £650 and the defendant executed a legal charge in respect of the property in favour of the plaintiff for £500 without interest. The charge provided that if the defendant performed the covenants and the power of sale had not arisen the plaintiff would not require repayment of the principal sum until 1965. By the same deed the defendant assigned an insurance policy to secure £500 in 1965 and covenanted to pay the premiums thereon. In 1958 there were negotiations for the plaintiff to purchase the property and the defendant ceased paying the insurance premiums. Negotiations broke down and in March, 1960 the plaintiff issued a summons for possession. In May, 1960 the defendant persuaded the plaintiff to agree to the reinstatement of the insurance policy and the defendant paid the overdue premiums. The plaintiff then sought an order for possession. *Held*, (i) the mortgagee's power of sale was exercisable at the date of the issue of the summons and the defendant, not having established that the arrangement regarding the reinstatement of the insurance policy was intended to affect the legal relationship between the parties, the plaintiff was not estopped from saying the power of sale was still exercisable;

(ii) since the defendant had done nothing towards making arrangements to pay off the mortgage during the four months since June, 1960 and was not living in the property, the court would not exercise its discretion in his favour and, therefore, the plaintiff was entitled to an order for possession. *Quaere* whether the power of the court, in its discretion to adjourn a mortgagee's summons for possession under R.S.C. Ord. 55, r. 5a, does not extend to the case of a mortgage which is not payable by instalments.

Bramwell's Contract, Re, Bramwell v. Ballards Securities Investments Ltd., [1969] 1 W.L.R. 1659   **[41]**

A contract for the sale of land incorporated Condition 12(1) National Conditions of Sale, 17th Edn., which provided: "The Purchaser shall admit the identity of the property with that comprised in the muniments offered by the vendor as the title thereto upon the evidence afforded by the descriptions contained in such muniments, and of a statutory declaration to be made (if required) at the purchaser's expense, that the property has been enjoyed according to the title for at least twelve years." It was impossible to identify the properties described in the root of title with those contracted to be sold. *Held*, despite the condition in the contract, the purchaser could not be compelled to complete. If the root of title was not shown to comprise the land agreed to be sold it could not be said to afford evidence of the identity of the property with that agreed to be sold.

Branca v. Cobarro, [1947] 2 All E.R. 101 (Court of Appeal)   **[42]**

The parties negotiated for the sale of a mushroom farm and signed a document containing the terms of their agreement which concluded: "This is a provisional agreement until a fully legalised agreement drawn up by a solicitor and embodying all the conditions herewith stated is signed." The purchaser sued for the return of his deposit and the vendor contended that their "provisional agreement" was a binding contract. *Held*, there was an immediately binding contract "until" the document was replaced by one expressed in more precise and formal language. If the parties had used the word "tentative" instead of "provisional" it would probably have been held otherwise, but each case depends on the intention of the parties as found by the court. (But see *Bonnewell* v. *Jenkins*.)

Brazil (Concrete), Ltd. v. Amersham Rural District Council (1967), 18 P. & C.R. 396 (Court of Appeal)   **[43]**

Before 1962 land was used for storage in connection with a building contractor's business. In 1962 Brazils acquired the land and applied for planning permission to use a shed on it and convert it for offices, a carpenter's shop, a plumber's store, an engineer's store and shop, and a garage for vehicles in connection with the building business. Planning permission was granted. At the same time, the company's subsidiary, Brazil Concrete, erected a ready-mixed concrete plant on the land, where they mixed concrete for their own building business and for sale. Large vehicles involved in the concrete business caused nuisance to neighbours. Three enforcement notices were served, two of which were found to be invalid. The third, as amended by the Minister, said there had been material change of use from a builder's business to that of concrete manufacturing and required discontinuance. The plaintiffs claimed that the whole user was that of an "industrial building" and there had been no change of use. *Held*, although articles were made in the carpenter's shop, that was incidental to the primary use as a builder's yard, and that purpose was not that of an industrial building. There had been change of use without permission from a builder's yard to premises of makers of concrete and the enforcement notice was valid.

Bridges v. Mees, [1957] 2 All E.R. 577   **[44]**

Bridges was the registered proprietor of No. 6 Priory Road, Surbiton. A company owned land at the rear of Nos. 6 and 8 and in April, 1936 Bridges agreed to purchase the land for £7. He went into occupation and paid the price by instalments, completing payment by the middle of 1937. He did not register his ownership. Mees became the registered proprietor of No. 8 Priory Road in September, 1935. In 1955 the company went into liquidation and Mees applied to the liquidator to purchase the piece of land occupied by Bridges. The company sold the plot to Mees for £5 and transferred the title to him as trustees. On April 13th Mees was registered as proprietor. Mees demanded possession from Bridges who brought an action for rectification of the register. *Held*, (i) the company having received the purchase price in 1937 became a bare trustee of the fee simple interest. Bridges had acquired title, as a beneficiary against the bare trustee, by virtue of possession for twelve years under the Limitation Act 1939, s. 10(1). Mees had therefore acquired his title subject to Bridges' rights which were overriding interests under s. 70(1)(f) of the Land Registration Act 1925; (ii) Mees' title was also subject to Bridges' interest as a person in actual occupation of the land, under s. 70(1)(g) of the Act being an overriding interest; by s. 59(6) overriding interests do not require to be protected on the register by caution; (iii) Bridges had an equitable interest under the contract of 1936 and right to specific performance. The company being a trustee for him could not transfer a better title than it had. Mees held as a trustee for Bridges and could be compelled to transfer to him.

Bridgett and Hayes' Contract, Re, [1928] 1 Ch. 163   [45]

Under the will of Caroline Stoneley her niece Thornley was on January 1st, 1926, and at the date of her (Thornley's) death, tenant for life of settled land, and one Jackson was the sole surviving trustee of the settlement. Thornley died on January 17th, 1926, by her will appointing Bridgett to be the sole executor thereof, and a general grant of probate of her will was duly made to him. On the death of Thornley the settlement came to an end, and Bridgett contracted to sell part of the land to Hayes. *Held*, Bridgett could, without the concurrence of Jackson, give a good title to the land contracted to be sold.

Brighton and Shoreham Building Society v. Hollingdale,   [46]
    [1965] 1 All E.R. 540

A house owned by H. was subject to two mortgages to the building society, one dated 1958 and the other 1961. In 1963 H. deserted his wife, leaving her in occupation of the matrimonial home. H. defaulted in his mortgage repayments and the building society issued an originating summons for sale and possession of the house. On May 6th, 1964 the district registrar ordered H. to deliver up possession. At that date the building society knew of Mrs. H.'s occupation and on May 21st asked her to vacate the house. On September 2nd she took out a summons asking that the order of May 6th should be set aside and that she be joined as a party to the proceedings. The registrar ordered that Mrs. H. be joined as a defendant, that execution be stayed pending further order and the hearing of the action be referred to a judge in chambers. Mrs. H. moved that the order of May 6th be set aside on the ground that it was irregularly made and the summons was void as she had not been served with it. *Held*, the order to deliver up possession should stand as (i) in proceedings by a mortgagee for possession it was not imperatively necessary to join as a defendant the person in actual occupation of premises but by virtue of R.S.C. Ord. 55 r. 5B only such persons, other than the mortgagor, as claimed independent right to stay in occupation as against the mortgagee need be joined as defendants: Mrs. H. did not claim such right; (ii) proceedings for delivery up of possession by a mortgagor, in which the mortgagee did not join as parties persons who might have independent rights to continue in occupation as against the mortgagee were not a nullity, but a person claiming an independent right was entitled to be heard and for that purpose to be joined as defendant. Accordingly the originating summons and the order of May 6th against H. were not void.

13

Brine and Davies' Contract, Re, [1935] All E.R. Rep 871   **[47]**

A vendor and purchaser entered into a contract for the sale of the vendor's freehold house which had title registered at H.M. Land Registry. The contract provided that if the purchaser did not raise objections within fourteen days of delivery of the abstract he should be deemed to have accepted the title. The abstract disclosed that the property was registered with possessory title and twenty-seven days after delivery of the abstract the purchaser objected to possessory title as being insufficient. *Held*, the purchaser was entitled to assume that the abstract would show absolute title. The fact that the vendor could only give possessory title should have been disclosed in the contract. The contract was misleading and therefore the vendor was not entitled to rely on the fact that objection to the title had not been taken within the stipulated time. The purchaser was entitled to a declaration that good title had not been shown in accordance with the contract and to have his deposit returned.

Britain v. Rossiter (1879), 11 Q.B.D. 123   **[48]**

Held, the doctrine of part performance, whereby a contract not enforceable by an action at law owing to the provisions of the Statute of Frauds, s. 4, was rendered enforceable in equity, was confined to suits as to the sale of land.

Brookes v. Flintshire County Council (1956), 6 P. & C.R. 140   **[49]**

Before "the appointed day" under the Town and Country Planning Act 1947 a field was used by a farmer in summer as a caravan site but for agriculture during the rest of the year. The number of caravans was increased without planning permission. The local authority served an enforcement notice requiring removal of all caravans. On appeal to the justices it was held that the notice must be varied to permit fifteen caravans. The justices refused to quash the notice as there had been unauthorised development by increase of numbers. The farmer appealed on the ground that on Bank Holidays before the coming into force of the 1947 Act there had been more than fifteen caravans. *Held*, the restriction on number went too far; instead there should be restriction as to area *i.e.* only that part of the land which originally had been used as a caravan site could continue to be so used. The unit is the matter of importance for the purpose of development in planning law, not the degree of user. (But see *Horwitz* v. *Rowson*.)

Brooks v. Gloucestershire County Council (1967),   **[50]**
    19 P. & C.R. 90

From 1962 a room in the appellant's house (otherwise used for dwelling purposes) was used as a shop. In 1965 two other rooms were used for the sale of furniture and service of meals to customers. The local authority served an enforcement notice requiring, *inter alia*, discontinuance of user as a restaurant. The appellant appealed on the ground that mere intensification of a shop use, which had been in existence for more than four years, did not amount to material change of use. The Minister dismissed the appeal and held that the shop use had increased in 1965 to such an extent that it imported a substantial second use of the building as a whole. The appellant appealed. *Held*, where two different uses were carried on concurrently it was a question of fact and degree whether the extension of one use to absorb the site to the exclusion of the other amounted to a material change of use of the premises as a whole. The latter was the proper unit for consideration in the present circumstances and the Minister's conclusion could not be interfered with.

Broomfield v. Williams, [1897] 1 Ch. 602   **[51]**

Held, a right to light passed on a conveyance by the "general words" implied under s. 6 Conveyancing Act 1881 (see now s. 62 Law of Property Act 1925) without necessity for diversity of occupation of the dominant and servient tenements prior to the disposition of the land. (But see *Long* v. *Gowlett*.)

Broughton v. Snook, [1938] 1 All E.R. 411   **[52]**

The plaintiff orally agreed to purchase the Bridge Inn and with the consent of the owner went into possession and made alterations and improvements to the value of nearly £200. *Held,* these actions were necessarily referable to the contract as the existence of the agreement was the only reasonable explanation for them: they constituted acts of part performance and the plaintiff was entitled to a decree of specific performance. (See also *Rawlinson v. Ames.*)

Brown v. Liverpool Corporation, [1969] 3 All E.R. 1345   **[53]**
(Court of Appeal)

A letting of a house included steps and an access path. Access from the road was by a gate, down four steps, and along a path 7 feet long to an entrance door which was below the road level. The steps were in a state of disrepair which caused the tenant to fall and sustain injury. *Held,* the steps and path were an integral part of the building as without them the building would have no access and could not be used as a dwellinghouse. Hence the steps were part of "the structure and exterior of the dwellinghouse" within s. 32(1)(a) of the Housing Act 1961.

Bryant and Barningham's Contract, Re (1890) 44 Ch.D. 218   **[54]**

Vendors contracted to sell land as trustees for sale. In fact, the trustees had no power of sale until the death of the existing life tenant. The tenant for life was willing to convey but the purchaser refused to enter into a new contract with the tenant for life. *Held,* the purchaser could not be required to contract with the tenant for life who was willing but not compellable. He was, therefore, entitled to rescind the contract and have his deposit returned with interest and the costs of investigating title. (But see *Re Baker and Selmon's Contract.*)

Buckingham County Council v. Callingham, [1952] 1 All E.R. 1166   **[55]**
(Court of Appeal)

A model village with houses 2 to 4 feet high was held to be a "structure or erection" and therefore "buildings" within s. 119(1) of the Town & Country Planning Act 1947. Therefore the building of the same was a building operation and hence "development" within s. 12(2) of the Act requiring planning permission. *Per* SINGLETON, L. J.: "There is no substance in the submission that because this is a model village, or because the buildings are small, neither is, or are, within the planning legislation."

Buckland v. Mackesy (1968), Sol. Jo. 841 (Court of Appeal)   **[56]**

The plaintiff instructed the first defendant to act for him as his solicitor in the purchase of a house and the second defendant to act as his surveyor. Both defendants knew the plaintiff would require a mortgage. The house was divided into two maisonettes, the plaintiff intending to occupy one and let or sell the other. The surveyor prepared drawings, to show the living accommodation available, which were to be attached to the lease or conveyance of the maisonette which was to be let or sold. He sent the drawings to the plaintiff and, in an accompanying letter, pointed out that as a matter of interest he had noticed some minor matters needing attention in the house. The plaintiff read this as indicating there was nothing else wrong with the property. The plaintiff signed the contract and paid £100 deposit before his application for a mortgage had been granted. The solicitor warned him that he would lose his deposit if contracts were exchanged but the purchase fell through but said that one had to take risks to get on in this world. The mortgage was not granted because the house was in a very poor condition. The plaintiff forfeited his deposit and had to meet fees from the surveyor and solicitor. He sued both for negligence but lost. He appealed. *Held,* there was no duty on the solicitor to ensure that a purchaser obtained a mortgage before exchanging contracts; it was sufficient that he warned his client of the risk. Accordingly the claim against the first defendant failed. But the surveyor had not given a proper report and had misled the plaintiff by his letter. Accordingly the second defendant must pay damages consisting of the lost deposit, that part of the solicitor's costs incurred after the date of the surveyor's letter and the greater part of the surveyor's fees.

Bucknell v. Bucknell, [1969] 2 All E.R. 998   [57]

A wife who had divorced her husband issued a writ of sequestration in respect of accumulated arrears of maintenance owed to her by her former husband. Barclays Bank, as mortgagee of a house standing in the husband's name, intended to exercise its power of sale under s. 101 of the Law of Property Act 1925. After sale there would be a substantial surplus which the bank would hold on trust for the husband. The bank maintained it was entitled to refuse to hand over the surplus to the sequestrators unless there was a court order specifically directing it to do so. *Held,* (i) the husband's interest in the surplus which was held on trust under s. 105 of the Law of Property Act 1925 amounted to an equitable chose in action and fell within "personal estate" in the writ of sequestration: hence the sequestrators were entitled to collect the surplus under the writ; (ii) the bank did not need the protection of a court order and should have paid over the money but its attitude was not unreasonable and no order as to costs would be made against the bank.

Bull v. Bull, [1955] 1 All E.R. 253 (Court of Appeal)   [58]

A house was conveyed into the name of a son but the purchase money had been provided by the son and his mother in unequal shares. *Held,* not only could the son not evict the mother from the house but the purchase had created an equitable tenancy in common and a statutory trust for sale. (Hence it would appear that on a sale of the property the son would be unable to make title without appointing an additional trustee.)

Bulstrode v. Lambert, [1953] 2 All E.R. 728   [59]

The plaintiff and his father were auctioneers. The father owned two semi-detached houses and premises at the rear which were used as an auction mart. In 1944 one house was sold, together with a yard and garage, to the defendant's predecessors in title. The conveyance reserved a right of way, with or without vehicles, to the auction mart. At the time of the conveyance it was impossible for large furniture vans to enter the yard owing to the width of the gates. The plaintiff's father died in 1950 and the plaintiff became the owner of the dominant tenement. In 1951 the defendant purchased the servient tenement and removed the gates. The plaintiff claimed a right to bring furniture vans into the yard to the auction mart. *Held,* (i) the reservation in the conveyance gave the plaintiff right to enter with vehicles of any size, which had not been prejudiced by failure to exercise the right for several years; (ii) the plaintiff was entitled to park his vehicles in the yard for such time as was necessary to load and unload, this being an incident of the easement and ancillary thereto.

Burgess v. Cox, [1950] 2 All E.R. 1212   [60]

The owner of a holiday camp (the vendor) and the defendant concluded an oral contract for the sale and purchase of the holiday camp, including certain chattels, consumable stock and deposits by intending guests. A document was drawn up and signed by the vendor incorporating all the material terms except that relating to the deposits, but after a few days the defendant wrote and signed a letter to the vendor in which he said "I am pleased we were able to mutually agree terms for the purchase of [the holiday camp] and shall look forward to taking over from you at an early date". The defendant was unable to raise the necessary money and the vendor's executrix sought damages for breach of contract. *Held,* her action could not succeed. Although the defendant's letter did not refer to the earlier document, it was proper to look at the document as recording the transaction referred to in the letter and, as it was clear on the face of the two documents that the same transaction was referred to, the defendant's signature to the letter could be incorporated in to the document and there was thus a sufficient signature by the party to be charged to satisfy s. 40 (1) of the Law of Property Act 1925. However, the omission of any reference in either document to the deposits was an omission of a material term of the agreement and the documents were thus insufficient to satisfy s. 40 (1) of the 1925 Act: the plaintiff could not concede this term in favour of the defendant so as to render the contract enforceable. (But see *Leeman* v. *Stocks*.)

Burgess v. Jarvis, [1952] 1 All E.R. 592 (Court of Appeal) [61]

A rural district council, as the local planning authority, served enforcement notices on the owners and occupiers of sixteen houses under s. 23 of the Town and Country Planning Act 1947. The notices required the owners to demolish the houses and restore the land to its condition before the houses were erected "within five years after the date of the service of this notice". The notice did not state the period at the expiration of which the notice would take effect, as required by sub-s. (3) of s. 23. *Held*, the notice was invalid because it specified no date for its coming into effect and it afforded no opportunity to any person who was aggrieved to challenge and appeal against it.

Burrows v. Lang, [1901] 2 Ch. 502 [62]

The owner of a mill and farm, whose cattle were watered to some extent by an ancient watercourse diverted from a stream and running on mill property alongside the farm, but constructed and maintained for the purpose of the mill, conveyed the farm without mention of a water right. *Held*, having regard to the temporary purpose (for the mill) for which the watercourse was constructed, the expense of maintaining it and the fact that it lay on mill property, the purchaser of the farm acquired no right by implied grant or under the "general words" of s. 6 of the Conveyancing Act 1881 (now s. 62 of the Law of Property Act 1925) to have the watercourse continued for his benefit. The watercourse was, therefore, precarious and a precarious easement is unknown to the law; hence the purchaser had no right to the use of the water.

Butler v. Mountview Estates, Ltd., [1951] 1 All E.R. 693 [63]

Vendors contracted to sell as beneficial owners three leasehold properties, subject to a condition that the "purchaser shall be deemed to purchase with full notice of the actual state and condition of the property" and a special condition in respect of one of the properties provided "the purchaser shall be deemed to have notice of the actual state and condition of the property and shall take the property as it is". The purchaser inspected the properties. In reply to requisitions the vendors' solicitors stated they were not aware of any breaches of the covenants and conditions in the leases and they produced receipts for the last rents paid. The assignments were "as beneficial owners" thereby impliedly covenanting under s. 76 (1) (b) of the Law of Property Act 1925 and Sched. II Part II that the leases were not void or voidable and that all the covenants and conditions on the part of the lessee had been observed and performed. The repairing covenants had not been fully complied with, in that the properties were not in a full state of repair at the date of assignment. The purchaser claimed damages for breach of implied covenants for title. *Held*, (i) the implied covenant that the lease was not void or voidable was merely a covenant of title and did not contain an obligation on the vendors in regard to the condition of the premises; the breach having been waived by the landlord's acceptance of rent, the lease was no longer voidable; (ii) the implied covenant that all the lessee's covenants had been observed gave the purchaser a right to claim damages for failure to keep in repair. As the covenant was unqualified it was immaterial that the purchaser knew of the state of repair; (iii) as the vendors' liability for damages in respect of

17

the implied covenants would be contrary to the intention of the parties under their contract, there would be rectification of the assignments to give effect to the true intention of the parties, even though the vendors had not counterclaimed for rectification. (See also *Page* v. *Midland Railway Co.*)

Buxton v. Minister of Housing and Local Government, [64]
[1961] 1 Q.B. 278

An appeal by a company against refusal of planning permission to develop land by digging chalk was allowed by the Minister. Owners of adjacent property applied to the High Court under s. 31 (1) of the Town and Country Planning Act 1959 to quash the Minister's decision on the ground that the proposed operations would injure their land and that they were persons "aggrieved" by the Minister's action. *Held*, the expression "person aggrieved" in a statute meant a person who suffered a legal grievance. Anyone given the right under s. 37 of the 1959 Act to have his representations considered by the Minister was a person aggrieved within s. 31 if his rights were infringed. But the applicants, although they would suffer from the proposed operations, did not have any legal rights in respect of the development unless there was trespass or nuisance or the like. Therefore the applicants had no rights under the statute and could not challenge the Minister's decision.

Byrne Road, Balham, 33, Re, Byrnlea Property Investments, [65]
Ltd. v. Ramsay, [1969] 2 All E.R. 311 (Court of Appeal)

A tenant served notice on his landlord of his desire to purchase the freehold of the property under the Leasehold Reform Act 1967. The form of notice gave an alternative to require either the freehold or an extended lease and printed in the margin were the words "Delete whichever is inapplicable". The tenant failed to delete either alternative. *Held*, a notice in the alternative was invalid and void for uncertainty.

Calabar Properties, Ltd. v. Seagull Autos, Ltd., [1968] 1 All E.R. 1 [66]

A lease for twenty-one years contained usual covenants, a covenant restrictive of user and a proviso for re-entry and forfeiture on breach of covenant. The landlords issued a writ for possession under the right of re-entry and sought injunctions, pending trial, to restrain further breaches of covenant. The tenants contended that the landlords could not seek injunctions to enforce the covenants as by claiming possession they were denying that the lease was still subsisting. *Held*, the landlords were entitled to seek injunctions as they might decide at the trial to abandon the claim for possession and proceed on the footing that the lease was still subsisting.

Cantor Art Services Ltd. v. Kenneth Bieber Photography Ltd., [67]
[1969] 3 All E.R. 843 (Court of Appeal)

A contract for the sale of an underlease was subject to the grant of a licence to assign. The contract provided "If the licence to assign is delayed beyond the date fixed for completion the purchaser shall on that date pay the balance of the purchase money to (a stakeholder) pending completion and the vendors shall thereupon allow the purchasers to enter into occupation pending completion and the purchasers shall as and from the date fixed for completion pay the rent and discharge all outgoings . . ." The vendors offered possession on the completion date but the purchasers did not go into possession as no licence to assign had been granted and it was indicated that the underlessors would object to the purchasers going into occupation. The purchasers did not go into possession until the licence to assign was granted several months later. *Held*, the purchasers were not liable for rent and outgoings between completion date and the granting of the licence to assign. The purchasers had not been allowed "to enter into occupation" on the completion date as that meant being lawfully allowed into possession with some binding assurance from the landlords and superior landlords giving apparent security of tenure.

Capital Finance Co., Ltd. v. Stokes, Re Cityfield Properties Ltd.,   [68]
[1968] 3 All E.R. 625. (Court of Appeal)

On July 27th, 1965 the first defendant agreed in writing to sell to the second defendant, a company, land for £37,900 on terms which included a provision that the vendor would leave 75% of the purchase money with the purchaser to be secured by first legal mortgage. On exchange of contracts £500 was paid. The first defendant conveyed the property on February 23rd, 1966 to the second defendant which paid the balance of the 25% of the purchase price. The second defendant charged the property to the first defendant on the same date by legal charge but the charge was not registered under s. 95 of the Companies Act 1948. By a debenture made on October 27th, 1966 the second defendant charged the property, with other assets, to the plaintiff. The plaintiff appointed a receiver and on October 3rd, 1967 an order for the compulsory winding-up of the second defendant was made on the ground of insolvency. The first defendant had retained possession of the property and the title deeds. It was admitted that if the first defendant were entitled to an unpaid vendor's lien on the property it would have priority over any charge created by the debenture. *Held*, (i) as the property was conveyed to the second defendant as purchaser, which then charged it by legal mortgage to the first defendant as vendor, the charge was created after the second defendant's acquisition of the land and thus fell within s. 95, not s. 97, of the Companies Act 1948, with the consequence that as particulars of the charge were not registered pursuant to s. 95 the charge was void as against the liquidator; (ii) the express covenant in the contract to create a legal mortgage in favour of the first defendant gave him an immediate equitable charge but that was registerable under s. 95 and so was void for want of registration as against the liquidator; the equitable charge, moreover, merged with the legal charge; (iii) although between contract and completion there was an equitable charge in the first defendant's favour on 75% of the purchase money, leaving room for a vendor's lien on the remaining 25%, such lien must have been abandoned on completion when the vendor got all that he had bargained for *i.e.* 25% of the purchase money and a legal charge for the balance.

Carter and Kenderdine's Contract, Re, [1897] 1 Ch. 776   [69]
Vendors derived title to property under conveyances by way of settlement. The purchaser objected that these conveyances, being voluntary, were liable to be avoided under s. 47 of the Bankruptcy Act 1883. *Held*, according to the true construction of s. 47 a voluntary settlement is not void against the settlor's trustee in bankruptcy from its date but is only void against the trustee from the time when his title accrues; so that, if before that time the property comprised in the settlement has been sold *bona fide* to a purchaser for value, the title of the purchaser will be good as against the trustee.

Cassel Arenz & Co., Ltd. v. Taylor (1968), 209 Estates Gazette 357   [70]
The plaintiffs, a bank, had a second legal charge on property owned by the defendants, subject to a prior legal charge to a building society. It was provided that the bank's powers as second mortgagees became immediately exercisable on default in observance of any of the mortgagor's covenants. One such was that on demand the mortgagors would pay the whole sum outstanding. Instalments not being met in May the bank demanded the whole amount then outstanding. In June the bank informed the building society of their intention to seek a possession order. The building society replied on October 17th that they had obtained a possession order on September 24th. On November 5th the building society wrote that, serious arrears on their account having been reduced, the proposed eviction of the borrowers had been suspended. On November 11th they wrote

that they had no objection to the bank obtaining a possession order. Hence the second mortgagees were entitled, as against the mortgagors, to possession. *Held*, a possession order would be granted to the second mortgagees with the words inserted "subject to the rights of the first mortgagee". When there was an order for possession already granted to a first mortgagee, that should be made clear in the possession order granted to the second mortgagee.

Castellain v. Preston (1883), 11 Q.B.D. 380; [1881–5] All E.R. Rep. 493   **[71]**

After a contract had been entered into for the sale of a house but before completion the house was damaged by fire. The house had been insured against fire risk by the vendors. The insurance company, unaware of the contract for sale of the property, paid the vendors for the fire damage. The purchase was completed and the vendors received the full amount of the purchase money. *Held*, the contract of insurance was a contract of indemnity only and, as the vendors were entitled to the full amount of the purchase money, they had sustained no loss and the insurance company was entitled to recover the amount they had paid to the vendors.

Cater v. Essex County Council, [1959] 2 All E.R. 213   **[72]**

The appellant began to use his land as a caravan site in 1954. He applied for planning permission and was refused. In 1956 the planning authority served an enforcement notice under s. 23 (1) of the Town and Country Planning Act 1947 requiring discontinuance of "the use of the said land comprising the said development" and reciting that a material change of use had been carried out without permission under the Act, "the said land being used for the purpose of a caravan site". The appellant relied on the Town and Country Planning General Development Order 1950, art. 3 (1) and Sched. 1, Class IV, para. 2, whereby permission was given for the "use of any land for any purpose on not more than twenty-eight days in total in any calendar year, and the erection and placing of movable structures on the land for the purpose of that use." *Held*, the enforcement notice was a nullity because the permission granted under the General Development Order 1950 was a permission granted under the 1947 Act in relation to the appellant's land when the caravans were first brought on to it and the recital in the enforcement notice was untrue. (See also *Francis v. Yiewsley and West Drayton Urban District Council* and *East Riding County Council v. Park Estate (Bridlington), Ltd.*)

Cato v. Thompson (1882), 9 Q.B.D. 616   **[73]**

T. contracted to sell to C. freehold properties and to make a good marketable title. Investigation of title showed the houses were subject to stringent restrictive covenants which made the title not marketable. T. refused to try to obtain a release of the covenants. C. sought to rescind the contract and recover his deposit. T. showed that C. knew of the covenants at the time of the contract. *Held*, this evidence could not be admitted to modify the terms of the express contract and C. was entitled to recover his deposit.

Catt v. Tourle (1869), 4 Ch. App. 654   **[74]**

The plaintiff, a brewer, sold land to the trustees of a freehold land society who covenanted that the plaintiff, his heirs and assigns, should have exclusive right to supply beer to any public house erected on the land. The plaintiff did not covenant to supply beer. The defendant, also a brewer, a member of the society, acquired part of the land with notice of the covenant and erected thereon a public house which he supplied with his own beer. *Held*, the covenant, although in terms positive, was negative in substance and was enforceable against the purchaser who took with notice. It was not void for uncertainty or want of mutuality or for being in unreasonable restraint of trade. An injunction would be granted to restrain the defendant from acting in contravention of the covenant.

(See also *Esso Petroleum* v. *Harper's Garage (Stourport), Ltd;* but see *Petrofina (Gt. Britain), Ltd.* v. *Martin.*)

Caunce v. Caunce, [1969] 1 All E.R. 722   [75]

A mortgagee, who had no constructive notice of the equitable interest of the mortgagor's wife, had priority over that interest. A house was in the husband's name although the wife had provided part of the purchase money, and, after the husband's bankruptcy, she had paid instalments to a building society. A bank had loaned money on mortgage on the property. *Held*, although both the husband's and wife's accounts were with the same bank, the bank had no duty to ascertain from the wife's account whether she had provided any payments towards the purchase of the property; such enquiry was not one which should have reasonably been made under s. 199 (1) (ii) of the Law of Property Act 1925. Moreover, where a vendor or mortgagor was in possession or occupation of a house, a purchaser or mortgagee was not affected with notice of the equitable interests of any other person resident there whose presence was consistent with the title offered. Therefore the presence of the wife being consistent with the title offered by her husband did not give the bank constructive notice of her equitable interest.

Chaney v. Maclow, [1929] 1 Ch. 461 (Court of Appeal)   [76]

An auctioneer who has knocked down property to the highest bidder at a sale has authority to sign a memorandum of the contract to satisfy s. 40 of the Law of Property Act 1925, during any period within which his signature can reasonably be held to be part of the transaction of sale. The defendant, who had had the property knocked down to him, refused to sign the memorandum on the ground that he had only just noticed that one of the particulars provided that the purchaser would be responsible for road charges. He did not repudiate the contract until a week later. The auctioneer had signed the memorandum on the defendant's behalf two hours after the sale, after leaving the sale room for his office. *Held*, the auctioneer had authority to sign the memorandum and the authority still persisted at the time of signature. (But see *Bell* v. *Balls.*)

Chatsworth Estates Co. v. Fewell (1931), Ch. 244; [1930],   [77]
      All E.R. Rep. 142

In 1897 a predecessor in title of the defendant had purchased a house on an estate, subject to a covenant that it was not to be used for any trade or business without a licence. The plaintiff had permitted erection of schools and an hotel on the estate and had allowed houses to be used as boarding houses, some with licence and some without. The defendant used his property as a boarding house and the plaintiff sought an injunction to restrain such use. *Held*, (i) where the defence was that the covenant should not be enforceable because there was such a change in the character of the area, the defendant must be able to show that there was no value left in the covenant and this the defendant had failed to do; (ii) in considering whether it was equitable to grant the plaintiff relief, the test was whether he had represented to the defendant that he was entitled to do as he was doing with the house. This the plaintiff had not, by his acts or omissions, done and therefore the defendant had persisted in committing a breach of covenant to which he knew the plaintiff objected. The plaintiff was entitled to an injunction although there was no evidence of substantial damage.

Cheshire County Council v. Woodward, [1962] 1 All E.R. 517   [78]

A coal-hopper and a conveyer on wheels were held not to be a structure and therefore not within the definition of "development" for the purpose of the Town and Country Planning Act 1947. It was said there is no one test to determine what physical characteristics constitute development. It depends on all the circumstances and the degree of permanency of the "building, engineering, mining or other operations". To constitute a building as defined by s. 119 (1) of the Act a "structure or erection" must form part of the realty and change the physical character of the land.

Chillingworth v. Esche, [1924] 1 Ch. 97; [1923] All E.R. Rep. 97   **[79]**
    (Court of Appeal)

By a document (referred to in a receipt for the deposit as an "agreement") the plaintiffs "agreed to purchase" land from the defendant "subject to a proper contract to be prepared by the vendor's solicitors". *Held,* in the absence of any further document there was no binding agreement and the plaintiffs were entitled to return of the deposit paid and (*per* Warrington, L. J.) the plaintiffs' solicitors were not agents so as to bind their clients when they agreed the terms of a contract with the defendant's solicitors. (But see *Branca* v. *Cobarro*.)

Chowood's Registered Land, Re, [1933] Ch. 574   **[80]**

Chowood, Ltd. purchased land and were registered as proprietor with absolute title. The land included strips of woodland to which an adjoining owner, Mrs. Lyall, had acquired title by adverse possession, unknown to the company. When the company took action against Mrs. Lyall for trespass, they failed and Mrs. Lyall's title was declared valid. The court ordered rectification of the register under s. 82 (1) of the Land Registration Act 1925, by removal of Mrs. Lyall's land from the title of the company. The company claimed indemnity from the Land Registry's insurance fund but this was refused on the ground that the company had suffered no loss. Mrs. Lyall had had an overriding interest at the time of the company's purchase so that the company took subject to it and was no worse after rectification than before. (But see *Re 139 High Street, Deptford*.)

Church of England Building Society v. Piskor, [1954] 2 All E.R. 85   **[81]**

In September 1946 the mortgagors had contracted to purchase leasehold property and in October were let into possession on payment of part of the purchase money. They immediately sublet various parts of the building to H. and others. On November 25th the lease was assigned to the mortgagors who charged their interest to the building society on the same day. The legal charge described the property as "vested in the mortgagors free of incumbrances". In January, 1947 H. sublet a room to X. on a weekly tenancy. The mortgagees claimed possession of the property including the room occupied by X. and it was agreed that X. was in the same position as H. *vis-a-vis* the mortgagees. *Held,* so soon as the mortgagors took the assignment of the leasehold interest they were the legal owners and the estoppel created by the grant of the subtenancy was fed by the legal interest of the mortgagors and became a legal interest in favour of the subtenants which was binding on the mortgagees. Notwithstanding that the assignment and the charge bore the same date, the assignment must have preceded the charge and, despite the recital in the charge, there was a period of time, no matter how short, when the legal interest of the subtenants was created. A purchase and a mortgage, even though part of the purchase money is provided under the mortgage, are not one transaction.

City Permanent Building Society v. Miller, [1952] 2 All E.R. 621   **[82]**
    (Court of Appeal)

M. agreed orally to grant a tenancy of a flat to Mrs. C. on October 15th, 1950. The next day he signed a document purporting to grant her a tenancy for three years from October 16th, 1950 and "thereafter on a weekly basis" and acknowledged receipt of £228, being rent in advance at 30s. per week. The property was registered land to which M. had no title at that date. On January 4th, 1951 the registered proprietor executed a transfer to M. and on the same day M. charged the property to a building society. The transfer and charge were registered on January 11th and Mrs. C. went into occupation on January 15th. Subsequently the building society sought possession of the premises. *Held,* (i) the document of

October 16th failed to create a lease as the term exceeded three years by at least one week and therefore required to be by deed under s. 52 (1) and (2) (d), s. 53 (1) (a) and s 54 (2) of the Law of Property Act 1925. No legal term had been created and, at the highest, Mrs. C.'s interest was only that of one who has a contract for a lease; (ii) Mrs. C.'s interest was not an overriding interest under s. 70 (1) (k) of the Land Registration Act 1925 which referred to "leases for any term or interest not exceeding 21 years, granted at a rent without taking a fine". This did not include an agreement for a lease as the word "granted" imported the actual creation of a term. The court did not find it necessary to decide whether the payment of rent in advance amounted to a fine. Mrs. C. had, therefore, no interest which took priority to the building society's charge and the building society was entitled to possession.

Clark v. Barnes, [1929] 2 Ch. 368   **[83]**

The plaintiff had purchased plots of land together with a right of way over other plots. Subsequently he purchased the other plots so that, having become the legal owner of the dominant and servient tenements, the right of way became merged. Later he sold the plots which had enjoyed the right of way to the defendant. In the draft conveyance a right of way was inserted for the defendant but this was struck out by the plaintiff's solicitors and the conveyance, as executed, did not contain a right of way. The defendant claimed a right of way as reputed to be enjoyed with the land. *Held*, the conveyance should be rectified to limit the implication of any right of way which might arise under s. 62 of the Law of Property Act 1925 as the evidence showed that the parties had not intended that any such right should pass.

Clark (H) (Doncaster), Ltd. v. Wilkinson, [1965] 1 All E.R. 934   **[84]**
(Court of Appeal)

The defendant's land was sold to the plaintiffs at auction. The defendant's solicitor was present at the auction and signed the contract. The defendant, who had tried to withdraw the property from the auction, claimed that his solicitor had no authority to sign the contract and therefore there was no written agreement for the purpose of s. 40 of the Law of Property Act 1925. The plaintiffs brought an action for specific performance and, at a hearing under R.S.C. Ord. 86, r. 1 for summary judgment, counsel for the defendant admitted that the solicitor had authority to sign the contract. The defendant sought to withdraw that submission. *Held*, an admission by counsel in the course of interlocutory proceedings could be withdrawn unless the circumstances gave rise to estoppel; the plaintiffs in this case had not been prejudiced and leave to defend the action would be given. *Per* DANKWERTS, L. J.: "A solicitor prima facie has no authority to sign a contract of sale and purchase on behalf of his client. He must either have express authority or the circumstances must be such that implied authority can be inferred from them." (But see *Gavaghan* v. *Edwards*.)

Clarke v. Pass, [1952] C.P.L. 420   **[85]**

The defendant agreed to purchase from the plaintiff the lease and goodwill of licensed premises. The contract was subject to the consent of the brewery company to the assignment. The plaintiff was to take all reasonable steps to assign the lease and various licences. Should the purchaser not complete his deposit was to be forfeited. The agreement contained a clause that should the brewery fail to accept the purchaser as a tenant "for any reason whatsoever" the agreement would be void, the deposit would be repaid and no compensation would be payable by either party. The defendant gave the plaintiff an I.O.U. for the deposit. The brewery company refused to accept the defendant as tenant. The defendant did not redeem the I.O.U. The plaintiff claimed damages for breach of contract and that he was entitled to forfeit the deposit. The jury found that, assuming there was an implied term that the purchaser should present himself to the brewery company for interview and refrain from doing anything to prevent the company from accepting him, he was in breach of that implied term but they found that, even if the defendant had complied with such a term, there was no reasonable likelihood that the brewery would have accepted him. Lynskey, J. held that to give business efficacy to the contract, there should be implied a term that the purchaser would co-operate with the vendor to obtain the brewery's consent. But the jury had found that there never was any chance that the brewery would give consent. The clause that the contract was void if the brewery did not consent was final. It was not possible to add to the words "for any reason whatsoever" the words "other than a breach of contract by the purchaser which does not cause the brewery to refuse their consent". *Held*, the contract was null and void and no claim would lie. (See also *Hinderer* v. *Weir*.)

Clarke v. Ramuz, [1891] 2 Q.B. 456; [1891–4] All E.R. Rep. 502   **[86]**
    (Court of Appeal)

A vendor of land remained in possession after a contract of sale had been entered into. The contract provided for completion on August 12th, 1889 but the conveyance was not executed until October 21st. In September a stranger removed quantities of soil without the knowledge or authority of the vendor or purchaser. *Held*, where a vendor of land remains in possession until completion he is in the position of a trustee for the purchaser to use reasonable care to keep the land in a reasonable state of preservation. The purchaser's action was maintainable notwithstanding that the conveyance had been executed as, not knowing of the position, the purchaser had not thereby waived his rights.

Cleveland Petroleum Co., Ltd. v. Dartstone, Ltd., [1969]   **[87]**
    1 All E.R. 201 (Court of Appeal)

The owner of a freehold garage and adjoining land leased the garage and covenanted that the adjoining land should not be used as a petrol filling station without the lessee's consent and subject to a condition that only motor fuels purchased from the lessee should be sold. On July 1st, 1960 the lessee subdemised the land for twenty-five years with covenants by the underlessee to carry on the business of a petrol filling station and to sell only motor fuels provided by the underlessor. Ultimately the underlease and the freehold interest in the garage and adjoining land became vested in Dartstone, Ltd. who took with notice of the covenants. *Held*, that although the burden of the covenant was annexed to the adjoining land, it was for the benefit of the demised land and was a covenant between lessor and lessee. It was therefore incapable of registration as a Land Charge Class D (ii) under the Land Charges Act 1925 and was binding on the company which took with notice. The covenant was not void as being in unreasonable restraint of trade and an injunction would be granted to enforce it. If a lessee takes a lease of land on terms that he is to tie his business to a particular supplier and is let into possession on those terms he has given up no previous rights and the tie is good. It is otherwise if he is already in possession when the tie is entered into.

Coleshill and District Investment Co., Ltd. v. Minister of   **[88]**
    Housing and Local Government, [1969] 2 All E.R. 525 (House of Lords)

Removal of protective embankments outside blast walls surrounding ammunition magazines was held to be carrying out of building, engineering or other operations within s. 12 (1) of the Town and Country Planning Act 1962 and therefore constituted development. It was held that removal of the blast walls would also constitute development requiring planning permission. These operations did not fall within the exemption of s. 12 (2) (a) of the Act as, although they were alterations to a building, they would materially affect the external appearance of the building. *Quaere* whether demolition of a building, as distinct from a demolition of part in such a manner as to alter its external appearance, would be development. *Held*, on the true construction of s. 12 (1), it depended on the particular facts as to whether demolition or removal operations constituted development. Since the Minister, after consideration of the facts, had decided that there was development, his decision disclosed no error of law.

Collard's Will Trusts, Re, Lloyds Bank, Ltd. v. Rees,   **[89]**
    [1961] 1 All E.R. 821

By his will a testator provided that the income of one moiety of his residuary estate should be held on protective trusts for his daughter for life, and subject thereto, on trust as to both capital and income for such of her children as should be living at the testator's death or be born thereafter and who should attain 21 or previously marry. At the date of the summons the daughter was past the age of child-bearing and had one son aged 21. A farm had been appropriated to the daughter's share of settled residue and her son carried on the farm business. The will provided that the power of advancement of capital under s. 32 of the Trustee Act 1925 should apply to the trusts but not for the purpose of setting up a beneficiary in business. It was asked whether trustees could convey the farm to the son with a view to avoidance of estate duty on the death of the testator's daughter. *Held,* (i) as the trustees could properly advance cash to the son and sell him the farm for that amount of cash, so they could exercise the power of advancement by conveying the farm to the son for its market value, treating the conveyance as an advancement of the amount of that value; (ii) the purpose of avoiding estate duty was not a purpose connected with the business of farming, therefore the trustees' power of advancement was not excluded by the words in the will.

Cook v. Cook, [1962] 2 All E.R. 811 (Court of Appeal)   **[90]**

A husband and wife purchased a freehold house as the matrimonial home, the conveyance being to the husband alone. The difference between the mortgage advance and the purchase price was contributed in cash by the husband and wife. Hence the husband held the house on a resulting trust in the wife's favour in respect of her contribution. *Held,* the conveyance to the husband constituted a post-nuptial settlement which fell within s. 25 of the Matrimonial Causes Act 1950, notwithstanding that the wife's beneficial interest in the proceeds of sale arose under a resulting trust.

Cook v. Wheeler, [1952] C.P.L. 537   **[91]**

In a conveyance of a plot of land to the plaintiff the defendant covenanted to make up a rectangle of land fronting the plaintiff's plot and extending to the centre of the road to the standard of a domestic road and to the satisfaction of the local authority. A hundred other plots were conveyed with similar covenants. The road was not taken over by the local authority. The plaintiff claimed that the defendant had not complied with the covenant and asked for specific performance or damages. The defendant denied non-compliance with the covenant. VAISEY, J. said that the local authority would never approve isolated plots of the road which had been made up as required by the covenant. The court would not order something which was useless so there would be no order for specific performance or damages.

Cooper v. Critchley, [1955] 1 All E.R. 520 (Court of Appeal)   **[92]**

The parties were joint tenants in fee simple of certain business premises which they held on trust for sale and on trust to hold the net proceeds of sale and the net rents and profits until sale for themselves as tenants in common in equal shares. They granted a lease of the premises to Sterlina Furnishers, Ltd., a company in which each of them held one-half of the total issued share capital and, with a view to severing their business association, certain negotiations took place whereby the plaintiff offered the defendant his interest in the property and his interest in the company, *i.e.,* his holding of shares. *Held,* even if a binding contract had been concluded (which, on the facts, it had not), a contract for the sale by the plaintiff of his interests to his co-owner would have been a contract for the sale of an "interest in land" within s. 40 (1) of the Law of Property Act 1925, and, as there was no sufficient memorandum in writing of the alleged contract, that section would have afforded the defendant a good defence. (See *Irani Finance* v. *Singh;* but see *Re Rayleigh Weir Stadium.*)

Cooper v. Phibbs (1876), L.R. 2 H.L. 149 (House of Lords)   **[93]**

The appellant sought to be relieved from an agreement whereby he contracted to take from the respondent a three-year lease of a salmon fishery. At the time of making the agreement the appellant believed that the fishery belonged to the respondent but it afterwards appeared that the fishery was the property of the appellant himself. *Held*, the appellant was entitled to have the agreement for the lease set aside subject to the respondent having a lien on the property in respect of money spent on purchasing certain fishing rights and improving the fishery. (But see *Bligh* v. *Martin.*)

Cordell v. Second Clanfield Properties, Ltd., [1968] 3 All E.R. 746   **[94]**

By a conveyance of March 10th, 1966 the plaintiff conveyed land to the defendant company, who were developers. The conveyance contained a provision "excepting and reserving to the vendor for the benefit of his adjoining land coloured grey on the plan a right of way over any of the estate roads constructed on the property hereinbefore (described) to obtain access to such adjoining land and also a right of drainage through any sewers or drains constructed thereon". The plaintiff claimed he was entitled to a right of way 28 feet wide over the defendants' land and asked for a mandatory injunction to pull down a building erected on the defendants' land and an interlocutory injunction to restrain further building. *Held*, since under s. 65 (1) of the Law of Property Act 1925 the reservation of an easement no longer requires execution by the purchaser or grantee and operates at law without any regrant by him, the rule that an exception out of a grant is to be construed against the grantor should be applied to reservations so that they will be construed against the grantor and in favour of the purchaser or grantee. Even if this were not so, the plaintiff's right of access over roads on the estate would not impose an obligation on the defendants to construct suitable roads for this purpose or to provide land for the plaintiff to do so. (But see *Bulstrode* v. *Lambert.*)

Cottrill v. Steyning and Littlehampton Building Society,   **[95]**
    [1966] 2 All E.R. 295

The defendants had granted to the plaintiff an option to purchase freehold land. The option included a term that the plaintiff should apply for planning permission and modification of a tree preservation order. The plaintiff applied for planning permission and modification of the tree preservation order and then went abroad for a month. The defendants wrongly treated the plaintiff's absence as repudiation and in breach of contract they sold the land to another. They knew that the plaintiff planned to develop the land for profit and had applied for planning permission. *Held*, damages should be assessed by reference to the profit the plaintiff had lost by not being able to develop the land and should not be restricted to the difference between the market price and the contract price. (But see *Diamond* v. *Campbell-Jones.*)

Courcier and Harold's Contract, Re, [1923] 1 Ch. 565   **[96]**

A freehold house was sold subject to a special condition of sale which provided that the land should not be used "for carrying on any trade or business nor as a school, hospital, nursing home, public workshop or otherwise than as a private dwellinghouse but not precluding the practice of a profession there". By mistake words had been omitted and instead of "public workshop" the restrictions should have read "or public institution or charity nor for holding public meetings nor for public worship". The general conditions provided that "If any error, mis-statement or omission shall be discovered in the particulars, the same shall not annul the sale, nor shall any compensation be allowed by the vendor in respect thereof". The purchaser objected that the restrictions had not been sufficiently disclosed. *Held*, (i) the restrictions had been sufficiently disclosed and (ii) even if they had not, the error fell within the general condition and the purchaser was not entitled to require the release of the omitted restrictions.

Cox and Neve's Contract, Re, [1891] 2 Ch. 109   [97]

Property described as "freehold" was sold by auction. The conditions of sale provided that the title should commence with a mortgage dated July 29th, 1852 and that the purchaser should, within fourteen days of delivery of the abstract, send all requisitions and objections as to the title, and subject thereto, the title should be deemed to be accepted. The purchaser's solicitor sent the requisitions within fourteen days, but not being satisfied with the replies, later sent further requisitions. By inquiries of a third party in respect of another matter, the purchaser discovered a restrictive covenant in a deed prior to the root of title but did not raise objection until the issue of a vendor and purchaser summons. *Held*, the purchaser having acquired notice of the covenant he would be bound by it; it formed a valid objection to the title and he was not too late in raising the objection and was entitled to rescind. *Semble* as the purchaser had agreed to accept less than forty years' title (under the Vendor and Purchaser Act 1874), he would, even had he not discovered the covenant, have had constructive notice and would have been bound by it.

Craddock Bros., Ltd. v. Hunt, [1923] 2 Ch. 136; [1923] All E.R. Rep.   [98]
394 (Court of Appeal)

If a written memorandum of an oral contract for the sale of land omits a term agreed upon, owing to the mistake of both parties, the court may, in one action, rectify the memorandum and grant specific performance of the agreement. Rectification can be granted of a written agreement on parol evidence of mutual mistake. When rectified the written agreement is to be read as though thus originally drawn and it is of that document of which specific performance will be decreed. *Held*, where a purchaser had acquired a legal estate in land under a conveyance which contained an error and with knowledge that another had a better claim to part of the land, he could not insist on his position at law but in equity would be treated as a trustee for the person rightfully entitled and, if necessary, ordered to convey to him.

Cresswell (Trustees of the Cobbett Settlement) v. Proctor   [99]
(Trustees of the Convent of the Holy Family), [1968] 2 All E.R. 682
(Court of Appeal)

An unsuccessful application by a covenantor to the Lands Tribunal under s. 84 (1) (c) of the Law of Property Act 1925 to discharge a restrictive covenant because circumstances had changed in the two years since the covenant was created. The Lands Tribunal held that, although the covenantor could establish that the persons entitled to the benefit of the covenant would not be injured by its discharge, the Lands Tribunal could refuse the discharge as the covenant had been entered into by the applicant himself only two years previously. The Court of Appeal held it was a proper exercise of the Lands Tribunal's discretion to take this fact into account.

Crisp from the Fens, Ltd. v. Rutland County Council   [100]
[1950] W.N. 72; 1 P & C.R. 48 (Court of Appeal)

A company obtained planning permission to change the use of premises under sections 12 and 14 of the Town and Country Planning Act 1947 by carrying on there the manufacture of potato crisps, subject to the condition that use of the buildings should be confined "to the manufacture of potato crisps or any use within Class III of the Town and Country Planning (Use Classes) Order 1948". The reason given was to ensure that the building should not be used for general industrial purposes which would be likely to be detrimental to the amenities of the locality. An enforcement notice was served on the ground that the condition had been broken, in that the company had caused detriment to amenities by noise, smell and smoke "contrary to the definition of use of a light industrial building as defined by Class III" of the Order of 1948, and discontinuance was required of the use of the buildings for the manufacture of potato crisps or any use which did not comply with the "conditions" in the permission. The company appealed to the justices under s. 23 (4) of the Act. The justices found that smell, noise and smoke were emitted and dismissed the complaint. The company appealed, contending that, as the wording of the permission was in the alternative *i.e.* "manufacture of potato crisps or any use within Class III", the manufacture did not infringe the condition, even if it was in violation of Class III. *Held,* the proper construction of the permission was that reference to Class III governed also the manufacture of potato crisps, so that permission to manufacture potato crisps was given subject to the manufacture being within Class III, with consequential preservation of amenities. *Per* SINGLETON, L. J.: The principle of *contra proferentes* did not apply to the construction of a permit. The local authority were not granting an easement and it would be wrong to construe the permit against them in view of the fact that they had a duty to the general public to preserve amenities. The decision of the Divisional Court was affirmed.

Cumberland Consolidated Holdings, Ltd. v. Ireland,   [101]
[1946] 1 All E.R. 284 (Court of Appeal)

In 1945 the respondents entered into a contract to purchase freehold property, including a warehouse. The contract provided for vacant possession on completion and included a term that the purchaser bought with full knowledge of the condition of the property and took it as it was. The warehouse had been disused for some time and damaged by fire. Underneath the property were cellars filled with rubbish, including bags of hardened cement. During negotiations the appellant vendor undertook to remove the rubbish but in fact the greater part was not removed. The respondents had the rubbish removed and successfully claimed in the county court for the cost. On appeal it was claimed that (i) the respondents could not object to the rubbish on the premises as the contract provided that they took the property in the condition in which it was sold and (ii) "vacant possession" meant that the property was transferred on completion free from right of possession by the vendor or any third person and the presence of chattels abandoned on the premises was not evidence of any such claim of right. *Held,* (i) the rubbish formed no part of the property sold and its presence was not covered by the state and condition of the property which related to the physical condition of the property itself; (ii) subject to the rule *de mininis* a vendor who left property of his own on completion could not be held to give vacant possession since he was claiming a right to use the premises as a deposit for his goods which was inconsistent with the purchaser's right on completion to undisturbed enjoyment; (iii) the right to unimpeded physical enjoyment was comprised in vacant possession and the existence of a physical impediment which interfered with enjoyment of a substantial part of the property stood in the same position as an impediment caused by the presence of a trespasser. The appellant had, therefore, failed to deliver vacant possession; (iv) pending completion the appellant was a quasi-trustee and by abandonment of the rubbish had committed a breach of trust for which an action would have lain for damages. (See also *Hissett* v. *Reading Roofing Co., Ltd.*)

Cumberland Court (Brighton) Ltd., v. Taylor, [1963] 2 All E.R. 536   [102]

The title to freehold land showed a legal charge made by a predecessor in title of the vendors. A receipt by the chargee had been endorsed on the charge but was dated two days later than a conveyance by the mortgagor which recited that the land was conveyed free from encumbrances. The purchaser contended that the effect of s. 115 of the Law of Property Act 1925 was that repayment of the charge by the mortgagor after the conveyance kept the charge alive and operated as a transfer. Therefore the purchaser maintained that he did not have to complete the purchase as there was an encumbrance on the title. The vendor served a notice to complete within twenty-eight days under the terms of the contract. The purchaser did not complete but registered the contract as a Land Charge Class C (iv). *Held*, even though under s. 115 of the Law of Property Act 1925 the receipt acted as a transfer, the doctrine of feeding the estoppel would apply and the mortgagee would be unable to exercise any legal rights he might have had under the charge; accordingly the objection did not go to the root of the title. Time having become of the essence of the contract under the notice to complete, or twenty-eight days' notice being reasonable in the circumstances, it was unnecessary to decide whether equity would have extended the period. The vendors, having been ready, able and willing to complete on the date in the notice, the purchaser was in default and the vendors were entitled to have the registration of the land charge vacated. (But see *Re Barr's Contract*.)

Curtis v. French, [1929] 1 Ch. 253   [103]

The plaintiff purchased a freehold house at an auction subject to the National Conditions of Sale, Clause 10 of which provided that no error, misstatement or omission in the particulars should annul the sale, nor should any compensation be allowed in respect thereof. The particulars stated the property was let to a tenant who was in occupation on sufferance and that vacant possession would be given on completion. The premises were in fact occupied by a sub-tenant who claimed to be a statutory tenant and refused to vacate. The purchaser refused to complete without vacant possession and sued the vendor for damages for breach of contract. *Held*, there was no breach of contract, the misstatement in the particulars falling within Clause 10, in respect of which the purchaser could not claim compensation. The purchaser was, however, entitled to rescind the contract and to have his deposit repaid with interest. (See also *Courcier and Harrold's Contract, Re*.)

Curtis Moffatt, Ltd. v. Wheeler, [1929] 2 Ch. 224   [104]

The defendant had an underlease containing a covenant not to assign without the underlessor's consent, such consent not to be withheld in the case of a responsible assignee. The defendant agreed to sell the underlease to the plaintiff company. The underlessor refused licence to assign to the company but stated that a licence would be granted for assignment in favour of a specified nominee. The defendant did not apply for the licence but returned the plaintiff's deposit. The company brought an action for specific performance. *Held*, the defendant could not be compelled to complete in favour of the specified nominee.

Dances Way, West Town, Hayling Island, Re. See Freehold Land in Dances Way, West Town Hayling Island, Hants, Re.

Daniel, Re, Daniel v. Vassall, [1917] 2 Ch. 405;   [105]
[1916–17] All E.R. Rep 654

The vendor, who had contracted to sell property which was subject to a mortgage, died before the title had been accepted by the purchaser. After the vendor's death, the purchaser accepted the title but the mortgagees refused to release the property and the executors were unable to pay off the mortgage as the vendor's estate was insolvent. *Held*, the vendor's incapacity to complete did not arise from a defect in title but from inability to convey. Hence the rule in *Bain* v. *Fothergill* did not apply and the purchaser was entitled to damages for the loss of his bargain.

Daniels v. Trefusis, [1914] 1 Ch. 788 [106]

There was an oral agreement for the sale of land and the vendor, at the request of the purchaser, gave notice to two tenants who, in consequence, gave up possession. The purchaser then contended that there was no sufficient written evidence under s. 4 of the Statute of Frauds and that the contract was not enforceable against him by action. *Held*, (i) The Statute may be satisfied by a note or memorandum signed by an agent providing the agent had authority to sign the particular note or memorandum; the fact that the agent is not authorised or intended to bind his principal is immaterial; (ii) giving notice to quit to weekly tenants to give up possession is an act of part performance which is sufficient to take the case out of the Statute. Hence in this case the vendor was entitled to specific performance of the contract even though there might be insufficient writing to satisfy the Statute. (See also *Broughton* v. *Snook*.)

Davies v. Sweet, [1962] 1 All E.R. 92 (Court of Appeal) [107]

The memorandum of an agreement for the sale of land was a receipt for the deposit given on the headed paper of estate agents in the following terms: "Received from Mrs. Iris Davies of 22 Mount Pleasant Street, Dowlais, a deposit of £5 for land on which Evans Row houses previously stood (bottom of New Road, Penydarren) sold at £75 subject to planning permission for petrol (station) to be built. F. A. Phillips & Son." Planning permission was obtained. *Held*, there was a sufficient memorandum for the purpose of s. 40 of the Law of Property Act 1925. The description of the land was adequate. It did not matter that the vendor was not named nor that the estate agents were not stated to be agents for some principal. Section 40 required that the memorandum should be signed by the party to be charged or his duly authorised agent. This memorandum being sufficient, specific performance of the contract would be ordered.

Davstone Estates, Ltd's Leases, Re. Manprop, Ltd. v. O'Dell, [108]
[1969] 2 All E.R. 849

The lease of a flat contained a covenant by the lessee to pay £15 per annum towards the lessors' expenses incurred in repairs and maintenance of the building, in performance of the lessors' covenants set out in Clause 3 of the lease, but if 1/10th of the expenses reasonably and properly incurred exceeded £15 the lessee was to pay the excess. The amount of the lessors' expenditure was to be certified by the lessors' surveyor "whose certificate shall be final and not subject to any challenge in any manner whatsoever". *Held*, the surveyor's certificate was not conclusive as to whether works done fell within the covenant; this was a question of law, being one of construction of the clause in the lease. On the wording of the clause this did not fall within the decision of the surveyor's certificate which was limited to the amount of the expenses. Had the clause been worded so as to make the surveyor's certificate conclusive on a matter of law, the clause would have been void as against public policy by ousting the jurisdiction of the courts and the objectionable part would not have been severable.

Day v. Singleton, [1899] 2 Ch. 320 [109]

The rule in *Bain* v. *Fothergill* is available only to an honest and reasonable vendor, so that where an assignment of a lease could not take place because no attempt had been made to obtain the lessor's necessary consent, the disappointed purchaser was entitled to damages for the loss of his bargain. (See also *Re Daniel*.)

Des Reaux and Setchfield's Contract, Re, [1926] Ch. 178 [110]

The respondent contracted to sell a house to the appellant under a contract which contained a condition that "If the purchaser shall insist on any objection or requisition which the vendor shall be unable, or on the ground of expense, unwilling to remove or comply with, the vendor may by notice in writing to be given to the purchaser, and notwithstanding any intermediate negotiation or litigation, rescind the contract . . . " The legal estate was not vested in the vendor but the vendor had hoped to make good the title with the concurrence of the trustee. The appellant required that the respondent should make application to the court to perfect the title. The respondent refused on the ground of expense and purported to rescind the contract. *Held*, the appellant was not entitled to rescind under the clause in the contract as he had acted carelessly and recklessly. He was bound to make the necessary application to the court.

Devotwill Investments Ltd. v. Margate Corporation, [111]
[1969] 2 All E.R. 97 (Court of Appeal)

Owners of land allocated as primarily for residential use applied for planning permission, it being accepted that if the whole of the land were developed twenty houses could be erected. Planning permission was refused on the ground that part of the land would be required for construction of a bypass road. A purchase notice was served under s. 129 of the Town and Country Planning Act 1962 and was accepted. The authority offered £8,200 compensation; the company claimed £16,000. The matter was referred to the Lands Tribunal which awarded £13,500. The authority appealed to the Court of Appeal who upheld the Land Tribunal's award, which was based on the assumption that if the land were not acquired and the proposed road were constructed elsewhere, the claimants' land would be capable of accommodating twenty houses. By virtue of s. 16 (7) of the Land Compensation Act 1961 the Lands Tribunal were entitled to take into account any planning permission which might reasonably be expected to be granted if no part of the owner's land were proposed to be acquired. [Leave to appeal to the House of Lords granted.]

Dewer v. Mintoft, [1912] 2 K.B. 373 [112]

A purchaser entered into a contract for the purchase of land which contained a clause forfeiting the deposit if the purchaser failed to complete. The purchaser paid no deposit and failed to complete. *Held*, the vendor was entitled to recover the amount which should have been paid by the purchaser by way of deposit, not merely the actual damage suffered by the vendor. (But see *Lowe* v. *Hope*.)

Diamond v. Campbell-Jones, [1960] 1 All E.R. 583. (1961) Ch. 22 [113]

The measure of damages on wrongful repudiation of a contract for the sale of land by the vendor was held to be the difference between the contract price and the market value at the date of the breach. The purchaser could not claim for loss of the profit he could have made by developing the property. Special circumstances were necessary to justify imputing to the vendor knowledge that the purchaser was likely to develop for profit; it was insufficient that the vendor knew the property was ripe for development or that it was the purchaser's business to convert property; he might have sold it in an unconverted state. (But see *Cottrill* v. *Steyning and Littlehampton Building Society*.)

Dibble (H. E.), Ltd. (trading as Mill Lane Nurseries) [114]
v. Moore (West, Third Party), [1969] 3 All E.R. 1465 (Court of Appeal)

A company conveyed land, used as a market garden, to W. W. granted to the company a licence to remain in occupation rent free subject to six months' notice. The holder of a debenture issued by the company appointed a receiver who purported to sell to D. two Dutch greenhouses which stood on their own weight on concrete dollies. W. claimed the greenhouses were part of the realty and should not be removed. *Held*, (reversing the county court decision) that the greenhouses were not included in the conveyance of the land by virtue of s. 62 (1) of the Law of Property Act 1925. They were not "erections" within the general words implied in a conveyance by that Section as they were not fixtures. The conveyance did not pass chattels so that ownership had not passed to W.

Dillwyn v. Llewellyn (1862), 4 De G.F. & J. 517   **[115]**

A testator owned land on which he allowed his second son to build himself a house, although the testator's will devised the land to the testator's wife. A memorandum was signed by the testator and his eldest son to the effect that, with the consent of the wife, the testator gave the land to the second son "for the purpose of furnishing himself with a dwellinghouse". *Held*, the second son was entitled to a conveyance of the fee simple. The expenditure of money in building the house constituted valuable consideration so that an enforceable contract arose between the testator and his second son. (See also *Inwards v. Baker*.)

Draper's Conveyance, Re, [1967] 3 All E.R. 853; [1968] 2 W.L.R. 166   **[116]**

A husband and wife held the matrimonial home on a joint tenancy. *Held*, the commencement of proceedings by the wife under s. 17 of the Married Women's Property Act 1882 in relation to the house severed the equitable joint tenancy, so that on the husband's death after the issue of the summons, the *jus accrescendi* did not apply to give to the wife the husband's share in the property.

Driver v. Broad, [1893] 1 Q.B. 744   **[117]**

It was held that an interest in land includes a mortgage or charge on land, whether specific or floating. Debentures issued by a company charged all its undertaking and property, whatsoever and wheresoever. The company owned leasehold land. *Held*, a contract for the sale of the debentures was a contract for the sale of land within s. 4 of the Statute of Frauds.

D'Silva v. Lister House Development Ltd., [1970] 1 All E.R. 858   **[118]**

The defendant company had covenanted with the headlessor that any sub-letting of property in Harley Street was to be subject to the licence of the head-lessor granted personally to the professional tenant. The defendant company inadvertently allowed the plaintiff, a doctor, into possession of a suite of rooms and had taken a quarter's rent in advance without obtaining the licence. *Held*, the plaintiff had a periodic tenancy within the Landlord and Tenant Act 1954, being "a tenant by agreement . . . for an underlease" within the definition of s. 69 (1) of the Act. It was also held that an effective lease had come into existence as both the lease and the counterpart had been executed and, although the lease was not sent to the plaintiff, there was a deed binding upon the parties under s. 74 of the Law of Property Act 1925. (See also *Beesly v. Hallwood Estates, Ltd.*)

Duce and Boots Cash Chemists (Southern), Ltd.'s Contract, Re,   **[119]**
      [1937] 3 All E.R. 788

A testator appointed his son executor and gave him freehold property on trust to permit the testator's daughter "to personally use and occupy" the same free of rent, rates and taxes, during her lifetime or spinsterhood and charged the property with payment of an annuity to the daughter. The son proved the will and assented to himself as beneficial owner. The daughter released the property from the charge for the annuity but there was no mention in the release of her right to occupy the property as beneficial owner. On a later sale it was contended that by reason of s. 36 (7) of the Administration of Estates Act 1925 the assent was binding on a future purchaser who must assume that the son was beneficially entitled to the property. *Held*, the words in s. 36 (7) "sufficient evidence" do not mean "conclusive evidence" but only that the assent is sufficient evidence until, on a proper investigation of title, facts come to the purchaser's knowledge which indicate the contrary. In this case the assent contained a recital of the daughter's interest which was inconsistent with the vesting of the property in the son as beneficial owner and showed the property to be settled land, so that the purchaser had notice of the error and was not protected by s. 36 (7).

Du Sautoy v. Symes, [1967] 1 All E.R. 25   **[120]**

A farm was sold by a vendor, D. B., to the second to fifth defendants with an option for the vendor to repurchase within twenty-one years on giving one month's notice and if the purchasers wished to sell they must first offer the property to D. B. who was to notify them within one month if he wished to purchase. D. B. registered the option as an estate contract under the Land Charges Act 1925 against the names of the purchasers, describing the land as "Ordnance Survey 174" in Tillingham, Essex. The conveyance described the land as "Reddings Farm" but did not refer to the option. D. B. sold adjoining property to the plaintiff and assigned to him separately the benefit of the option. Notice of the assignment was given to the second to fifth defendants. In 1962 the latter proposed to sell to the first defendant the land they had purchased from D. B. and also two fields, Nos. 87 and 118 in the adjoining parish of Asheldham. Enquiry was made of the plaintiff as to whether he wished to exercise his right to purchase but he did not reply. The first defendant searched against the names of the second to fifth defendants in the Land Charges Register describing the land as "O.S. Field Nos. 87 and 118, Asheldham and Reddings Farm, Tillingham", and obtained a clear certificate of search. He completed his purchase. The plaintiff, out of time, served notice to exercise his option to purchase. He then claimed specific performance against the first defendant and damages against the second to fifth defendants. *Held,* (i) there were two rights, option and pre-emption and the personal liability of the second to fifth defendants remained after parting with the land; (ii) the first defendant was not protected by s. 17 (3) of the Land Charges Act 1925 unless application for a search gave no scope for misunderstanding; this application did not and therefore the plaintiff was not debarred from relief against the first defendant. (*Stock* v. *Wanstead and South Woodford Corporation,* [1962] 2 Q.B. 479 applied.); (iii) despite his delay the plaintiff was entitled to specific performance but he must choose his remedy and if he chose specific performance against the first defendant he could not have damages against the others.

Eagon v. Dent, [1965] 3 All E.R. 334   **[121]**

Property was sold by a contract subject to the National Conditions of Sale 17th Edition and to a tenancy agreement which contained an option to renew. The tenant, having failed to register the option as an estate contract, could not enforce it against the purchaser. The tenant successfully claimed damages from the vendor who was the grantor of the option. *Held,* the vendor was entitled to indemnity from the purchaser under Condition 18 (3) of the National Conditions, *viz.* "The purchaser shall keep the vendor indemnified against all claims by the tenant for compensation or otherwise, except in respect of a tenancy which expires or is determined on or before the completion date or in respect of an obligation which ought to have been discharged before the date of the contract."

E. & G. C. Ltd. v. Bate (1935), 79 L.J. 203   **[122]**

By a deed of 1909 B. conveyed land to S. and covenanted that when required by S. his heirs and assigns and provided that half of a new road had been made, he would construct the other half. Both parties' land abutted on the proposed road. The plaintiffs were assignees of the land of S. and the benefit of the covenant. The defendant was a devisee under B. The plaintiffs claimed damages for breach of the covenant to construct the road. *Held,* the burden of a positive covenant does not run at law and the claim failed. (See *Austerbery* v. *Oldham Corporation.*)

East Barnet Urban District Council v. British Transport   **[123]**
    Commission, [1961] 3 All E.R. 878; [1962] 2 Q.B. 484

Where in law no planning permission is necessary for development because permission was already given by Art. 3 (1) Sched. 1 Class XVIII A of the Town and Country Planning General Development Orders 1948 and 1950 (movement of traffic by rail carried out by railway undertakers or their lessees in, on, over or under the operational land), the fact that further permission had been asked for and given subject to a condition did not prejudice the applicants.

East Riding County Council v. Park Estate (Bridlington), [124]
     [1957] A.C. 223; [1956] 2 All E.R. 669 (House of Lords)

Land had been used for a holiday camp since 1934. In 1951 an enforcement notice was served alleging that development was "in contravention of planning control" and requiring that the land be used only for agricultural purposes. The notice referred to s. 23 of the Town and Country Planning Act 1947 relating to development since July 1st, 1948, but not to s. 75 relating to development prior to that date. *Held*, the enforcement notice should be quashed as, on its true construction, it alleged breach of planning control by development since 1948 but the development, having been prior to the date when the 1947 Act came into effect no planning permission was required. The enforcement notice was invalid because it did not allege that the development contravened previous planning control *i.e.* prior to July, 1948, nor did it specify the nature of the alleged contravention.

Eastwood v. Ashton, [1915] A.C. 900 (House of Lords) [125]

The vendor conveyed land, as beneficial owner, to the purchaser. The parcels clause in the conveyance stated "the premises are more particularly described in the plan endorsed on these presents and are delineated and coloured red in such plan". The plan showed to be included a small strip of land which had formerly formed part of the property but to which, at the time of the conveyance, an adverse title had been acquired by adjoining landowners. *Held*, the description by reference to the plan prevailed and the failure of the vendor to prevent acquisition of adverse title was a breach of the covenant for good right to convey implied by s. 7 (1) (A) of the Conveyancing Act 1881 where the vendor conveys as beneficial owner.

Eccles v. Bryant, [1947] 2 All E.R. 865 (Court of Appeal) [126]

The parties agreed to the sale and purchase of a house, subject to contract, and the vendors' solicitors wrote to the purchaser's solicitors: "Our clients have now signed their part of the contract herein and we are ready to exchange." The purchaser's solicitors sent their client's part of the contract, duly signed, to the vendor's solicitors but the vendors changed their minds and did not send their part in exchange. *Held*, in transactions conducted in this way (*i.e.*, by the customary method of exchanging the two parts of the contract), until such exchange took place, notwithstanding that both parts were signed, there was no contract. (And see *King* v. *O'Shea* and *Sim* v. *Griffiths*; but see *Property and Bloodstock, Ltd.* v. *Emerton*.)

Ecclesiastical Commissioners for England's Conveyance, Re, [127]
     [1936] Ch. 430; [1934] All E.R. Rep. 118

By a conveyance of 1887 a freehold house and land were conveyed by the Ecclesiastical Commissioners to G who covenanted for himself and his assigns and to the intent to bind all future owners and tenants of the land or of any part, and so that the obligations should run with the land and every part, with the Commissioners and their successors, and also as a separate covenant with their assigns, owners for the time being of lands adjacent or adjoining, to observe certain restrictive covenants. *Held*, the restrictive covenants might be enforced if they were expressed to be for the benefit of any particular parcel of land clearly indentified. Land mentioned in the deed was land "adjacent to" the land conveyed, which meant land lying near but not in actual contact with the land conveyed and under s. 56 (1) of the Law of Property Act 1925 the owners of such adjacent land could sue on the covenants although the original covenantees, under whom they derived title, were not parties to the conveyance.

Elliot v. Pierson, [1948] 1 All E.R. 939   **[128]**

E. was entitled to the leasehold interest in a roadhouse and its furniture and fittings, the freehold being vested in a company in which E. had the controlling interest. He contracted in his own name to sell the property, together with the good will of the business and the assets, "lock, stock and barrel". The purchaser objected that the title to the land was in the company, with which he had not contracted. *Held*, E. was entitled to specific performance as, having the controlling interest in the company, he was able to compel the company to convey. The words "lock, stock and barrel" did not extend to articles which were not assets of, or devoted to the purposes of the business.

Elliston v. Reacher, [1908] 2 Ch. 665 (affirming [1908] 2 Ch. 374)   **[129]**

Where restrictive covenants are taken from purchasers on sale of plots of land under a "scheme of development" the covenants are mutually enforceable between the purchasers. The essentials of such a scheme were explained by PARKER, J. as (i) the plaintiffs and defendants should derive title under a common vendor; (ii) before selling the land to which the plaintiffs and defendants are respectively entitled, the vendor should have laid out his estate, or a defined portion thereof, including the plaintiffs' and defendants' land, for sale in lots subject to restrictions intended to be imposed on all the lots and consistent only with some general scheme of development; (iii) these restrictions should be intended by the vendors to be, and should be, for the benefit of all the lots sold; (iv) both plaintiffs and defendants, or their predecessors in title, should have purchased their lots from the vendor upon the footing that the restrictions subject to which the purchases were made were to enure for the benefit of the purchasers of other lots included in the general scheme. (See also *Reid* v. *Bickerstaff*.)

Engall's Agreement, Re, [1953] 2 All E.R. 503   **[130]**

Vendors contracted to sell land to the purchaser, completion to be on September 30th, 1952. The purchaser failed to submit the draft conveyance in the time provided by the contract. On October 21st, 1952 the vendors served notice to complete by November 5th. On October 29th the draft conveyance was submitted On November 4th the purchaser registered a Land Charge Class C (iv). Completion did not take place on November 5th and the vendors purported to forfeit the deposit under the terms of the contract. The purchaser refused to withdraw the registration of the Land Charge and the vendors applied under s. 10 (8) of the Land Charges Act 1925 for its removal. *Held*, the application was misconceived, being an attempt to use the machinery of the Land Charges Act to obtain adjudication on the existence or non-existence of a contract.

England v. Public Trustee (1967), 205 Estates Gazette 651; 112   **[131]**
Sol. Jo. 71 (Court of Appeal)

The will of a testatrix, who died in 1918, appointed her husband executor and the Public Trustee her trustee. She gave twelve cottages to her sister, Mrs. R., for life and after her death upon trust to sell and divide the proceeds between six nieces. The testatrix's husband died in 1929, having executed a vesting assent in favour of Mrs. R. In 1955 Mrs. R. decided to sell the cottages and gave notice to the Public Trustee, who raised no objection. The cottages, which were all subject to protected tenancies, sold at auction for £2,750, part of which money was used to discharge a mortgage. Mrs. R. died in 1964 and the beneficiaries then became aware of their rights. One of them claimed against the Public Trustee for negligence and breach of trust in relation to the sale. *Held*, the sale was in the hands of the tenant for life and s. 97 of the Settled Land Act 1925 gave such protection to trustees that, unless they were fraudulent, it was almost impossible to sue them for anything they might or might not have done. In view of the rise in value of landed property since 1955 the sale appeared improvident and imprudent but the beneficiaries had no legal rights as a result of the provisions of the 1925 Act.

Englefield Holdings, Ltd. and Sinclair's Contract, Re. Rosslyn   [132]   and Lorimer Estates, Ltd. v. Englefield Holdings, [1962] 3 All E.R. 503

A vendor's leasehold interest in two flats was sold by auction on December 13th, 1961. On October 12th, 1961 the vendor had been served with a certificate of disrepair under the Rent Act 1957 in respect of one flat. This resulted in the rent payable being reduced from 28s. 3d. to 15s. 7d. per week until repairs were carried out. The particulars of sale gave the rent as 28s. 3d. The conditions of sale provided that no representation or warranty was made that the rent receivable was the rent properly chargeable under the Rent Acts and the purchaser should not make any requisition with regard thereto. *Held*, the vendor having failed to disclose the certificate of disrepair was not entitled to specific performance of the contract at the contract price. It was declared that unless the vendor obtained discharge of the certificate of disrepair before completion the contract should be completed with an abatement of £520 in the price.

English v. Cliff, [1914] 2 Ch. 376   [133]

By a settlement of May 13th, 1892 the settlor conveyed real property to trustees in fee simple to stand possessed of the premises for twenty-one years and "at the expiration of the said term of twenty-one years" to sell the premises. On June 20th, 1913 the trustees contracted to sell to the defendant. He objected that the trust for sale was void for remoteness. *Held*, the determination of the term and the commencement of the trust for sale arising at the same moment, the trust was not void for remoteness on the ground that it was limited to take effect "at the expiration of the term". Also the term under the settlement commenced from midnight on May 12th and therefore the trust for sale was not void for remoteness on the ground of exceeding a term of twenty-one years from its creation.

Esdell Caravan Parks v. Hemel Hempstead Rural District   [134]   Council, [1966] 1 Q.B. 895; [1965] 3 All E.R. 737 (Court of Appeal)

A field had been used as a caravan site before the Town and Country Planning Act 1947 came into force and the use was continued thereafter. There were never more than twenty-four caravans. As a result of s. 17 (3) of the Caravan Sites and Control of Development Act 1960 planning permission was deemed to be granted for use as a caravan site, unrestricted to any particular number of caravans. A site licence was granted limiting the number of caravans to twenty-four. Under the Model Standards the maximum number was twenty per acre. This site was 4·8 acres. *Held* (i) the licensing authority had jurisdiction under s. 5 of the 1960 Act to impose conditions on granting a site licence and a condition restricting the total number of caravans stationed on a field could be validly imposed; (ii) in determining whether a condition should be imposed under s. 5 (1) on granting a site licence or on appeal under s. 7 (1) of the 1960 Act, which was a question of fact not law, there should not be taken into consideration factors which were solely planning factors but there might be taken into consideration factors which were properly site licensing considerations *e.g.* public health, educational considerations, transport problems and upsetting the social balance between villagers and caravan dwellers; (iii) since one of the factors which had been taken into account, *i.e.* that the land was zoned as a green belt, was solely a planning factor, the magistrates' determination would be remitted to them for consideration. The magistrates were bound to accept that there was an existing right to use this site as a caravan site although it was in a green belt.

Essex County Council v. Essex Incorporated Congregational   [135]   Church Union, [1963] 1 All E.R. 326 (House of Lords)

A Nonconformist chapel, being a place of worship not liable to be assessed for rates (Rating and Valuation (Miscellaneous Provisions) Act 1955 s. 7) was entered as "exempt" in the local valuation list without mention of a "nil" or other value.

The owners served notice requiring the Council to purchase their interest under s. 39 (2) of the Town and Country Planning Act 1959. The Council served a counter notice under s. 40 (1) (f) that the owners had not made reasonable endeavours to sell their interest. This objection was referred to the Lands Tribunal. After time for serving counter notices had expired, the Lands Tribunal was asked to decide as a preliminary point of law whether the building qualified for "blight" protection under s. 39 of the 1959 Act, whereby a qualifying interest must be an interest in a hereditament whose annual value "does not exceed" £250 per annum. The Tribunal decided that as no annual value was shown in the valuation list because the hereditament was exempt, the annual value was nil and so did not exceed the £250 maximum specified and the purchase notice was valid. This was upheld by the Court of Appeal. The House of Lords held that the ground of objection that the owners' interest was not qualified for protection not having been raised in the Council's counternotice, the Lands Tribunal had no jurisdiction to consider it and accordingly neither the Court of Appeal nor the House of Lords had jurisdiction to give a decision on the preliminary point of law. *Per curiam*: a hereditament which is exempt from rating is not a hereditament whose "annual value does not exceed" £250 within s. 39 (4) (a) of the 1959 Act. The decision of the Court of Appeal (sub nom, *Essex Incorporated Congregational Church Union* v. *Essex County Council*, [1962] 2 All E.R. 518) not sustained and, *obiter*, disapproved.

Esso Petroleum Co., Ltd. v. Harper's Garage (Stourport), [136] Ltd., [1967] 1 All E.R. 699 (House of Lords)

The respondents, the owners of Corner garage, charged the same by way of legal mortgage to the appellants to secure the repayment of a principal sum of £7,000 and covenanted to repay the £7,000 with interest by quarterly instalments over twenty-one years and during the continuance of the mortgage to purchase exclusively from the appellants all motor fuels which they might require for consumption or sale at Corner garage. The mortgage further provided that the respondents were not entitled to redeem the security otherwise than in accordance with the covenant as to repayment. *Held*, the mortgage stipulation relating to the purchase of fuel was within the ambit of the legal doctrine relating to covenants in restraint of trade, it was unenforceable as being in unreasonable restraint of trade and the respondents were entitled to redeem the mortgage. (But see *Cleveland Petroleum Co., Ltd.* v. *Dartstone Ltd.*)

Fay v. Miller, Wilkins & Co., [1941] 2 All E.R. 18 [137] (Court of Appeal)

The memorandum of a contract for the sale of a house incorporated certain conditions of sale in which it was stated: "The vendor will convey as personal representative." *Held*, this was a sufficient description of the vendor to satisfy the requirements of s. 40 of the Law of Property Act 1925. "If the vendor's name does not appear on the face of the contract, the contract will not suffer from insufficiency on that score if it indicates the vendor by a description sufficient to preclude any fair dispute as to identity" (*per* CLAUSON, L.J.).

Fawcett Properties Ltd. v. Buckingham County Council, [138] [1961] A.C. 636; [1960] 3 All E.R. 503 (House of Lords)

A condition was attached to a grant of planning permission that occupation of houses to be erected was to be "limited to persons whose employment or latest employment is or was employment in agriculture as defined by s. 119 (1) of the Town and Country Planning Act 1947, or in forestry, or in an industry mainly dependent upon agriculture and including also the dependants of such persons as aforesaid". An argument that the condition was not sufficiently certain to be valid failed as the language employed in the condition had been taken from the Housing Acts, which had a definite and ascertainable meaning. *Held*, the condition was not *ultra vires* as the wording of the condition, though open to criticism, was fairly and reasonably related to the permitted development, the inclusion of the area in a green belt in the future being envisaged. Neither was the condition spent, being a continuing one.

Fernandez v. Walding, [1968] 1 All E.R. 994 (Court of Appeal)   **[139]**

A factory building, constructed in three sections, was partly occupied by the landlord and partly let on a business tenancy. The landlord served notice to determine the tenancy and that he would oppose a new tenancy on the ground that he intended to extend the factory by building operations which included the part of the premises occupied by the tenant. The county court granted a new tenancy but excluding that part of the building on which an additional storey was to be constructed. The Court of Appeal held that a new tenancy must be refused if the work cannot reasonably be done without possession of the "holding", as defined in s. 23 (3) of the Landlord and Tenant Act 1954. A new tenancy can only be granted of the "holding" and this did not include part only of the "holding". (But see s. 7 of the Law of Property Act 1969.)

Finkielkraut v. Monahan, [1949] 2 All E.R. 234   **[140]**

The vendor under a contract for the sale of land served notice making time of the essence of the contract. The purchaser was ready and able to complete on the date fixed for completion in the notice but the vendor was not. *Held*, the vendor was also bound by the date in the notice and was, therefore, in breach of contract and not entitled to specific performance. Hence the purchaser could rescind and reclaim his deposit.

Fison's Will Trusts, Re, Fison v. Fison, [1950] 1 All E.R. 501   **[141]**

A testator died in 1920 and by his will gave his son the option of purchasing certain properties which were subject to a mortgage and an equitable charge. *Held*, if the son exercised the option, he elected to become a purchaser and was not a devisee under the will and, therefore, s. 1 of the Real Estate Charges Act 1854 (now s. 35 of the Administration of Estates Act 1925), did not apply: it followed that the son would be entitled to a conveyance of the properties free from any encumbrances.

Flight v. Booth (1834), 1 Bing N.C. 370   **[142]**

A vendor will be unable to enforce a contract if there is substantial misdescription. Misdescription is substantial if it affects the subject matter of the contract so far that it is reasonable to suppose that the purchaser would not have entered into the contract but for the misdescription. A purchaser was able to rescind the contract and obtain return of his deposit with interest and costs where the vendor of a lease had given only an incomplete disclosure of the trades prohibited under the terms of the lease.

Foley v. Classique Coaches Ltd., [1934] All E.R. 88 (Court of Appeal)   **[143]**

An agreement for the sale of land included a term that the purchasers would buy their petrol from the vendor at a price to be agreed from time to time, with an arbitration clause if the price could not be agreed. The agreement was acted on for three years before the purchasers argued that the petrol agreement was void for uncertainty. *Held*, that so long as the vendor offered petrol at a reasonable price the purchasers must buy from him. A reasonable price could be fixed by arbitration if necessary.

Foundling Hospital v. Crane, [1911] 2 K.B. 367   **[144]**

H. signed and sealed an undated document purporting to be an assignment of a lease and gave it to his solicitor to hold in escrow until instructions were sent to complete it, but if H. died the document was to be considered to have been completed before his death. H. never gave any further instructions and continued to occupy the property which was the subject of the document. Later he was party to a deed, reciting that the leasehold was vested in him, by which the lessors gave him consent to make structural alterations to the property. *Held*, the document was never legally delivered during H.'s lifetime either as a deed or in escrow and was, therefore, inoperative. *Per* FARWELL, L.J.: "I doubt if a deed can be delivered as an escrow at all subject to an overriding power in the grantor to recall the deed altogether." A document purporting to be a deed of conveyance delivered on condition that it shall become operative on death is a testamentary document and cannot take effect as an escrow. This document was not attested so as to satisfy the requirements of the Wills Act 1837 so that it was ineffective. Applied in *Windsor Refrigerator Co., Ltd.* v. *Branch Nominees, Ltd.* Distinguished in *Vincent* v. *Premo Enterprises (Voucher Sales), Ltd.* (See also *Beesly* v. *Hallwood Estates, Ltd.*)

Fowell v. Radford (1969), 213 Estates Gazette 757 (Court of Appeal)   [145]

It was held that husband and wife do not necessarily have the same main residence. For the purpose of rights under the Leasehold Reform Act 1967 there was nothing to prevent a wife, even though happily married, from having a separate main residence from her husband. In this case the wife was only able to spend occasional weekends at her husband's residence as her occupation in running a guest house obliged her to live in a flat next door to the guest house. This flat was, therefore, her "main residence" within s. 1 (2) of the 1967 Act.

Fowley Marine (Emsworth), Ltd. v. Gafford, [1968] 1 All E.R. 979   [146]
(Court of Appeal)

The plaintiff company claimed £5 per annum for a permanent mooring put down in Fowley Rythe, a tidal creek. The defendant having refused to pay, the plaintiffs claimed in trespass. The plaintiffs claimed possession and ownership of the bed and banks of the creek. The company had purchased the creek and part of the foreshore in 1963. There was some evidence that the creek and part of the foreshore had been included in a grant in 1628 by the Crown and it was contended that that grant, coupled with subsequent conveyances, in particular a conveyance of 1918 which was a good root of title, showed the paper title was vested in the company. The company also alleged a possessory title as against the Crown by sixty years' adverse possession. The defendant denied the company had sufficient possession to found trespass and challenged the company's title. *Held*, that acts done by the company and its predecessors in title such as letting of the Rythe from 1907 to 1913 and laying and giving permission to lay moorings, had when viewed in the light of the paper title, the quality of assertions of ownership, and, coupled with the paper title, showed possession by the company and its predecessors sufficient to maintain trespass against the defendant. The acts of the defendant and others in laying moorings were referable to an erroneous belief that there was some general right, such as a right of navigation, entitling them to lay moorings, rather than to an assertion of possession of the Rythe. In making title to property such as the foreshore, which must have originally lain in the Crown, it is necessary to show a Crown grant to some subject or to show a possessory title acquired against the Crown; it is not sufficient merely to show a good root of title sixty years old.

Francis v. Yiewsley and West Drayton Urban District Council,   [147]
[1958] 1 Q.B. 478 (Court of Appeal)

An enforcement notice is not invalidated by failure to refer to the contravening development so long as the act constituting the contravening development is stated in the enforcement notice. However, the enforcement notice in this case was invalidated by reason that it failed to state that planning permission had been granted for a limited period (which had expired at the date of service of the notice) but instead referred to development without planning permission. Mere reference to development contravening planning control is insufficient. The owner of the land, on being served with the notice, did not apply to a court of summary jurisdiction under s. 23 (4) of the Town and Country Planning Act 1947 but that did not debar him, by reason of s. 23 (4) or otherwise, from applying to the court for relief. *Held*, the landowner was entitled to a declaration that the enforcement notice was ineffective. (See also *Miller-Mead* v. *The Minister of Housing and Local Government*.)

Freehold Land in Dances Way, West Town, Hayling Island,   [148]
Hants, Re, [1962] 2 All E.R. 42 (Court of Appeal)

By a conveyance of June 20th, 1939 the respondent conveyed freehold land to the appellant, "excepting and reserving full right of way for all persons entitled to the same their heirs and assigns . . . and all other persons having occasion to use the same . . . through and over . . ." a strip of land about 40 feet wide traversing the land conveyed. The respondent retained adjacent land but the reservation did not identify the dominant tenement. The appellant subsequently sold parts of the land. In 1959 the appellant registered the remaining land with absolute title but a note was entered pursuant to s. 70 (2) of the Land Registration Act 1925 in the property register of the title that registration took effect subject to the reservation, on the ground that it created an easement. The appellant applied for rectification of the register and the entry was cancelled on the ground that it did not benefit the respondent's adjoining land. The Chancery Division held that the exception and reservation operated by way of regrant to create a right within s. 70 (2) of the Act. The appellant appealed. *Held*, the cancellation should stand as (i) *Per* Lord EVERSHED, M.R. and UPJOHN, L.J., the Chief Land Registrar had not been shown to have exercised his discretion wrongly; (ii) *per* DIPLOCK, L.J., the Chief Land Registrar had jurisdiction to determine the question of the construction of the exception and reservation and his decision that it did not create an easement was right. *Per* Lord EVERSHED, M.R. and UPJOHN, L.J. (DIPLOCK, L.J. dissenting), the Chief Land Registrar's decision would not give rise to *res judicata* on the construction of the exception and reservation.

Frewen, Re, [1926] Ch. 580   [149]

Property was settled with a direction that two-thirds of the income should be paid to the tenant for life and the balance accumulated in trust, after the death of the tenant for life, for his first and other sons in tail. The powers of a tenant for life under the Settled Land Acts were declared to be exercisable by the trustees. *Held*, the tenant for life did not have the powers of a tenant for life under the Settled Land Act 1925, not being entitled to the income of the settled land within s. 20 (1) (viii) of the Act. The trustees had such powers by virtue of s. 23 (1) of the Act and under the terms of the settlement.

Fuller v. De Ritter, [1963] Ch. D. (*The Times*, April 15th.)   [150]

The plaintiff was persuaded by the woman with whom he was living to execute a transfer of the registered title of his house to her. He pleaded *non est factum*, claiming that he did not know that he had made a deed of gift and thought that "as settlor" in the transfer meant "as settler" and that he could remain in the property. *Held*, to establish a plea of *non est factum* the plaintiff must show the misrepresentation leading to the execution of a deed was as to its character and class; it was not sufficient to have misunderstood the contents. However, on the facts, the transfer would be set aside as having been obtained under undue influence. (But see *Gallie* v. *Lee*.)

Fyson v. Buckinghamshire County Council,]1958] 2 All E.R. 286   [151]

Land used for the storage of scrap metal before "the appointed day" under the Town and Country Planning Act 1947 continued to be so used until 1949. From

1949 to 1956 the land was unoccupied, then used again for storage of scrap metal. The local authority served an enforcement notice requiring discontinuance of the use on the ground that there had been a material change of use requiring planning permission. The Divisional Court held that resumption of a former use does not constitute a material change of use and therefore no planning permission was necessary. (But see *Postill* v. *East Riding County Council*.)

Gable Construction Co., Ltd. v. Inland Revenue   **[152]**
   Commissioners, [1968] 2 All E.R. 968

Two long leases were varied by deed to increase the rents reserved. The deed of variation was assessed to Stamp Duty by charging *ad valorem* duty on the amount of the increase in the average rents on the basis that it operated as a surrender of the existing leases and grant of new leases for terms equal to the unexpired residues of the original terms. *Held*, the deed of variation did not act as a surrender. The deed was chargeable under the heading "Bond, Covenant, etc." in the Stamp Act 1891 Schedule 1, but the amount chargeable was limited by s. 77 (5) as if the deed were a lease or tack, as s. 77 (5) was a relieving provision. Alternatively, the reference in s. 77 (5) to rent reserved by lease or tack applied to the rent reserved by the original leases as varied by the deed of variation.

Gallie v. Lee, [1969] 1 All E.R. 1062 (Court of Appeal)   **[153]**

Mrs. Gallie owned a leasehold house which she intended to give to her nephew. She had already given him the title deeds when the nephew and his friend, Lee, called on her and she was persuaded to execute a deed without reading it. Lee told her it was a deed of gift of the house to the nephew but it was in fact an assignment to Lee. Lee told the nephew he would pay £25 per month to Lee's mistress to support a business in which Lee and the nephew were engaged. The nephew gave Lee the title deeds. Lee then obtained £2,000 from a building society on a mortgage of the house. He defaulted in the mortgage repayments and the building society claimed possession. Mrs. Gallie applied for a declaration that the assignment was a nullity. She succeeded at first instance in a plea of *non est factum* as it was held that an assignment on sale to A. is an instrument of entirely different character from deed of gift to B. The decision was reversed by the Court of Appeal. It was held: (i) Mrs. Gallie could not say the deed of assignment was not her deed; it was obviously a legal document and the building society had advanced money on the faith of its being her document; she could not now disavow her signature; (ii) the evidence was not sufficient to establish the necessary minimum facts to support a plea of *non est factum* and to discharge the burden of proof necessary to establish the plea. To establish a plea of *non est factum* the deed must be of a totally different character from that intended to be signed; (iii) the plaintiff had failed to establish that had she known the true character of the document of transfer she would not have executed it nor that she had been induced to sign by anything the first defendant had told her. Neither a mistaken belief that the document transferred the property as a free gift nor a mistake as to the identity of the transferee could amount to a mistake as to the character or class of a document for the purpose of a plea of *non est factum*. (See also *National Provincial Bank of England* v. *Jackson* and *Fuller* v. *De Ritter*.)

Gardner v. Coutts & Co., [1967] 3 All E.R. 1064   **[154]**

The owner of a house contracted (i) not to sell without giving right of first refusal to his neighbour to purchase at £3,000; (ii) not to let the property except on the neighbour's approval and (iii) that the neighbour should have the right to purchase from the owner's personal representatives should the property still be in the owner's possession at his death. The owner gave the house to his sister before he died. The neighbour succeeded in action against the owner's estate for breach of contract. *Per* CROSS, J.: ". . . it is implicit in a grant of first refusal that the person who has to offer the property to the other party should not be entitled to give the property away without first offering to sell it to the person with the benefit of the right of first refusal."

Garland v. Minister of Housing and Local Government (1968),   [155]
112 Sol. Jo. 841 (Court of Appeal)

The applicant carried out building operations on his house by building on an extra storey which increased the cubic content by some 25% in excess of that permitted under Class II of Schedule 1 to the General Development Order 1963. Before the work was completed the local authority served two enforcement notices alleging development without planning permission and requiring the building to be demolished. The applicant's appeal to the Minister was dismissed after an inquiry and report by one of the Minister's Inspectors. The applicant appealed to the Q.B. Divisional Court on the ground that the notices were invalid in that they charged him with developing without permission, whereas he should have been charged with failure to comply with the limitation imposed by Class 1/1 of the Order. His appeal was dismissed and he appealed to the Court of Appeal. *Held*, the permission given under Class I/1 of the Schedule to the 1963 Order was not permission subject to a limitation but permission to do the particular thing specified *i.e.* to enlarge a dwellinghouse to the permitted extent of the cubic content of the original house plus 1750 cubic feet or 1/10th, whichever was the greater. Where there was a substantial difference between what was permitted and what was done, the whole was done without permission. Where the maximum permitted was exceeded by some 25% that was not an excess over a limitation but a difference in substance between what was permitted and what was done. Accordingly this was development without permission and the enforcement notices were valid.

Gartside v. Silkstone and Dodworth Coal and Iron Co. (1882),   [156]
21 Ch.D. 762

Where two deeds are executed on the same day the court must enquire which was executed first but if there is anything in the deeds to show an intention that they shall take effect *pari passu* or even that the later deed shall take effect in priority to the earlier, the court will presume the deeds were executed in such order as to give effect to the manifest intention of the parties. (See also *Weg Motors, Ltd.* v. *Hales.*)

Gavaghan v. Edwards, [1961] 2 All E.R. 477 (Court of Appeal)   [157]

The vendor and purchaser orally agreed the sale and purchase of a house. They both signed a contract which was a sufficient memorandum for the purpose of s. 40 of the Law of Property Act 1925 except that it provided that "the date fixed for completion is to be agreed between the parties". The parties orally agreed a date for completion. The same solicitors were acting for both parties. The solicitors wrote to the purchaser that the vendor had informed them that the date for completion was to be January 31st, 1959. The purchaser telephoned his confirmation. The purchaser did not wish to complete. He claimed there was breach of contract because no date had been fixed for completion or, if there was a contract, it was unenforceable because it did not satisfy s. 40 of the Law of Property Act. *Held*, the contract was enforceable because the solicitors' letter signed with the firm name was sufficient to complete the memorandum for the purpose of s. 40. Where a solicitor acts for both parties and the parties are agreed the solicitor has authority to complete a memorandum so as to bind either or both of his clients.

Georgiades v. Edward Wolfe & Co., Ltd., [1964] 3 All E.R. 433   [158]
Owners of a restaurant employed estate agents to sell their leasehold interest in the land and the business. A written contract provided for payment of commission to the agents on their introducing a person who made an offer to purchase

for a certain amount and subject to certain qualifications if the sale was not completed. A clause in the contract provided that the owners "hereby charge the deposit paid and the purchase moneys with payment . . . of the commission due . . ." The agents claimed commission on the introduction of a purchaser whose offer was accepted but which failed to result in a sale. The estate agents registered a Land Charge Class C (iii) under s. 10 (1) of the Land Charges Act 1925 *i.e.* a general equitable charge imposed by the contract. *Held*, the charge should be vacated as the charge given in the contract took effect only on the deposit and purchase moneys and was not a charge on land within s. 10 of the Act of 1925.

Gilliat v. Gilliat (1869), L.R. 9 Eq. 60   [159]

When land is sold at auction under conditions stating that the sale is subject to a reserved bidding, it is illegal to employ a person to bid up to the reserved price unless there has been an express stipulation for the right to do so. Where it transpired that the auctioneer had employed a person to bid, the sale was set aside.

Gloag and Miller's Contract, Re. (1883), 23 Ch.D. 320   [160]

The vendor of land knew it was subject to restrictive covenants. The purchaser was aware of the covenants but the contract did not provide that he should take subject to them. The purchaser went into possession before completion and made structural alterations. *Held*, that by going into possession the purchaser had waived objection to irremovable defects of title of which he was aware. *Per* FRY, J.: "When the contract is silent as to the title to be shown by the vendor, and the purchaser's right to a good title is merely implied by law, that legal implication may be rebutted by showing that the purchaser had notice before the contract that he could not make a good title."

Goding v. Frazer, [1966] 3 All E.R. 234   [161]

An estate agent who, when negotiating on behalf of his principal a sale of land "subject to contract", accepts from the proposed purchaser a deposit, does so as agent for the vendor in the absence of some other agreement (*e.g.* as stakeholder). When a deposit is so accepted as agent the vendor remains liable throughout for its return, notwithstanding the fact that the purchaser may himself have a right of action, in certain circumstances, against the estate agent. Accordingly, when an estate agent so accepted a deposit and subsequently became insolvent, the vendor was liable to repay to the purchaser the amount of the deposit when the proposed purchase did not proceed. *Per curiam*: Even if the agent nominated by the vendor were regarded as stakeholder, the risk of insolvency while holding the deposit should fall on the vendor as he had selected the agent.

Goel v. Sagoo, [1969] 1 All E.R. 378 (Court of Appeal)   [162]

Although less than 7% of the rent was attributable to the use of furniture the Court of Appeal held the property in question to be furnished and outside Rent Act protection for unfurnished property. It was said that the court should take a commonsense view and not be bound by percentages. The tenant had not supplemented the furniture and had previously invoked the assistance of a Rent Tribunal on the basis that the premises were furnished. The Court of Appeal dismissed the appeal from the county court decision, holding that the county court judge was entitled to take these matters into consideration. *Per* HARMAN, L.J.: "It would be an abuse if a tenant were allowed first of all to invoke the assistance of the Rent Tribunal on the footing that his tenancy was a furnished one and so get his rent reduced, and then seek the protection of the Rent Acts, when he was sued in the county court, on the footing that the tenancy was an unfurnished one." (See also *Klassnick* v. *Allen*.)

Golden Bread Co., Ltd. v. Hemmings, [1922] 1 Ch. 162   [163]

Where, by reason of the purchaser's default, a contract for the sale of premises and the goodwill of a business being carried on thereon, is not completed on the date fixed for completion, the vendor is entitled to carry on the business at the purchaser's risk and to be indemnified for loss incurred providing he has informed the purchaser promptly that he is carrying on the business at a loss.

Golden Lion Hotel (Hunstanton), Ltd. v. Carter,   [164]
[1965] 1 W.L.R. 1189

By two leases L. demised two plots of land, "A" and "B", for 99 years from September 29th, 1871 and covenanted that no building (save as expressed) should be erected on a plot adjacent. In 1898 L. leased the servient plot to a predecessor in title of the plaintiff company, which subsequently purchased the reversion with knowledge of the restrictive covenant. In 1948 the successor in title of the lessee of plot "A" purchased the freehold reversion and in 1949 the lease was expressly merged in the freehold on a conveyance on sale of that plot (which was subsequently purchased by the defendant). In 1916 L. conveyed the freehold reversion of plot "B" to the then lessee and the freehold and leasehold were thereupon merged. That plot also was subsequently acquired by the defendant. *Held*, although so long as the leases of plots "A" and "B" subsisted the covenant would have been enforceable by either of the lessees aginst the reversioner and, after the ownership of the burdened land had passed to the plaintiff company, against the company as well, when the leases were extinguished by merger the right to enforce the covenant was lost.

Goldsmith (F.) (Sicklesmere), Ltd. v. Baxter, [1969] 3 All E.R. 733   [165]

A contract for the sale of land was entered into by Goldsmith (Sicklesmere) Coaches Ltd. The purchaser's search in the Companies Register showed that no such company existed and the purchaser refused to complete. It was established that by error, when the land was purchased in 1966, the conveyance had been taken in the wrong name. The vendors perfected the title by means of a supplemental conveyance from the 1966 vendors to F. Goldsmith (Sicklesmere) Ltd. The purchaser refused to complete on the ground that the contract was invalid because the vendors were not identified for the purpose of s. 40 (1) of the Law of Property Act 1925. *Held*, the contract was binding as the vendors could be identified, the address of the registered office being correctly given, the name of the director who signed the contract being correctly stated and the property correctly named. The court will look at the agreement as a whole and its circumstances to decide if parties to it can be identified. (See also *Allen & Co., Ltd.* v. *Whiteman*.)

Goody v. Baring, [1956] 2 All E.R. 11   [166]

A solicitor acted for both vendor and purchaser of a leasehold house. The two upper floors were each let at 25s. per week inclusive of rates. The plaintiff purchaser was told by the defendant solicitor that there had been increases in rates since 1950 and it was possible that the rents could be increased. The plaintiff purchased the property and then sought to increase the rents. The tenants applied for a reduction in rents and the standard rents were reduced by the county court to 17s. 6d. and 18s. 4d. per week respectively. The plaintiff had to make repayment of overpaid rent to the tenants. He claimed damages for negligence. *Held*, the defendant was liable in negligence as he had accepted the information given by the vendor as to the rents without ascertaining what were the standard and recoverable rents of the property and because he had failed to advise the plaintiff that he could not rely on the rents which were being paid being recoverable rents. *Per curiam*: Although full enquiries before contract have been made, it is still the duty of the purchaser's solicitor to make requisitions and enquiries after contracts have been exchanged, even if the preliminary enquiries have been so complete that it is only necessary to ask if the answers are still complete and accurate.

Grace Rymer Investments, Ltd. v. Waite, [1958] 2 All E.R. 777   [167]
(Court of Appeal)

By a contract dated November 28th, 1955 W. agreed to purchase freehold property from G.S. for £2,300, part of which was to be left on mortgage. In October W. had agreed to let to H. at a weekly rent of £2 0s. 6d. a flat in the property in which, at that date, W. had no interest. H. paid to W. 156 weeks' rent in advance. W.'s purchase of the freehold was completed by execution of a registered transfer on December 30th, 1955 and on the same day the property was mortgaged to the plaintiffs by registered charge. The charge did not exclude or limit the purchaser's power of leasing. In July, 1956 instalments on the charge being in arrear, the plaintiffs took proceedings against W. and H. for possession. *Held*, the plaintiffs were not entitled to possession for the following reasons :– (i) Even if rent in advance was an unlawful premium under the Landlord and Tenant (Rent Control) Act 1949 s. 2., H. was not debarred from asserting rights under a contract of tenancy; (ii) Payment in advance did not lose its character as rent and become a mere premium so as to enable the plaintiffs to say no rent had been paid; (iii) H. acquired "an interest in land by virtue of taking possession" within the Law of Property Act 1925 s. 55 (c) and there being a moment of time on December 30th, 1955 when W. was absolute beneficial owner, W. was estopped from denying H.'s right as a tenant to remain in occupation for the period for which rent had been paid; (iv) the plaintiffs were in no better position than W. because the Land Registration Act 1925 s. 27 (3) did not render the plaintiffs' legal charge effective from the date of execution so as to override H.'s interest, which was an overriding interest within s. 70 (1) (g) of the land Registration Act, to which the plaintiffs' charge was made subject by s. 20 (1).

Greaves v. Wilson (1858), 25 Beav. 290   [168]

A public house was put up for sale by auction subject to a condition that the vendor could rescind the contract if the purchaser should "show any objection of title, conveyance or otherwise and should insist thereon". *Held*, the condition did not entitle the vendor to rescind without answering the requisitions. Even though some of the requisitions were untenable he was bound to answer them and give the purchaser the opportunity of waiving them or insisting upon them. Also the vendor was bound to comply with a requisition that a mortgagee of the property should be paid off and concur in the conveyance. Conditions of sale must be construed strictly against the person who frames them.

Greswold-Williams v. Barneby (1900), 83 L.T. 708; 17 T.L.R. 110   [169]

The plaintiffs agreed in writing to purchase freehold property and in the agreement it was warranted that the property was in first-class condition. After the conveyance was taken it was found that there were serious defects in the drainage system. *Held*, the contract had merged in the conveyance and, in the absence of fraud, no action could be maintained in respect of errors in the particulars in the contract, which did not appear in the conveyance. (But see now Misrepresentation Act 1967 s. 1.)

Griffiths v. Young (1969), 212 Estates Gazette 1137   [170]

The plaintiff agreed in April, 1963 to purchase some of the defendant's land and to guarantee the defendant's overdraft at the bank after contract and until completion, which was to be on September 29th, 1964. On May 2nd, 1963 the purchaser's solicitors wrote setting out the offer, subject to contract. On May 2nd the vendor was being pressed to repay his overdraft. The solicitors for both parties had telephone conversations and the purchaser's solicitors made an oral offer to buy. The vendor's solicitors wrote on May 3rd that they were instructed to sell. In February, 1964 the vendor called off the sale and the purchaser sued for specific performance. *Held*, the intention to bind the parties by the usual exchange of contracts (recognised as standard practice in *Eccles* v. *Bryant* [1948] 1 Ch. 93) had been cast aside. There was an agreement to sell and s. 40 of the Law of Property Act 1925 was satisfied by reading together the letters of May 2nd and 3rd. The vendor's solicitor had been instructed to sell and could bind his client.

Grist v. Bailey, [1966] 2 All E.R. 875   [171]

Both vendor and purchaser mistakenly believed a house to be subject to a statutory tenancy. The contract for sale provided that the house was sold "subject to the existing tenancy thereof" at £850. Between contract and completion the vendor discovered that the property was not subject to the Rent Acts and the occupier was about to vacate. With vacant possession the property was worth about £2,250. The purchaser was refused specific performance of the contract on the basis that there was common fundamental mistake. The vendor was entitled to rescission on condition that a new contract would be offered to the purchaser at a price taking into account the availability of vacant possession.

Gross v. Lewis Hillman, Ltd., [1969] 3 All E.R. 1476   [172]
(Court of Appeal)

The defendants contracted to sell to G. Ltd. the freehold reversion of shop premises let to S. Ltd. for a term of twenty-one years. The defendants' agents (who managed the property) made representations as to the stability of S. Ltd., including that it was an old-established company and had paid-up capital of £5,000. The company had been dormant for years and its former shareholders had taken and divided its capital between them. G. Ltd. recommended the property to the plaintiff and allowed him to have the benefit of their contract on payment of commission. Accordingly the defendants conveyed the reversion to the plaintiff in 1965. On discovering the true position the plaintiff brought an action against the defendants and their agents alleging fraudulent misrepresentation and claiming damages against both and rescission against the defendants. All the relevant events having occurred before the Misrepresentation Act 1967, the plaintiff was prima facie bound by the rule that rescission is not available after completion in respect of an innocent misrepresentation. *Held*, (i) the statements taken together, amounted to misrepresentation even though none of them taken singly was false; (ii) the right to rescind a conveyance for misrepresentation did not run with the land. The representations were made to, and the contract with, G. Ltd., not the plaintiff and any misrepresentation was spent when G. Ltd. entered into the contract. Therefore the plaintiff would not be entitled to rescission of the conveyance as against the defendants on account of fraudulent misrepresentation made to G. Ltd. by the defendants; (iii) the court would not disturb the finding of the trial judge that the defendants' agents did not know the representations were false or made them recklessly. *Per* Cross and Widgery, L.JJ.: Possibly if the misrepresentation had been fraudulent the plaintiff could have rescinded after completion: it would have been sufficient that the false statement, though not made to the plaintiff, had been made to an expert (G. Ltd), on whose recommendation the plaintiff had relied.

Guildford Rural District Council v. Penny, [1959] 2 All E.R. 111   [173]
(Court of Appeal)

Land was being used before the "appointed day" under the Town and Country Planning Act 1947 as a site for eight caravans. The number was gradually increased until there were twenty-seven. In 1948 planning permission had been granted for twenty-one caravans. The local authority served an enforcement notice, alleging material change of use. On appeal to justices it was found that the increased number of caravans did not constitute material change of use. An appeal to the Court of Appeal failed as the court held the justices' finding was one of fact, not of law, and the Court of Appeal would not disturb it. It would appear that whether intensification of user amounts to material change of use depends on the circumstances in every case.

Gurasz v. Gurasz, [1969] 3 All E.R. 822 (Court of Appeal)   [174]

A husband and wife were joint owners of the matrimonial home. The wife was forced to leave the house and take the children away because of the husband's behaviour. Under s. 1 of the Matrimonial Homes Act 1967 an order was made for the husband to vacate the house and for the wife and children to return. The husband appealed. *Held,* s. 1 of the Act of 1967 gives no rights to a wife who already has a proprietory, contractual or statutory right to occupy the home but an innocent wife, who is joint owner of the matrimonial home, has a right, if in occupation, not to be evicted or excluded by the other spouse except by order of the court and, if not in occupation, a right by order of the court to enter and occupy. The wife's personal right entitled the court to interfere with the husband's right to possession. The court also held that it could affirm the order on the ground of the court's inherent jurisdiction.

Haedicke and Lipski's Contract, Re, [1901], 2 Ch. 666   [175]

Where a condition precluding a purchaser making requisitions or objections to the title is inserted in a contract for sale of land, the purchaser is bound only if he is made aware of the risk he is accepting, based on proper disclosure by the vendor. An agreement for the sale of leaseholds contained a stipulation that "the vendor's title is accepted by the purchasers". The leases contained onerous and unusual covenants of which the purchasers had not had notice. *Held,* the condition as to acceptance of the title did not affect the vendor's general duty of disclosure and the purchasers were entitled to rescission and return of the deposit with interest. (See *Becker* v. *Partridge.*)

Hall & Co., Ltd. v. Shoreham-by-Sea Urban District   [176]
Council, [1964] 1 All E.R. 1. (Court of Appeal)

A condition attached to planning permission which required the landowners not only to build a road on their land but also, in effect, to grant a public right of way over it without compensation, was held to be unreasonable and *ultra vires* while a more regular course for constructing a road at public expense, under which compensation for compulsory acquisition of land was open to the local authority under the Highways Act 1959. (But see *Westminster Bank, Ltd.* v. *Minister of Housing and Local Government.*)

Halsall v. Brizell, [1957] 1 All E.R. 371   [177]

In 1851 forty acres of land were purchased by O. and J. and sold in 174 building plots. Purchasers of the plots covenanted to contribute to the upkeep of the roads and promenade by the sea wall and maintenance of the sewers under the roads. The deeds recited that the roads and promenade were vested in O. and J. on trust to permit the same to be used and enjoyed for ever by the purchasers, their heirs and assigns and the occupiers of the plots and the houses to be erected thereon. The purchasers covenanted for themselves, their heirs, executors administrators and assigns with O. and J. and their heirs and assigns to pay "a due and just proportion in respect of the plot" marked on an annexed plan. In 1931 F. purchased a dwelling house subject to the covenants of 1851 and let the house to several tenants. In 1951 a resolution was passed that the trustees be empowered to make an additional call for payment under the covenant in respect of any house divided into more than one dwelling. F. had died and his executors denied the validity of the resolution. *Held,* (i) although the covenant was a positive one and the burden did not run with the land and the particular provisions of the 1851 deed offended the rule against perpetuities, nevertheless the defendants were bound to accept the burden of contribution in the deed of

1851 if they wished to take the benefit of the use of the roads and sewers; (ii) the resolution was invalid; the true construction of the 1851 deed was that the contribution was in respect of each plot of land, not in respect of the user. Hence the amount payable by the defendants was that computed under the 1851 deed, not under the 1951 resolution.

Hamilton-Snowball's Conveyance, Re, [1959] Ch. 308; [1958]   **[178]**
2 All E.R. 319

H., who was in occupation of a requisitioned dwellinghouse contracted to purchase it subject to the requisitioning. On the same day he agreed to sell to the purchaser, no reference to the requisitioning being in the contract. After H. had taken a conveyance of the house and before he conveyed it to the purchaser, the house was derequisitioned and compensation became payable to H. under the Compensation (Defence) Act 1939 s. 2 (1) (b) and 2 (3). The purchaser claimed that H. was a trustee of the compensation for her. *Held*, the purchaser was not beneficially entitled to the compensation as H. did not contract to sell it to her and though after contracting to sell the house H. became a trustee of it for the purchaser, yet he was a trustee for her only of that which he had contracted to sell, viz. the house.

Hancock v. B. W. Brazier (Anerley), Ltd., [1966] 2 All E.R. 901   **[179]**
(Court of Appeal)

A contract for the sale of a house in the course of erection provided that prior to completion the vendor would "in a proper and workmanlike manner erect . . . a dwellinghouse in accordance with the plan and specification" and that "if the purchaser shall discover any structural defects in the said house and works within six months from the date of completion and shall notify . . ." the builder such defects would be made good at the builder's expense. Unsuitable materials were used in the construction, both before and after the contract was entered into and substantial damage arose two years later. The purchaser brought an action for breach of the obligation to build in a proper and workmanlike manner. *Held*, the purchaser was entitled to a three-fold warranty in the contract for sale: (*a*) that the work would be done in a proper and workmanlike manner; (*b*) that the materials would be good and proper and (*c*) that the house would be reasonably fit for habitation. Warranty (*b*) included materials used before the contract was signed. (See also *Jennings* v. *Tavener* but see *Greswolde-Williams* v. *Barneby*.)

Hargreaves Transport, Ltd. v. Lynch, [1969] 1 All E.R. 455   **[180]**
(Court of Appeal)

The defendant applied for outline planning permission to erect a transport depot. While the application was pending he agreed to sell the site to the plaintiffs who paid a deposit. The balance was to be paid on April 1st, 1966, subject to a condition that the plaintiffs should obtain planning permission to use the site as a transport depot and develop it by erection of buildings. Planning permission was to be deemed not to have been received if it was subject to a condition which the plaintiffs reasonably considered unacceptable. On April 1st, 1966 the plaintiffs submitted detailed plans for approval. On April 5th outline planning permission was granted. Following objections by local residents, on June 13th the local authority refused approval of the detailed plans. On June 14th the plaintiffs gave notice to rescind the contract. The defendant refused to return the deposit. *Held*, the plaintiffs were entitled to rescission and the return of their deposit as: (i) although in planning law outline permission was the permission, it was insufficient for the plaintiffs' purpose because they could not erect buildings and accordingly outline permission was not the permission required by the contract; (ii) the plaintiffs had done everything reasonable to obtain detailed planning permission and could not reasonably be expected to appeal to the Minister, which could postpone completion for six months or more.

Once detailed plans were submitted to the authority and a final decision obtained on them, the plaintiffs were entitled to end the contract. (But see *Richard West & Partners (Inverness), Ltd.* v. *Dick.*)

Harris v. Swick Securities, Ltd., [1969] 3 All E.R. 1131   [181]
    (Court of Appeal)

The leaseholder of premises under a tenancy which was a long tenancy at a low rent within the Leasehold Reform Act 1967 occupied the basement and sublet the other three floors to tenants. *Held*, the leaseholder was entitled to acquire the freehold because under s. 1 (2) of the Act of 1967 a person was entitled to say he occupied the house as his residence when he occupied part only and sublet the rest.

Hartley v. Minister of Housing and Local Government,   [182]
    [1969] 3 All E.R. 1658 (Court of Appeal)

Up to 1961 land was used as a petrol filling station and for the display and sale of cars. It was then taken over by a Mr. Fisher who died shortly after and his widow and nineteen-year old son ran the business. The petrol filling station business continued but very few cars were sold, the widow not wishing the son to sell cars as he was inexperienced. In 1965 Mr. Hartley bought the property and commenced selling cars in a big way. The planning authority served an enforcement notice requiring the site to be used only for the sale of petrol. The Court of Appeal upheld the decision of the Queens Bench Division that there had been abandonment of the car sales use between 1961 and 1965 and that resumption of that use was a material change of use for which planning permission was required; hence the planning authority was entitled to serve the enforcement notice.

Harvey v. Facey, [1893] A.C. 552 (Privy Council)   [183]

The appellants telegraphed "Will you sell us Bumper Hall Pen? Telegraph lowest cash price." The respondents telegraphed "Lowest cash price for Bumper Hall Pen £900". The appellants telegraphed "We agree to buy Bumper Hall Pen for £900 asked by you. Please send us your title deeds so that we may get early possession." *Held*, there was no contract. The final telegram was not an acceptance of an offer to sell land for none had been made. It was an offer to buy, the acceptance of which must be expressed and could not be implied.

Hawkins v. Price, [1947] 1 All E.R. 689   [184]

A vendor and purchaser reached agreement for the sale of a bungalow and the vendor gave the following receipt in respect of the payment by the purchaser of £100 deposit: "Received of [the purchaser] the sum of £100 being deposited on bungalow and ground named 'Oakdene', Station Road, Stoke Mandeville, Bucks., sold for £1,000." The receipt made no mention of the fact that vacant possession was to be given by a certain date. The purchaser sought a decree of specific performance. *Held*, a decree would not be awarded as the contract was not evidenced by a sufficient note or memorandum as required by s. 40 of the Law of Property Act 1925, in that the receipt made no mention of the agreement as to vacant possession. This agreement was a material term of the contract of benefit to both parties, so that it could not be waived by the purchaser to enable him to proceed on those terms of the agreement evidenced by the receipt. (See also *Burgess* v. *Cox* and *Gavaghan* v. *Edwards*.)

Hayward v. Challoner, [1967] 3 All E.R. 122 (Court of Appeal)   [185]

Before 1938 a small piece of land was let to the Rector of a church at 10s. per annum for use as a garden. No rent was paid after 1942 when a year's rent was paid in advance. The land was used as an adjunct to cottages on glebe land. In 1955 the plaintiffs bought a farm including the piece of land. The defendant was inducted in April, 1962. In 1966 the plaintiffs brought an action for possession. *Held*, there having been a periodic oral tenancy to the Rector as such he ceased to be a tenant when the period covered by the last payment of rent expired and subsequent possession was adverse possession. Accordingly the plaintiffs' right of action to recover the land was barred by s. 4 (3), 9 (2) and 10 (1) of the Limitation Act 1939 by reason of more than 12 years' adverse possession.

Healey v. Hawkins, [1968] 3 All E.R. 836 [186]

The plaintiff owned the fee simple of a dwellinghouse and land having a driveway on the north-east side. The defendant owned land adjoining the driveway. In 1928 C., a predecessor in title of the defendant, built a bungalow and used as access to it for his motor cycle, a narrow pathway along the plaintiff's drive. In 1935 C. acquired a three-wheeled car and widened the pathway but in wet weather he used the plaintiff's drive with permission given from time to time. In 1938 C. acquired a larger car and regularly used the plaintiff's drive until his death. C.'s son thereafter used the plaintiff's drive for his car when visiting the widow until her death in 1961. In 1961 the defendant purchased the property and let it to tenants who regularly used the drive until they left in 1966. From 1966 until the issue of the writ in March, 1967 the land was unoccupied while a new house was being built by the defendant. The plaintiff applied for an injunction to prevent the defendant from using his drive. The defendant claimed a right under the Prescription Act 1832. *Held*, (i) once permission had been given the user must remain permissive and was not capable of ripening into a right save where the permission was oral and user had continued for 40 or 60 years, unless and until, having been given for a limited period only, it expired or, being general, it was revoked, or there was a change of circumstances from which revocation could be implied; (ii) the user, though permissive in origin, changed its character in 1938 when C. began to use the plaintiff's drive regularly and became non-permissive. That user continued under C.'s widow and the defendant's tenants and therefore the plaintiff's drive had been regularly used by the defendant and his predecessors in title for upwards of 20 years next before the issue of the writ and the defendant had acquired a prescriptive right.

Herklots' Will Trusts, Re. Temple v. Scorer, [1964] 2 All E.R. 66 [187]

A testatrix, by will, gave her residue, including a house, to trustees on trust for sale. The trustees were to pay the income to G. during life "without prejudice to the trust for sale herein contained and shall permit her to reside in the house for so long as she wishes". Subject thereto, the residue was as to one third for T. and two thirds to others. By a codicil the testatrix directed the trustees to transfer to T. "absolutely if he desires my house in part settlement of the one third share to which he may become entitled". *Held*, G. could not sell the house without T.'s consent. On the construction of the will there was an immediate binding trust for sale but only exercisable with the consent of G. and T.

Hesketh v. Willis Cruisers Ltd., (1968), 206 Estates Gazette 1193 [188]
(Court of Appeal)

In 1941 Miss S. conveyed Nye Meadow on the bank of the Thames and Rose Eyot, an island connected to Nye Meadow by a footbridge, and two other islands to Mrs. B. Under the conveyance Mrs. B. acquired a corporeal fishery, the fee simple in the bed of the river. Mrs. B. was registered as the first proprietor of the fee simple at H.M. Land Registry. The result of rule 278, Land Registry Rules 1925 (the boundaries rule) was to include in the registered title the whole of the bed of the river between the islands and between the river bank and the islands. In 1950 Mrs. B. sold Rose Eyot, another island and the eastern strip of Nye Meadow to Mrs. Hesketh's predecessor in title. Where the owner of land, which includes the bed of a river, transferred land on one side of the river and retained the opposite bank, in the absence of an express provision, there was a presumption that the transfer included the bed of the river adjacent to the land transferred up to the median line between the banks of the land transferred and the land retained. The title was transferred to Mrs. Hesketh in 1954. Mrs. Hesketh was awarded damages in the county court for trespass by wrongful mooring of holiday cruisers at Nye Meadow and demolition of a concrete post belonging to her. The defendants appealed. *Held*, the acts of trespass alleged were in waters beyond the median line. Mrs. Hesketh had no greater rights than her predecessor in title and had failed to rebut the presumption that she owned the river bed only to the median line. The appeal against finding of trespass therefore succeeded. The county court judge had found that the concrete post was on Mrs. Hesketh's land, although the defendants had reasonably believed that it encroached on their land. That was a finding of fact and the court would not upset it.

Hewitt v. Leicester City Council, [1969] 2 All E.R. 802   **[189]**
(Court of Appeal)

In May, 1965 the Corporation, acting under a compulsory purchase order, sent notice to treat by recorded delivery to the owner of a house. The letter was returned marked "gone away" and "returned undelivered". In December, 1965 the notice was sent to the claimant's appointed agents. Compensation payable at the date of the service of the notice to treat was £1,100 if service was effected in May but £1,500 if effected in December. *Held*, the letter having been returned it could not have been served and could not be deemed "to have been effected at the time at which the letter would be delivered in the ordinary course of post" within the Interpretation Act 1889. Hence the notice to treat was not served until December, 1965.

Hewson v. Shelley, [1914] 2 Ch. 13   **[190]**

Land was sold by the administratrix of a deceased's estate who had obtained a grant of letters of administration on the footing that the deceased had died intestate. Later a will was found appointing another person executor and devising the land. The grant of letters of administration was revoked. *Held*, the purchaser of the land was not prejudiced by the revocation of the grant and had a good title. (See now Administration of Estates Act 1925, s. 37.)

Heywood v. B.D.C. Properties, Ltd., [1963] 2 All E.R. 1063   **[191]**
(Court of Appeal)

The correspondence commencing the transaction contained the words "subject to contract". It was held that these words attached to the whole transaction with the result that no binding contract came into existence. Hence registration of a Land Charge Class C. (iv) under s. 10 (1) of the Land Charges Act 1925 must be vacated. It was held that an order for vacation of the registration could be made under s. 10 (8) of the Act of 1925 on application by interlocutory motion, even though the relief claimed in the action was merely a declaration that no contract existed. (See also *Sim* v. *Griffiths*; but see *Re Engall's Agreement*.)

High Street, Deptford, No. 139, Re, Ex p. British Transport   **[192]**
Commission, [1951] 1 All E.R. 950

In 1948 land at Deptford was conveyed to a purchaser, being described as "all that shop and dwellinghouse situate at and known as No. 139 High Street, Deptford". No plan was annexed either to the contract or conveyance. Both vendor and purchaser believed that the property included a piece of land to the south of the vendor's land, to which access was possible only over the vendor's land. In fact this piece of land belonged to the adjoining owners, the British Transport Commission. The purchaser was registered at H.M. Land Registry as first registered proprietor with absolute title. The plan annexed to the land certificate showed included in the title the piece of land which belonged to the British Transport Commission. Later the British Transport Commission discovered the error and applied to the court for rectification of the register by exclusion from it of the land wrongly included. *Held,* the applicants were entitled to rectification, even against a registered proprietor in occupation because the purchaser had contributed to the error in the register within s. 82 (3) (a) of the Land Registration Act 1925 by putting forward a misleading description of the property. However, the purchaser, not having been fraudulent, would not be precluded from claiming indemnity. (But see now Land Registration Act 1966, s. 1 (4).)

Highett and Bird's Contract, Re, [1903] 1 Ch. 287   [193]

A purchaser entered into an open contract to purchase a leasehold house. The purchaser knew that the lease contained a covenant to keep in good repair and that he was buying at a reduced price because the house had not been kept in repair. The vendor produced a receipt for the last rent paid. *Held,* production of the receipt for the last rent paid is not, under the Conveyancing Act of 1881 s. 3 (4), conclusive evidence of due performance of the covenants in a lease but only "unless the contrary appears". Therefore the purchaser can deduce evidence of non-performance as a ground for resisting specific performance. The vendor's obligation to make good title was not removed by the knowledge of the purchaser that the title was bad by reason of the breach of covenant and hence the expense of complying with a dangerous structure notice fell upon the vendor. (But see *Butler* v. *Mountview Estates, Ltd.*)

Hillingdon Estates Co. v. Stonefield Estates, Ltd.,   [194]
[1952] 1 All E.R. 853

The plaintiffs agreed to purchase building land from the defendants, the land to be taken up in three portions. After the first two portions had been taken up Middlesex County Council made a compulsory purchase order in respect of the third portion and served notice to treat on both parties. The plaintiffs contended that the contract had been frustrated. The defendants counterclaimed for specific performance. VAISEY, J. said there was absence of authority that frustration applied to contracts for the sale of land. Contracts having been exchanged the purchasers became owners in equity and therefore they were the party affected by the compulsory purchase order. The position had not been altered in such a catastrophic way as to justify the court in saying that the contract was frustrated. The land could be conveyed subject to the notice to treat and the plaintiffs would be entitled to the compensation money payable on compulsory purchase. The defendants were entitled to an order for specific performance.

Hinderer v. Weir, [1953] C.P.L. 164 (Court of Appeal)   [195]

The plaintiff agreed to purchase from the defendant a leasehold interest for £1,200. The lease contained a covenant against assignment without the landlord's licence. The contract provided that the purchaser should produce all references required by the landlord. The plaintiff produced references from a bank, solicitors and a householder. The bank's reference stated that he was a respectable person but they had no knowledge of his resources. The solicitors' reference stated he was respectable and responsible and should be able to pay the rent. The landlord refused his licence. The defendant sold the property for £800 and refused to return the plaintiff's deposit of £120. The plaintiff claimed rescission of the contract and the return of his deposit. The defendant counterclaimed £400 damages for breach of contract, alleging that the plaintiff had failed to supply the references as required by the landlord. *Held,* the plaintiff was only required to do his best and, although the bank's reference was unsatisfactory, he had complied with his obligation under the contract and was entitled to rescind and to the return of his deposit.

Hissett v. Reading Roofing Co., Ltd., [1970] 1 All E.R. 122   [196]
[1969] 1 W.L.R. 1757

A contract for the sale of land included a special condition that vacant possession would be given on completion. The contract also incorporated Condition 33 of the Law Society's Conditions of Sale 1953 which provided that "notwithstanding the completion of the purchase any general or special condition . . . to which effect is not given by the conveyance and which is capable of taking effect after completion . . . shall remain in full force and effect." The property sold included a flat occupied by a protected tenant and vacant possession of this could not be given on completion. *Held*, the vendor was liable in damages for breach of contract by failure to give vacant possession of the whole of the property on completion. Notwithstanding that the condition as to vacant possession was to be performed on completion, it fell within Condition 33 as a "condition capable of taking effect after completion". Even apart from Condition 33, the provision of vacant possession still subsisted after completion. It did not merge in the conveyance as it was not a matter with which the conveyance was concerned. (See also *Cumberland Consolidated Holdings, Ltd.* v. *Ireland.*)

Holland v. Tolley [1952], C.P.L. 34 (Court of Appeal)   [197]
Following negotiations an offer was made by telegram on April 12th to purchase freehold premises and a tobacconist's business for £7,800. The offer was accepted by telegram. On the same day the vendor signed a memorandum that he accepted the offer subject to completion on May 20th and the terms of the contract being agreed by the parties' solicitors. The purchaser confirmed his offer in writing to the vendor and the vendor's agents. A draft contract was submitted by the vendor's solicitors to the purchaser's solicitors. On May 1st the purchaser wrote that he did not intend to proceed. *Held*, the parties had agreed the material terms of the contract when they exchanged telegrams and that a concluded agreement had then arisen. What had followed was by way of reducing the terms of the agreement to writing in a formal way. The purchaser was, therefore, in breach of contract and the vendor could claim damages. (See also *Branca* v. *Cobarro*.)

Horwitz v. Rowson, [1960] 2 All E.R. 881   [198]
A lease contained a covenant "not to suffer or permit material change of use" without the landlord's consent. The premises consisted of a ground floor shop and a basement on the other side of the street. The shop was used for the sale of flowers and seeds and the basement for storing plants and bulbs and making and repairing seed boxes and trays. The tenant sublet the basement as a store, workshop and warehouse for a printing business. The question was whether the premises as a whole had a primary use as a shop or whether there had been mixed user as a shop and a workshop which had been severed by the sublease. *Held*, the premises could not be regarded as a shop as a whole but there could be light industrial user as a whole. Hence the user of the basement for other light industrial purpose was permitted by the Use Classes Order and did not constitute development so as to cause breach of covenant in the lease. (But see *Brookes* v. *Flintshire County Council*.)

Hotchkys, Re. Freke v. Calmady (1886), 32 Ch.D. 408   [199]
A testator by will gave "all my real and personal estate" to trustees in fee simple "upon trust at their discretion to sell all such parts thereof as shall not consist of money". *Held*, the will created a mere power of sale and there was no trust for sale of the land.

Household Fire and Carriage Accident Insurance Co. v.   [200]
     Grant (1879), 4 Ex.D. 216; (1874–80) All E.R. Rep. 919

Where an offer has been made to a person who is expressly or by implication authorised to accept it by post, then, as soon as a letter containing an acceptance is posted correctly addressed to the offeror, the contract is complete, even though the letter never reaches the offeror. (But see *King* v. *O'Shee*.)

Howatson v. Webb, [1908] 1 Ch. 1   [201]

The defendant, a solicitor, signed deeds having been told they were deeds of transfer of land. One of the deeds was a mortgage containing a covenant for payment of principal and interest. In an action by a transferee of the mortgage the defendant pleaded *non est factum*. *Held*, the plea failed as the misrepresentation was only as to the contents of a deed known by the defendant to deal with the property and the defendant was liable on the covenant. (See also *Gallie* v. *Lee*.)

Hughes v. Griffin, [1969] 1 All E.R. 460 (Court of Appeal)   [202]

The testator owned a freehold house and lived there with his wife. In 1951 he conveyed the property to his nephew without telling his wife or his nephew. Later he informed the nephew and in 1959 handed him the title deeds. In 1960 the testator offered to give up occupation but the nephew told him to stay. The testator's will, made in 1965, referred to the conveyance and to the nephew's not having required occupation. The testator died in 1965 and the widow remained in occupation. The nephew claimed possession but the widow contended his right of action was barred by s. 4 (3) of the Limitation Act 1939 as more than twelve years had elapsed since the conveyance of 1951. *Held*, the nephew's claim succeeded as the testator had been in possession as the nephew's licensee and there had been no adverse possession. *Per curiam*: Had the testator's possession been adverse, the handing over of the title deeds in 1959 or the conversation in 1960 created a tenancy at will which would have interrupted the limitation period.

Hughes v. Waite, [1957] 1. W.L.R. 713   [203]

A prospective purchaser of land agreed to grant various leases. Before the tenants went into possession the purchaser was registered as proprietor of the land at H.M. Land Registry and executed a mortgage which was also registered. *Held*, the mortgagees were not bound by the tenancy agreements which had not been protected by registration and which were not overriding interests under s. 70 of the Land Registration Act 1925 as the tenants were not in occupation at the time the mortgagees acquired their interest. (But see *Grace Rymer Investments, Ltd.* v. *Waite*.)

Hunt (Charles), Ltd. v. Palmer, [1931] 2 Ch. 287   [204]

Leasehold premises were described in auction particulars as "valuable business premises". The sale was subject to the National Conditions of Sale, a clause in which provided that leases or copies thereof could be examined before the sale and that the purchaser was deemed to purchase with notice of the contents thereof. The purchaser only became aware of the sale on the day it was to be held. He was not supplied with a copy of the National Conditions and, relying on the particulars, successfully bid at the auction. On investigation of title it was discovered that the covenants in the lease of a shop limited the user to one trade only. *Held*, (i) that shop premises so limited could not be accurately described as "valuable business premises" and (ii) such a misleading statement was a misrepresentation which disentitled the vendors, despite the condition in the contracts to specific performance. The purchaser was entitled to rescission and recovery of his deposit.

Hunt v. Luck, [1902] 1 Ch. 428 (Court of Appeal)   [205]

Occupation of land by a tenant is constructive notice to a purchaser of the tenant's rights but not notice of the lessor's title or rights. Actual knowledge by the purchaser that rents are paid to someone whose receipt of them is inconsistent with the title of the vendor is constructive notice of that person's rights. Knowledge that rents are paid to an estate agent does not affect a purchaser with such notice.

Inwards v. Baker, [1956] 1 All E.R. 446 (Court of Appeal)   [206]

In 1931 a father suggested to his son, who wanted a piece of land on which to build a bungalow, that the son should build the bungalow on a piece of his, the father's land. The son gave up the idea of purchasing other land and built the bungalow on the father's land. The father made no contractual arrangement or promise as to the terms on which the son should occupy the land or for how long he should remain in occupation, but the son believed that he would be allowed to remain there for his life time or for so long as he wished. The father died in 1951. Under his will, made in 1922, the land vested in trustees for the benefit of persons other than the son. In 1963 the trustees sought possession of the bungalow. *Held,* where a person spends money on the land of another in the expectation, induced or encouraged by the owner of the land, that he will be allowed to remain in occupation, equity will protect his occupation of the land in such manner as the court will determine. The son was permitted to remain in occupation of the bungalow for so long as he desired. (See also *Ives (E.R.) Investments, Ltd.* v. *High*.)

Irani Finance, Ltd. v. Singh, [1969] 3 All E.R. 1455;   [207]
     [1970] 2 W.L.R. 117

In 1964 T.S. and G.S. purchased a house as beneficial joint tenants with the aid of a building society mortgage. The building society assigned their interest to M. Ltd. In 1968 the plaintiffs obtained judgments against both T.S. and G.S. and then obtained charging orders against the interest of each in the property. The plaintiffs sought a declaration against M. Ltd. that they were entitled to redeem the mortgage on payment of whatever was owing to M. Ltd. on the taking of the account. *Held,* the plaintiffs were not entitled to redeem the mortgage as the charging orders were ineffective because when the charging orders were made the debtors, T.S. and G.S., as joint tenants holding the land on trust for sale had merely an interest in the proceeds of sale of the property. They did not have any "land or interest in land" as required by s. 35 (1) of the administration of Justice Act 1956. On the true construction of the Section the interests of joint tenants in realty to which they were both legally and beneficially entitled did not fall within the expression "interest in land" and accordingly charging orders made under the Section did not create any charge of the joint tenants' interests in the realty. (See also *Re Rayleigh Weir Stadium*.)

Iveagh v. Harris, [1929] 2 Ch. 142   [208]

An action by a reversioner to recover possession of leasehold land under a power of re-entry for breach of a restrictive covenant contained in a lease, is not a "proceeding by action . . . to enforce a restrictive covenant" within s. 84 (9) of the Law of Property Act 1925. Accordingly, the court will not stay the action to enable the lessee to apply to the Lands Tribunal for an order modifying or discharging the restriction.

Ives (E.R.) Investments, Ltd. v. High, [1967] 1 All E.R. 504   [209]
     (Court of Appeal, Civil Division)

The plaintiffs' predecessor in title, one Westgate, and the defendant bought adjoining building sites, and the foundations of Westgate's block of flats encroached at least twelve inches into the defendant's land. The defendant objected to the trespass, but he and Westgate agreed (evidence of the agreement was contained in letters which passed between them) in 1949 that the foundations could remain and that the defendant could have a right of way across the yard of the block of flats. Westgate sold his land in 1950 to a Mr. and Mrs. Wright and

in 1959 the defendant built a garage on his land so positioned that access to it
could only be gained over the yard. The Wrights watched the garage being built
and complimented the defendant on it. In 1960 the defendant contributed one-
fifth of the cost of re-surfacing the yard and in 1963 the Wrights conveyed their
land to the plaintiffs subject "to the right (if any) of the owners and occupiers of
[the defendant's property] as now enjoyed to pass and repass with or without
vehicles over the open yard". The right of way was never registered as a land
charge. *Held*, the defendant had in equity a good right of way across the yard
by virtue of the principle *qui sentit commodum sentire debet et onus* and by virtue
of equitable estoppel or acquiescence of the plaintiffs' immediate predecessors in
title, and neither of these rights was an estate contract or equitable easement
within Class C (iv) or Class D (iii) of s. 10 (1) of the Land Charges Act 1925, with
the consequence that neither right was invalidated for want of registration.

Jackson v. Andrew, [1952] C.P.L. 396   [210]

The owner of two adjoining houses occupied one and sold the other to the
defendant. On the day she signed the contract for sale the vendor wrote to the
defendant that, in consideration of his purchase, should she at any time decide to
sell the other property she would give him first option to purchase at £4,000. On
her death, her trustees took out a summons asking whether they were bound by
the option. Upjohn, J. said the extent of the option depended on whether the
decision to sell had to be reached in the lifetime of the deceased or whether it
could be reached by her personal representatives. *Held*, the defendant was given
an option to purchase only if the owner herself decided to sell and therefore the
option was limited to her lifetime and was no longer exercisable.

Jameson v. Kinmell Bay Land Co., Ltd. (1931), 47 T.L.R. 593   [211]

An estate company, by their agent, orally promised an intending purchaser of
a building plot that a road, marked on a plan shown to him and giving access to
the plot, would be constructed within a reasonable time. The purchaser entered
into a written contract to purchase the plot and took a conveyance which did not
mention the road. Two years later the road had not been constructed and the
purchaser claimed damages for breach of contract. The company alleged the
claim was an attempt to vary a written contract by parol evidence and that such
a promise required writing to satisfy s. 40 (1) of the Law of Property Act 1925.
Held, (i) the oral promise did not form part of the contract to purchase but was a
separate contract and evidence of its terms could be given without contravening
the rule that parol evidence may not be given to vary a written agreement; (ii) a
promise to construct a road was not a "contract for the sale or other disposition,
of land or any interest in land" within s. 40 (1) of the Law of Property Act 1925,
so that action would lie upon it although the contract was oral.

Jaques v. Lloyd D. George & Partners, [1968] 2 All E.R. 187   [212]
(Court of Appeal)

The plaintiff orally agreed with the defendants, estate agents, for the sale of
his café and leasehold premises at £2,500. He signed a printed form of particulars
of sale including the clause "should you be instrumental in introducing a person
willing to sign a document capable of becoming a contract to purchase at a price,
which at any stage of the negotiations has been agreed by me, I agree to pay you
a commission of £250". The defendants introduced S. who signed a contract
subject to S. supplying satisfactory references and the landlord granting licence to
assign the lease. S. paid £250 deposit to the defendants but his references were
unsatisfactory and the landlord refused licence to assign. S. recovered his £250
from the plaintiff who sought to reclaim it from the defendants but they counter-
claimed for commission. *Held*, the defendants were not entitled to commission as
either the meaning of the clause was so uncertain as not to be enforceable or the
meaning of the clause had been misrepresented to the plaintiff. *Sheggia* v.
Gradwell distinguished.

Jeffkin's Indentures, Re, [1965] 1 All E.R. 608   **[213]**

By an originating summons the plaintiffs applied to the court for a declaration under s. 84 (2) of the Law of Property Act 1925 that neither of two properties owned by the plaintiffs was affected by any of the restrictive covenants contained in three indentures, dated respectively July 15th, 1873, November 11th, 1875 and June 18th, 1877, each made by George Jeffkin and another and that such restrictive covenants were not enforceable by any person. The third indenture included some land not belonging to the plaintiffs. The thirty-seven defendants did not appear and were not represented. *Held,* the declaration asked for, although followed the wording in the Act, was too wide in this case because it might operate for the benefit of other people besides the plaintiffs. The proper declaration was simply to declare that the two properties belonging to the plaintiffs were not affected by any of the restrictive covenants.

Jelbert v. Davis, [1968] 1 All E.R. 1182 (Court of Appeal)   **[214]**

In 1961 land was conveyed to the plaintiff with the benefit of a right of way over a metalled track on the defendant's land "at all times and for all purposes . . . in common with all other persons having a like right." In 1966 the plaintiff opened a site for a maximum of 200 caravans, having obtained planning permission for this use. The defendant objected to the excessive use of the track by caravans. *Held,* the plaintiff's use of the track was inconsistent with the terms of the grant. Although such an easement would permit user by vehicles other than those being used at the date of the grant, it would not entitle the grantee to excessive use outside reasonable contemplation at the date of the grant. (But see *McIlraith* v. *Grady*.)

Jelson v. Minister of Housing and Local Government: **[215]**
Wimpey (George) & Co., Ltd. v. the Same, [1969] 3 All E.R. 147
(Court of Appeal)

In 1954 owners were granted permission to develop their land for residential purposes, with the exception of a strip proposed to be the site of a ring road. The proposal for the road was abandoned in 1962. Housing had by then been constructed on the greater part of the land. The owners served a purchase notice under s. 129 of the Town and Country Planning Act 1962 in respect of the undeveloped strip. The purchase notice was confirmed and the owners applied under s. 17 (4) (a) of the Land Compensation Act 1961 for a certificate of appropriate alternative residential development. Planning permission could not be granted for any beneficial purpose for the strip of land, owing to its shape and the proximity of the houses erected. Had application for planning permission been made before the ring road proposals, planning permission could well have been granted for the whole of the land including the strip. *Held,* a certificate of alternative development could be refused as the planning authority had to determine what planning permission could reasonably have been granted at the date of the deemed notice to treat. At that date the Minister was entitled to find that planning permission could not reasonably have been granted for residential development.

Jennings v. Tavener, [1955] 2 All E.R. 769   **[216]**

The plaintiff's husband agreed in writing to purchase a bungalow which was in course of erection. The defendant was building it according to plans prepared by an architect but not under the architect's supervision. The purchase was completed and the plaintiff and her husband moved into the bungalow, which subsequently developed cracks owing to withdrawal of moisture from the soil by the roots of poplar trees some 30 to 40 feet from the bungalow. The husband died and the plaintiff sued for damages for breach of contract that the house should be fit for habitation. *Held,* the warranty implied in a contract for the sale of a house in the course of construction that, when completed, the house shall be fit for habitation, extends to the foundations below ground. As these had not been constructed in a manner which ensured they did not settle in consequence of extraction of moisture from the soil by the roots of neighbouring poplars, the defendant was liable in damages for breach of the warranty. (See also *Miller* v. *Cannon Hill Estates* and *Perry* v. *Sharon Development Co., Ltd.*)

Jennings' Trustee v. King, [1952] 2 All E.R. 608   **[217]**

The defendant agreed to sell land to J. for £3,750 by a contract dated August 29th, 1951, with completion on November 30th, 1951. J. paid 10% deposit and went into possession. He did works on the land to the value of £700. On November 29th J. committed an act of bankruptcy. On December 3rd the defendant's solicitors wrote to repudiate the contract and claiming forfeiture of the deposit. J. was adjudicated bankrupt on December 5th and the plaintiff was appointed his trustee in bankruptcy on December 21st. In January, 1952 the defendant contracted to sell the property to another purchaser for £4,900, completion to be in March, 1952. In February, 1952 the plaintiff registered the contract as an estate contract but cancelled the registration in March. The plaintiff brought an action for breach of contract, contending that his title as trustee related back to the first act of bankruptcy. The defendant alleged that notice of an act of bankruptcy was a repudiation of the contract which he had accepted before adjudication; hence on December 3rd he was entitled to forfeit the deposit and retain the work executed on the land by J. He alleged that the plaintiff had wrongly interfered with his contractual relations with the other purchaser and counter-claimed for damages. HARMAN, J. held that a vendor could not treat an act of bankruptcy before the date of completion as anticipatory breach. The legislature had made acts of bankruptcy available to creditors for three months; the vendor must either await that period to see if he could safely complete or file a petition in bankruptcy if no other creditor took that step in the interim. The defendant's purported rescission was invalid and there would be judgment for the plaintiff.

Johnson v. Clarke, [1928] Ch. 847   **[218]**

A testator who died in 1911 devised his real estate to executors and trustees on trust for sale with power to postpone sale and lease any unsold property. In 1927 the trustees contracted to sell part of the property. The premises had been occupied for some years by R., who was described in the contract as a tenant from year to year. R. produced a letter of 1915, signed by one of the trustees, purporting to give R. an indefinite option to purchase or to take a lease for any term and an undertaking that so long as R. remained sole tenant the rent would not be increased. The purchaser refused to complete on the ground that R. had a tenancy for life at a fixed rent. *Held*, R. was only a tenant from year to year and any greater right could not have been given to him as it was beyond the powers of the vendors as personal representatives. The agreement of 1915 was, therefore, no defence to an action for specific performance of the contract of sale. The court is bound to decide questions of law, involving construction of a document of doubtful meaning, as between vendor and purchaser, even though the decision may not bind a third party interested. It will not refuse to do so on the ground of any former rule that the title is too doubtful to force upon a purchaser. (See also *Smith* v. *Colbourne*.)

Johnson and Tustin, Re. (1885), 30 Ch.D. 42   **[219]**

A vendor of land is bound to produce to a purchaser a proper abstract of title, either for the statutory period, or for such other period as may be agreed upon. Under an open contract, the vendor must bear the expense of procuring and making an abstract of any deed not in his possession forming part of the statutory title.

Johnstone v. Holdway, [1963] 1 All E.R. 432   **[220]**
(Court of Appeal)

A vendor agreed to sell certain land to a company and by a conveyance reciting this agreement the vendor as trustee and the company as beneficial owner conveyed part of the land to a purchaser excepting and reserving to the company a right of way "for all purposes (including quarrying)" shown on a plan drawn on the conveyance. Although the vendor and the company were owners of land adjoining the land conveyed, the dominant tenement was not identified precisely in the conveyance. *Held*, this fact did not defeat the exception and reservation of the right of way as it was a question of the construction of the deed by which it was created (*i.e.*, the conveyance) and, in all the circumstances, and especially because at the time of the conveyance the purchaser would have been aware of the original agreement and the plan annexed thereto showing that the vendor and the company retained land adjoining including a quarry, the dominant tenement was sufficiently identified. Further, the easement created by the reservation to the company, which operated by way of re-grant, was a legal easement although at the date of the conveyance the company had only an equitable title to the dominant tenement.

Joliffe v. Baker (1883), 11 Q.B.D. 255; 48 L.T. 986   [221]

A vendor of land during negotiations for sale made representations to the purchaser, *bona fide*, that the land contained approximately three acres. After completion and execution of the conveyance the purchaser found the land to be little more than two acres. He sought to recover damages for false representation. *Held*, after completion compensation was not recoverable unless there had been fraud or breach of some condition or warranty contained in the conveyance. There is no such thing as "legal" fraud in the absence of moral fraud. (But see *Palmer* v. *Johnson* and see now Land Registration Act 1966 s. 1 (4) and Misrepresentation Act 1967 s. 1 and 2.)

Jones v. Challenger, [1960] 1 All E.R. 785 (Court of Appeal)   [222]

A husband and wife bought a lease of a house, and provided the purchase money in equal shares; they held on trust for sale, with power to postpone sale and to hold the proceeds on trust for themselves as joint tenants. The marriage broke up, the husband divorced the wife on the ground of her adultery, and the wife remarried. He remained in the former matrimonial home, and she applied under s. 30 of the Law of Property Act 1925 for an order for sale of the house and equal division of the proceeds. *Held*, different considerations arose on applications under s. 30 of the Law of Property Act 1925 and s. 17 of the Married Women's Property Act 1882 as in the latter case the marriage still subsisted. Here, the house had been bought as the matrimonial home, and that purpose had ended; the duty to sell under the trust for sale accordingly prevailed. The house was ordered to be sold, and the proceeds divided equally. "The true question is whether it is inequitable for the wife, once the matrimonial home has gone, to want to realise her investment . . . in my judgment it clearly is not" (*per* DEVLIN, L.J.).

Jones v. Lipman, [1962] 1 All E.R. 442   [223]

A vendor agreed to sell freehold land with registered title for £5,250. Between contract and completion the vendor sold and transferred the title to a company which he had acquired. The company had capital of £100 and the vendor and his solicitor's clerk were sole shareholders and directors. The purchase price of the property to the company was £3,000 of which £1,564 was borrowed on bank loan and the rest was owing to the vendor. Specific performance of the first contract was granted to the purchaser against both the vendor and the company, since the company was a cloak for the fraud of the vendor and the vendor, having the controlling interest in the company, could compel the company to transfer. (See also *Elliot* v. *Pierson*.)

J. W. Cafes, Ltd. v. Brownlow Trust, Ltd., [1950] 1 All E.R. 894   [224]

The defendants, who had the head lease of a shop, agreed with the plaintiffs to grant them a sublease, the lease to be in the form of a draft annexed to the agreement. This contained only one restrictive covenant but previous leases of the property by the defendant's predecessors in title had contained several restrictive covenants in accordance with a scheme for the neighbourhood which ran with the land. After taking counsel's advice, the defendants refused to execute the lease in the agreed form unless they were given an indemnity by the plaintiffs in respect of breach of any of the restrictive covenants affecting the property. The plaintiffs refused the indemnity and brought an action for breach of covenant. *Held*, the defendants' failure to complete was due to a defect in title and the rule in *Bain* v. *Fothergill* applied so that the plaintiffs were entitled only to return of their deposit with interest and their expenses incurred in investigating the title. (But see *Re Daniel*.)

Kelly v. Barrett, [1924] 2 Ch. 379 (Court of Appeal)   [225]

The defendant purchased two houses subject to a covenant not to use except as private residences. She was a medical practitioner and proposed to use the properties as a nursing home. The plaintiff was the successor in title to the land for the benefit of which the covenant was originally imposed but the only land retained was the roadway. The surface of the road had been taken over by the local authority. *Held*, the benefit of restrictive covenants can be validly annexed to the site and soil of a road so as to run with it even after it has been dedicated to the public but if the surface is taken over by the local authority the restrictions do not touch and concern the subsoil which the owner retains.

Kent County Council v. Kingsway Investments (Kent), Ltd.   [226]
The same v. Kenworthy, [1970] 1 All E.R. 70 (House of Lords)

The House of Lords, by a majority, held that a condition, attached to outline planning permission that it "shall cease to have effect" after three years unless the planning authority within that time had approved and notified their approval of detailed plans submitted by the developers, was *inta vires* the Town and Country Planning Act 1947 and the General Development Order 1950. This reversed the decision in the Court of Appeal which had held the condition unreasonable and invalid because it was outside the developers' control. The Court of Appeal had held that the condition could be severed, leaving the planning permission intact. Lords Donovan and Upjohn agreed with that but Lords Reid, Morris of Borth-y-Gest and Guest allowed the appeal on the ground that the condition did not cut down the developers' right of appeal to the Minister if they acted reasonably within the three-years period or such an extended period as was allowed by the authority. It was said that the essence of an outline application was that the applicant knew that permission would be conditional on later approval of reserved matters and time considerations might be highly relevant.

King's Motors (Oxford), Ltd. v. Lax, [1969] 3 All E.R. 665   [227]

A lease contained an option to renew for a further term of seven years "at such rental as may be agreed between the parties". The lease contained no arbitration clause. *Held*, the option was void for uncertainty and unenforceable at law. It was a mere agreement to agree.

King v. O'Shee (1951), 158 Estates Gazette 83   [228]

The vendor and purchaser had each signed their respective parts of a contract for the sale of land preparatory to exchange by post. The plaintiff's part was posted to the defendant's solicitors who received it on June 2nd. On June 2nd the plaintiff telephoned the defendant's solicitors to say that he withdrew from the contract. The defendant's part not having been posted before the telephone call was received, it was held there was no concluded agreement as either party could withdraw before exchange took place. (See also *Eccles* v. *Bryant*.)

King's Will Trusts, Re, Assheton v. Boyne, [1964] 1 All E.R. 833   **[229]**

A testatrix appointed three executors of whom two were also to be trustees. The will was proved by the two executor-trustees, power being reserved to the third executor, J. On the death of one of the proving executors, the other, C., by deed appointed J. a co-trustee of the trust property. On the death of C., J. appointed the plaintiff by deed to be a co-trustee. C.'s will was proved by the sixth defendant. J. died, leaving the plaintiff as sole surviving trustee. The action was brought to determine whether the legal estate in the trust property was vested in the plaintiff as trustee or in the sixth defendant as personal representative of the last surviving proving executor of the estate of the testatrix, or in any other person. *Held*, that since 1925 as a result of s. 36 (4) of the Administration of Estates Act 1925, a written assent is essential to vest the legal estate in land in a trustee or beneficiary, even though the person holding the legal estate as personal representative is the same person as the trustee or beneficiary. Hence the land had been held by the executors of the testatrix as personal representatives and had not been vested in them as trustees. Section 40 of the Trustee Act 1925 would not apply to vest the legal estate in J. or the plaintiff as trustees unless the signature on the deeds of appointment had been by trustees. These deeds had not been executed in the capacity of trustee. Neither could a deed of appointment replace an assent under s. 36 of the Administration of Estates Act. Thus the legal estate had remained with the executors as personal representatives and passed to the sixth defendant as executor by chain of representation.

Klassnick v. Allen, [1969] 3 All E.R. 1278 (Court of Appeal)   **[230]**

In 1961 a basement flat was let furnished on a weekly tenancy to Mr. and Mrs. A., as joint tenants. Subsequently the rent was reduced in consideration of their taking on housekeeping duties. In 1963 Mr. A. deserted his wife and Mrs. A. continued alone in the flat. From time to time much of the landlord's furniture was removed with the landlord's consent and replaced by the tenant's own furniture but the landlord refused to reduce the rent on account of the substitution of furniture. In 1968 the landlord terminated Mrs. A.'s employment as housekeeper and served notice to quit. *Held*, the tenancy had not become an unfurnished tenancy within the protection of the Rent Act 1968. The tenancy had commenced as a furnished letting and the landlord's furniture was still available to the tenant; the landlord had clearly refused an alteration in the character of the letting.

Ladyman v. Wirral Estates, Ltd., [1968] 2 All E.R. 197   **[231]**

An agreement for a business tenancy provided for a term of three years from May 1st, 1963 with rent payable quarterly in advance on May 1st, August 1st, November 1st, and February 1st each year, the first payment to be on May 1st, 1963. *Held*, payment of rent on May 1st, 1963 was strong indication that the tenancy was intended to commence *on* May 1st, 1963. Hence notice under the Landlord and Tenant Act 1954 terminating the tenancy on April 30th, 1966 was valid as stating a date not earlier then the lease would have come to an end, apart from Part II of the Act, by effluxion of time.

Lake v. Bennett, [1970] 1 All E.R. 457 (Court of Appeal)   **[232]**

The plaintiff sought to purchase from the defendant the freehold reversion of a property under the Leasehold Reform Act 1967. She occupied the top two floors and basement for living purposes but had sublet the ground floor to a book-maker and now it was a licensed betting office. The defendant contended the property was not a "house" within s. 2 of the Act of 1967 which provides that "house includes any building designed or adapted for living in and reasonably so-called, notwithstanding that the building is not structurally detached, or was or is not solely designed or adapted for living in, or is divided horizontally into flats or maisonettes." *Held*, the building was a "house" within the Act and the plaintiff was entitled to purchase the freehold. If a building was lived in by a tenant who used the ground floor for business purposes it would be a "house" within the Act; it made no difference if the tenant sublet the ground floor for business purposes.

Landi, Re, Giorgi v. Novani, [1939] Ch. 828   [233]

The testator and one, Fantoni, in 1915 purchased in equal shares leasehold premises in their joint names. From 1915 to 1923 they were in joint possession. From the end of 1923 until his death in 1935 the testator was in sole possession, taking all the rents and profits and not accounting to Fantoni. On the death of Fantoni his widow claimed half the rents and profits from the end of 1923 to the death of the testator. *Held*, the claim from 1923 to January 1st, 1926 was barred under the Statutes of Limitations, Fantoni's interest being a legal interest as tenant in common at law. But on January 1st, 1926 the testator and Fantoni became trustees on the statutory trust for sale imposed by s. 36 of the Law of Property Act 1925 and a fiduciary relationship arose so that the Statutes of Limitations no longer applied. Hence the testator was a trustee for Fantoni and the claim for rents and profits from January 1st, 1926 to the death of the testator should be allowed.

Lawrence v. Cassel, [1930] 2 K.B. 83   [234]

The defendant contracted in writing to sell to the plaintiff a plot of land on a building estate with a house in course of erection and to complete the house in accordance with the plans of other houses and with fittings similar in all material particulars to those in other houses erected on the estate. The land was conveyed by deed which contained no reference to the building of the house. The plaintiff claimed the defendant was in breach of his agreement, having failed to carry out the builder's work in a proper and efficient manner and having failed to use fit and proper materials. *Held*, the agreement to complete the house was collateral to the deed of conveyance and had not merged. The plaintiff, having proved breaches of the building agreement, was entitled to damages. (See also *Hancock v. B. W. Brazier (Anerley), Ltd.*)

Leachman v. L. K. Richardson, Ltd., [1969] 3 All E.R. 20   [235]

The parcels clause in a conveyance did not refer to a plan but a plan was bound up in the conveyance. *Held*, the plan formed part of the conveyance and reference could be made to it to resolve ambiguity in the parcels. *Wyse* v. *Leahy* (1875), I.R.9 C.L. 384 distinguished.

Lee v. Barrey, [1957] 1 All E.R. 191 (Court of Appeal)   [236]

The vendor was the registered proprietor of land of which the road frontage and rear boundary were parallel. The west boundary was at right angles. The east boundary started at right angles from the road but bent inwards to the west. The vendor divided the land into five plots, their side boundaries having an angle following the eastern boundary. In 1949 the defendant purchased Plot No. 4. The plan on the contract and transfer showed the side boundaries having an angle. The plan on the land certificate indicated the side boundaries by dotted lines running straight from back to front of the plot. It was stated on the certificate that the land had been plotted from the transfer plan and were subject to revision after erection of fences. The defendant erected a house on the assumption that the boundary was straight with the result that his building projected at the point of the angle on to Plot No. 3 which was purchased by the plaintiff in 1951. The defendant laid out his garden on the same assumption. The plaintiff claimed a declaration that his north-east boundary was what was, in effect, shown as the south-west boundary on the plan on the transfer to the defendant, and he claimed damages and an injunction. *Held*, (i) it was not a property dispute in the sense of the wrong property having been conveyed to the defendant but a boundary dispute; (ii) by s. 76 of the Land Registration Act 1925 and r. 284

of the Land Registration Rules the boundaries on the filed plan were not intended to be more than indicated and were not precisely defined. The plan on the defendant's land certificate could not be set up to overturn the bargain made with the vendor and recorded in the transfer and the plaintiff was entitled to relief.

Lee v. Gaskell (1876), 1 Q.B.D. 700   [237]

The tenant of premises having become bankrupt, his trustee in bankruptcy sold the tenant's fixtures to the plaintiff who sold them to the defendant, the landlord. There was no agreement in writing. *Held*, the sale was not within s. 4 of the Statute of Frauds as the sale of an interest in land, nor within s. 17 as a sale of goods and chattels and therefore an action on the contract was maintainable despite lack of writing. A contract by a tenant to sell removable fixtures to his landlord is a surrender of his right to remove them.

Lee v. Rayson, [1917] 1 Ch. 613   [238]

A contract provided for the sale of thirteen freehold houses which were let on leases for 99 years at ground rents totalling £72. One pair of houses was described as let at £11 10s., four pairs at £11 and the last three houses at £16 10s. The title shown was for twelve houses at £5 10s. and one at £6, each secured by one of the thirteen houses instead of the six rents in the agreement. There was a provision in the contract that there should be no compensation for error in description and that the contract should not be annulled. *Held*, that although the total of the rents was £72, the property was substantially different from that contracted for and the purchaser was entitled to rescission and return of his deposit.

Leeman v. Stocks, [1951] 1 All E.R. 1043   [239]

The vendor's house was offered for sale by auction and the purchaser was the highest bidder. Before the sale began the auctioneer wrote "W. E. Stocks" (the vendor's name) in the appropriate place on a printed form of agreement, entered the date for completion and particulars of the property and affixed a 6*d*. stamp. When bidding was completed the auctioneer inserted the purchaser's name and address, a description of the premises, the purchase price and the name of the purchaser's solicitor. The purchaser signed the document over the 6*d*. stamp but neither the auctioneer nor the vendor signed it in the usual way. *Held*, the agreement had been "signed by the party to be charged [the vendor] or by some other person thereunto by him lawfully authorised" within s. 40 of the Law of Property Act 1925, as evidence showed that neither party intended any other signature to be added to the document and that it was their intention that the agreement should be the final written record of the contract.

Lehmann v. McArthur (1868), 3 Ch. App. 496   [240]

A lessee contracted to assign his lease to a purchaser, subject to his landlord's licence. The landlord refused his licence because he wished to buy up the lease in order to rebuild. The lessee surrendered his lease to the landlord for the same price as he had contracted to sell to the purchaser. The purchaser sought specific performance of the contract. *Held*, the vendor was only bound to endeavour to obtain his landlord's consent; he did not have to go into the question of whether refusal of consent was unreasonable or to take legal action to obtain the consent. (See also *Lipman's Wallpapers, Ltd. v. Mason and Hodghton Ltd.*)

Lehmann and Walker's Contract, Re, [1906] 2 Ch. 640   [241]

Documents of title showing the title to, and the extinguishment of an easement formerly appurtenant to the land sold, over a servient tenement retained by the vendor, relate to the servient tenement and the vendor has a right to retain them because deeds relating to an easement relate to land.

Le Strange v. Pettefar (1939), 161 L.T. 300 [242]

The plaintiff leased to the defendant a bungalow. Prior to the lease the defendant had a sublease of the property. For some years he had parked his car on a roadway owned by the plaintiff and giving access to bungalows and the foreshore owned by the plaintiff. Members of the public also parked their cars there. The plaintiff had not objected. In 1937 the plaintiff made a car park at the end of the roadway for the use of which there was a small charge. The defendant refused to pay the charge, contending he had a right to park his car as a "liberty, privilege, right or advantage" appurtenant to his bungalow and comprised in his lease by virtue of s. 62 of the Law of Property Act 1925. *Held*, the words in s. 62 connote some right which is the subject of individual or class enjoyment as opposed to general enjoyment. The defendant's position was no different from that of any other members of the public as no right to park appertained to the bungalows.

Lipmanns Wallpapers, Ltd. v. Mason and Hodghton, Ltd., [243]
[1968] 1 All E.R. 1123

A contract for the sale of an underlease provided: "The sale is subject to the reversioner's licence being obtained where necessary . . . if the licence cannot be obtained the vendor may rescind the contract on the same terms as if the purchaser had persisted in an objection to the title which the vendor was unable to remove." The vendor failed to obtain the reversioner's licence. *Held*, the vendor could rescind and the purchaser, having no right to waive the condition and demand an assignment without the licence, was not entitled to notice of the vendor's intention to rescind (as in the purchaser's objection to matters on the title) as it would be pointless to give the purchaser time to consider a matter on which he was not entitled to make a decision. (But see *Basma v. Weekes*.)

Lock v. Bell, [1931] 1 Ch. 35 [244]

It was held that in a contract for the sale of a public house time was of the essence because of the nature of the property. Failure to complete on the due date entitled the vendor to rescind and to forfeit the deposit of £120. However, a clause in the contract providing for payment of £200 on failure by either party to perform any part of the contract was not damages but a penalty and therefore not recoverable.

London Borough of Enfield v. Lavender Garden Properties Ltd., [245]
[1968] 2 All E.R. 401 (Court of Appeal)

The company owned twelve acres of land zoned for allotment purposes. They were refused planning permission and obtained a certificate of alternative development which stated that planning permission might reasonably have been expected to be granted for residential development of a density comparable with that of neighbouring development. This density was agreed to be fifty-five habitable rooms per acre. The company made a further application for planning permission and, on refusal, served a purchase notice which was accepted. The price agreed was £240,000. Subsequently the Council were given permission by the Minister to erect 12-storey blocks of residential accommodation with a density of one hundred habitable rooms per acre. The company applied for further compensation under s. 23 (1) of the Land Compensation Act 1961. *Held*, the development by the Council constituted additional development within s. 23 (1). It was a question of fact for the Lands Tribunal as to whether a buyer in the open market, after the Minister's decision, would have estimated his chances of obtaining planning permission above fifty-five habitable rooms per acre, higher than they were before the Minister's decision. The Tribunal had decided that a buyer would have taken that view. Hence the company were entitled to additional compensation.

London County Council v. Allen, [1914] 3 K.B. 642   [246]

In 1906 the defendant, Allen, a builder, applied to the Council for permission to lay out certain land on which he had an option to purchase. He obtained permission on condition that he covenanted not to build on part of the land which was likely to be required for proposed streets. In a deed of 1907 he covenanted for himself, "his heirs and assigns and other the persons claiming under him" that he would not build on this part of the land and that he would give notice of the covenant on any dealing with the land. In 1908 the land was conveyed to Allen who mortgaged it. On the mortgage being redeemed the land was reconveyed, not to Allen, but to his wife, who erected three houses on the plot and mortgaged the land. The Council contended that the covenant was binding on Mrs. Allen and her mortgagee and sued for damages, an injunction and a demolition order. *Held*, the Council was only entitled to nominal damages against Allen. The covenant could not be enforced against Mrs. Allen and her mortgagee as the Council owned no land in the immediate neighbourhood. SCRUTTON, J. reviewed the development of restrictive covenants since *Tulk* v. *Moxhay* (1848), 2 Ph. 774 and held that the benefit of a restrictive covenant can only be enforced if some land, for the benefit of which the covenant was taken, remains in the possession of the covenantee or his assigns. (But see now Town and Country Planning Act 1962, s. 37, as amended by the Town and Country Planning Act 1968 s. 108 and Sched. 11.)

Long v. Gowlett, [1923] 2 Ch. 177; [1923] All E.R. Rep. 335   [247]

In 1911 the defendant, owner of a water mill situated on a river, failed in an action against the predecessors in title of the plaintiff, an upper riparian owner, for an injunction to restrain interference with free flow of water to the mill and a declaration that the defendant was entitled to pass and repass along the river banks to repair the banks and cut weeds. In 1921 the plaintiff began an action for an injunction to restrain the defendant from trespassing on the river and its banks. The defendant pleaded in defence the same rights as he had claimed in 1911. Both the mill and the higher riparian land had at one time been in the same ownership and occupation. The two lots were sold at auction in 1845 simultaneously, although the conveyance of the defendant's land was executed a week earlier than that of the plaintiff's land. The conveyance of the defendant's land included "full and free liberty of the stream watercourse and river there running and over which the said mill now stands as the same is now or has been used and occupied with the said mill". *Held*, an estoppel by record operates in respect of the whole right claimed, not merely in respect of the particular claim which failed and because of the earlier action the defendant's claim was *res judicata*. A purchaser will not acquire a right within s. 6(2) of the Conveyancing Act 1881 (now s. 62 (2) of the Law of Property Act 1925) unless there has been some diversity of ownership of the two closes. The only exceptions to this rule appear to be ways of necessity and of continuous and apparent easements. (*Broomfield* v. *Williams*, [1897] 1 Ch. 602 was distinguished on the ground that a right to light is on a different footing from other rights.) The two conveyances of 1845 must be treated as simultaneous, having arisen from the same auction sale. The words in the conveyance of the defendant's land did no more than prevent the grantor from interfering with the stream and gave no definite right to the grantee to go on the banks or river to repair or to cut weeds or do other acts to preserve the flow of water. The plaintiff was granted a declaration and injunction and 40s. damages for the defendant's trespass.

Long v. Millar (1879), 4 C.P.D. 450   [248]

An estate agent, the defendant, contracted to sell the land of one of his clients. The plaintiff signed an agreement and paid a deposit in return for which he was given a receipt signed by the defendant. *Held*, there was a sufficient memorandum for the purposes of s. 4 of the Statute of Frauds (now s. 40 of the Law of

Property Act 1925) as the agreement and the receipt should be taken together. (But see *Timmins* v. *Moreland Street Property Co., Ltd.*)

Longlands Farm, Long Common, Botley, Hants, Re.   [249]
Alford v. Superior Developments, Ltd., [1968] 3 All E.R. 552

The plaintiff owned fifty-seven acres of agricultural land. On April 2nd, 1964 he and the defendants executed a document stating the defendants "were agreeable to purchase" the land at £114,000, subject to the defendants obtaining planning permission to their entire satisfaction for development of the land and approval of the title. The plaintiff signed a receipt for £5 "in consideration of my holding the property for you". The defendants registered the document as a contract under the Land Charges Act 1925 s. 10, Class C (iv). In March, 1967 the plaintiff called on the defendants within twenty-eight days to apply for planning permission or vacate the registration of the Land Charge. The defendants replied that they considered a planning application premature in the circumstances of local conditions but, at the plaintiff's insistence, they applied in April, 1967 for planning permission to develop and were refused planning permission in July, 1967. The plaintiff took out a summons for an order that the Land Charge be vacated. *Held*, (i) the document of April 2nd, 1964 was not an option despite the £5 consideration but was a conditional contract which would become absolute if the defendants obtained planning permission to their satisfaction and approved the title; (ii) since the document did not state a time in which the condition relating to planning permission was to be satisfied, the defendants were given a reasonable time determined at the date of contract and judged by an objective test applicable to both parties; (iii) in all the circumstances, particularly the absence of any provision tying up the land for five years, for which the defendants might well have had to pay more than £5, the period which had elapsed was more than reasonable and the plaintiff was entitled to treat the contract as at an end and have the registration vacated. (See also *Aberfoyle Plantations, Ltd.* v. *Khaw Bian Cheng.*)

Lovesy v. Palmer, [1916] 2 Ch. 233; [1916–17] All E.R. Rep. 1034   [250]

In agreeing the terms of a lease the solicitor acting for the proposed lessee, Mr. Lovesy, referred to "my clients" as Mr. Lovesy intended to form a company to take the lease. *Held*, the agreement was unenforceable as it failed to identify the lessee for the purpose of s. 4 of the Statute of Frauds. (But see *Allen & Co., Ltd.* v. *Whiteman.*)

Lowe v. Hope, [1969] 3 All E.R. 605   [251]

The defendant agreed to purchase the plaintiff's house for £6,295, and to pay 10% by way of deposit to the plaintiff's solicitors. The defendant paid only £40 and then refused to complete the contract. The plaintiff rescinded the contract and claimed the balance of the deposit. *Held*, the plaintiff was entitled to rescind but was not entitled to payment of the balance of the deposit after rescission. (But see *Dewar* v. *Mintoft.*)

Luganda v. Service Hotels Ltd., [1969] 2 All E.R. 692   [252]
(Court of Appeal)

The plaintiff occupied a furnished bed-sitting-room in premises known as the Queensborough Court Hotel in return for a weekly payment. The premises consisted of rooms "let" to "tenants". The plaintiff had a Yale key to his room. The room contained a gas-ring and he prepared his own meals. Bedding and services were provided by the defendants. The defendants proposed to increase the "rent" and on the plaintiff's refusal to pay they gave the plaintiff two days' notice to vacate his room. When he failed to do so, the defendants changed the lock and let the room to another. The plaintiff claimed a mandatory injunction ordering the defendants to allow him back and a further injunction restraining them from interfering with his access to the room. *Held*, Part VI of the Rent Act 1968 applied to the contract, as for the purposes of the Act, a building which is used as a hotel is a house whether it was purpose-built or not. Persons taking a room in a hotel do not usually occupy as a residence but on the facts of this case, where the plaintiff had occupied the room for three years, he was entitled to occupy the premises as a residence. "Exclusive occupation" in s. 70 (2) of the Act of 1968 is not synonymous with exclusive possession. The plaintiff was entitled to security of tenure up to a period of six months under s. 77 of the Act and had been unlawfully excluded from the premises. He was, therefore, entitled to a mandatory injunction pending the trial of the action, having made out a prima facie case.

Lynch v. Thorne, [1956] 1 All E.R. 744 (Court of Appeal)   **[253]**

A builder agreed to sell a plot of land together with a house in the course of erection thereon and to complete the building in accordance with a plan and specification attached to the contract. The specification provided that the south wall to the house was to be a nine-inches solid brick wall. After completion rain penetrated the south wall so as to make one room uninhabitable. The purchaser claimed damages for breach of an implied warranty that the house should be completed so as to be fit for human habitation. It was found that a nine-inches solid brick wall, in that position, would not be weatherproof. *Held*, a warranty that the house, when completed, would be fit for human habitation should not be implied, since there was an express contract between the parties as to the construction of the building and the provisions of the contract had been complied with. (But see *Perry* v. *Sharon Development Co., Ltd.*)

Macara (James), Ltd. v. Barclay, [1945] 1 K.B. 148;   **[254]**
     [1944] 2 All E.R. 31, 589 (Court of Appeal)

A contract for the sale of land provided that vacant possession would be given on completion. It also provided that if the plaintiffs should fail to complete the purchase the deposit would be forfeited, unless the contract otherwise directed. Between contract and completion a notice was served under the Defence (General) Regulations 1939 requisitioning the property. Before the completion date the plaintiffs gave notice that they rescinded the contract on the ground of the defendant's inability to give vacant possession. The defendant contended that, no entry having yet been made under the requisitioning order, vacant possession could be given or, if vacant possession could not be given on the date fixed for completion, the stipulation as to the date for completion was not of the essence of the contract and the plaintiffs were not entitled to rescind, and their deposit should be forfeited. *Held*, (i) since actual entry was not necessary to exercise a power given by the 1939 Regulations, the serving of the requisition notice on the defendant was sufficient to show intention to enter into possession; (ii) hence, the vendor was not able to give vacant possession; (iii) the vendor having offered vacant possession, completion on the date in the contract, though not of the essence, could not be disregarded. The plaintiffs were entitled to repudiate the contract and recover their deposit. (But see *Hillingdon Estates Co.* v. *Stonefield Estates, Ltd.*)

McIlraith v. Grady, [1968] 1 Q.B. 468; [1967] 3 All E.R. 625   **[255]**
     (Court of Appeal)

The plaintiff was the owner of a grocer's shop which was separated from adjoining premises by a yard leading to the back of the premises. The plaintiff enjoyed a right of way created by a conveyance of 1901 "to pass and repass through over and along the yard to the back of the premises". Later the shop included a sub-post office and from 1953 post office vans used the yard for loading and unloading. The Court of Appeal held that owing to circumstances existing at the time of the grant *i.e.* that there must have been deliveries to the grocer's shop, the easement impliedly included a right to park while loading and unloading delivery vehicles. (See also *Jelbert* v. *Davies*.)

McManus v. Cooke (1887), 35 Ch.D. 681   [256]

The parties, who owned adjoining houses, orally agreed that they would pull down and rebuild a party wall and that each of them would be entitled to build a lean-to resting on the new wall and inclining upwards and outwards to the respective houses. The plaintiff carried out his part of the agreement but the defendant erected a lean-to which did not comply with its provisions as to height. *Held*, the oral agreement had given each party an easement of light over the other's land and the plaintiff was entitled to have it enforced. While the agreement was one to which s. 4 of the Statute of Frauds (now s. 40 of the Law of Property Act 1925) applied, the doctrine of part-performance also applied and "the defendant having obtained all the advantages which this agreement was intended to give him, it would be a fraud on his part to refuse to carry out his part of the agreement, and to resist an attempt to compel him to do so by insisting on the Statute of Frauds" (*per* KAY, J.). (See also *Rawlinson* v. *Ames*.)

Maddison v. Alderson [1883], 8 App. Cas. 467   [257]
(House of Lords)

Thomas Alderson induced the appellant to serve him for many years without wages as his housekeeper by making an oral promise to leave her a life estate in his land. Alderson did in fact make a will which purported to carry out his promise but it was of no effect as it was not properly attested. The appellant sought a decree of specific performance in respect of the intestate's oral promise. *Held*, her plea would be rejected as her acts in serving the intestate until his death were not unequivocally, and in their own nature, referable to some such agreement as that alleged and therefore would not constitute such part performance as to take the case beyond the provisions of s. 4 of the Statute of Frauds (now s. 40 (1) of the Law of Property Act 1925). The fact that the Statute had not been complied with rendered the contract unenforceable but not void. (But see *McManus* v. *Cooke* and *Wakeham* v. *Mackenzie*.)

Manchester Diocesan Council v. Commercial and General   [258]
Investments, Ltd., [1969] 3 All E.R. 1593

Land was advertised for sale by the Council and it was stated that offers to purchase were to be made by tender. A tenderer, whose offer was accepted, would be notified by post to the address stated in the tender. The price had to be approved by the Secretary for Education and Science. The vendors' surveyor wrote to the Investment Company on September 1st, 1964 that he recommended acceptance of their tender of August 25th, and would write when he had received formal instructions. On September 15th the vendors' solicitor wrote to the company's surveyor that the sale had been approved by the governing board and consent was being applied for. On December 23rd the solicitor wrote that consent having been received, there was a binding contract. On January 5th, 1965 the company's solicitors wrote to deny that there was a binding contract as the vendors' acceptance had not been notified to the purchasers at the address given in their tender. On January 7th the vendors' solicitors formally accepted the offer of August 25th. The company contended that owing to delay the offer had lapsed and could not be accepted. *Held*, the conduct of the vendors between August, 1964 and January, 1965 showed no intention of rejecting the offer and hence the offer had remained alive and, if a binding contract had not come into existence of September 15th, 1964, it was made by the letter of January 7th, 1965.

Manning v. Turner, [1956] 3 All E.R. 641   [259]

A house was sold at auction on October 14th, 1954. The defendants sold as beneficial owners. The root of title was a conveyance of September 7th, 1931.

Completion was to be "1954". The abstract of title showed the defendant's title depended on a deed of gift to them dated October 16th, 1953 by a donor who was still living. The plaintiff's solicitors required an insurance policy to be provided to indemnify the plaintiff against Estate Duty on the property which might arise if the donor died before October 16th, 1958. The defendants offered a covenant of indemnity. On November 8th the plaintiff's solicitors informed the defendants' solicitors that unless an insurance be provided the plaintiff would rescind. On December 9th the defendants' solicitors wrote that they had been instructed, without prejudice, to ascertain on what terms an insurance company would issue an indemnity policy. No more was heard and on December 21st the plaintiff rescinded the contract and claimed return of the deposit. The defendants then offered an insurance policy and served notice to complete. The plaintiff brought an action for rescission and return of the deposit. The defendants counterclaimed for specific performance. *Held*, the contract had been validly rescinded and the plaintiff was entitled to return of the deposit since (i) specific performance of the contract would not have been decreed unless the defendants effected an insurance policy with a reputable company giving indemnity against liability of the property for Estate Duty; and (ii) the plaintiff had repudiated the contract so soon as the defect in title had been discovered and had allowed reasonable time to the defendants to provide the insurance policy.

Marshall and Salt's Contract, Re, [1900] 2 Ch. 202   [260]

The vendor was the lessee of a public house. The lease contained a covenant against assignment without the lessor's consent. The vendor agreed under an open contract to sell to brewers. The lessor refused his consent on the ground that he wished the house to remain a free house. The vendor refused to give an indemnity against action by the lessor. *Held*, although a lessee can assign without consent such a title will not be forced on a purchaser.

Marten v. Flight Refuelling, Ltd., [1961] 2 All E.R. 696   [261]

The first plaintiff was the present owner in fee simple of a large agricultural estate known as Crichel Estate. By a conveyance dated March 25th, 1943, the second plaintiffs, who were at that time the owners in fee simple of the Crichel Estate as the special executors of the first plaintiff's father (the first plaintiff being then an infant) conveyed a part of the estate called Crook Farm to a purchaser. The conveyance contained a covenant by the purchaser with "the vendor and its successors in title" that no part of the land conveyed should at any time thereafter be used for other than agricultural purposes without the previous consent of "the vendor or its agent". In 1958 a part of Crook Farm which, since 1942, had been requisitioned by the Air Ministry under statutory powers for an aerodrome, was conveyed to the Ministry by the purchaser's executors, subject to the restrictive covenant so far as it was valid, and this land was occupied by the defendant company, under licence from the Ministry, and, in addition to maintaining the airfield for the Ministry, used part of the land for industrial purposes. In 1950, the first plaintiff having attained her majority, the second plaintiffs assented to the vesting of the Crichel Estate in her in fee simple, but the assent contained no reference to the restrictive covenant. *Held*, the plaintiffs were entitled to the benefit of the restrictive covenant because an intention that it should be for the benefit of the Crichel Estate could and should be found from the surrounding circumstances (it was not necessary that the intention should be expressly stated or that the land to be benefitted should be specifically identified) and the Crichel Estate was capable of being benefitted by the covenant. Although the first plaintiff was not an express assignee of the benefit of the restrictive covenant, she, as the person for whose benefit in equity the covenant was made, and the second plaintiffs, as the original covenantees, were entitled together to enforce it, but not so as to restrict the use of the land

69

by the Ministry or the defendants for the statutory purposes for which it had been compulsorily acquired, *i.e.*, an aerodrome for the Royal Air Force.

Maryon-Wilson's Instruments, Re, Blofield v.   **[262]** Maryon-Wilson, [1969] 3 W.L.R. 575

Land was settled in succession for P. for life and his sons in tail, for H. for life and his sons in tail male, on G. for life and his sons in tail. In 1959 H. assigned his life interest to the trustees of the settlement to merge and be extinguished for the benefit of other persons beneficially entitled to the settled land. P. died childless in 1965. H. had no child and was aged 80. *Held*, s. 104 of the Settled Land Act 1925 applied and the powers of the tenant for life did not pass to the assignee. Section 105 did not apply as G. was not "the next person entitled" owing to the intervening limitation to the sons of H. Therefore H. was still entitled to exercise the powers of a tenant for life.

Maynard v. Maynard, [1969] 1 All E.R. 1   **[263]**

This was an appeal by a wife from a refusal of the registrar to grant a mandatory injunction ordering her husband to leave, or to restrain him from continuing to live in, the matrimonial home, of which the statutory tenancy was to be transferred to the wife under the Matrimonial Homes Act 1967 s. 7 (3) as from the date of the decree absolute of divorce. *Held*, (1) s. 7 of the 1967 Act did not by itself enable the court to order the husband out of the matrimonial home; (ii) s. 1 of the 1967 Act did not supply the remedy omitted from s. 7 and the wife had, at best, a future right to occupy from the decree absolute; alternatively, if she had rights of occupation against her husband, the statutory tenant, there was no authority to give a registrar power to make an injunction ancillary or incidental to relief under s. 7, nor did s. 1 enable a registrar or the court to do so.

Mayson v. Clouet, [1924] A.C. 980 (Privy Council)   **[264]**

A contract for the sale of land provided that a deposit was payable immediately and two instalments of cash, being 10% of the balance of the purchase price, should be paid at certain dates. The final balance of the purchase price was to be paid within ten days of production of a certificate that the building was completed. Failure to comply with the conditions would cause forfeiture of the deposit. The purchaser paid the deposit and the two instalments but failed to pay the balance of the purchase money within the stipulated time. The vendor rescinded the contract. *Held*, the deposit was forfeited but the two instalments paid were recoverable, although the purchaser was in default, since the contract provided for forfeiture of the deposit and distinguished between the deposit and the instalments.

Mead v. Chelmsford Rural District Council, [1953] 1 Q.B. 32   **[265]**

An enforcement notice under s. 23 (1) of the Town and Country Planning Act 1947 is not valid unless it specifies the date on which it is to become effective and the date by which the work must be carried out. If the person on whom the notice is served fails to appeal to the justices and the ground on which he objects to the validity of an enforcement notice is one which could be raised on an appeal to justices, he cannot thereafter question the validity of the notice in subsequent proceedings against him. The court, finding that the notice was bad, referred the case back to Quarter Sessions from which there had been an appeal by case stated. (See also *East Riding County Council* v. *Park Estate* (*Bridlington*).)

Merritt v. Merritt (1969), *Times*, May 15th   **[266]**

A husband purchased the matrimonial home with the aid of a building society mortgage. In 1966 the husband and wife agreed that the house should be vested in them both as joint tenants at law and in equity and the transfer to effect this was registered in June, 1966. In May, 1966 the husband had left the wife. The husband agreed to pay the wife £40 per month, the wife to pay off the mortgage, and the husband would transfer the house to her. The husband contended that all that had been intended was that the wife should have a bare legal estate. *Held*, the parties had intended to create legal relations. The wife's undertaking to pay off the mortgage was sufficient consideration to support the husband's promise. It could not be supposed that the wife should be entitled only to a bare legal estate when she had undertaken to pay off the mortgage. The wife was entitled to a declaration that she was now sole beneficial owner of the property and the husband would be ordered to transfer it to her.

Metropolitan Properties Co. (F.G.C.), Ltd. v. Barder, [267]
[1968] 1 All E.R. 536 (Court of Appeal)

In 1951 a tenant took a lease of a flat and a new lease for fourteen years was granted to him in 1963. In 1955 he had been granted a quarterly tenancy of a bedroom adjacent to his flat, on terms that it was for the occupation of a domestic servant. The flat came within the Rent Act 1965. It was held in the County Court that the room was an extension of the flat and therefore also fell within the Act. The Court of Appeal held that the lettings of the flat and the room were distinct and separate and therefore the room was not part of the existing accommodation and not within Rent Act protection. Moreover, the single room was not a "dwelling-house" within the Rent Acts. (But see *Wimbush* v. *Cibulia*.)

Metropolitan Properties Co. Ltd. v. Noble, [1968] 2 All E.R. 313 [268]

In an application for fixing a fair rent for a block of flats there can be included in a landlord's claim for cost of services, both a management charge and Selective Employment Tax for residential and non-residential staff employed in providing services for the tenants.

Miles v. Bull (No. 2), [1969] 3 All E.R. 1585 [269]

It is fatal to a wife's claim to rights of occupation under the Matrimonial Homes Act 1967 if she has failed to register a Land Charge under s. 2 (6) of the Act, or, if the title to the house is registered, has failed to protect her interest by notice or caution under s. 2 (7) of the Act. It makes no difference that the wife was unaware of her husband's intention to sell the property. Equity would not set aside a sale by the husband as fraudulent merely because exchange of contracts and completion took place on the same day and even though one of the objects of expediting the transaction was to complete before the wife registered her interest. A purchaser is not affected by notice that the wife is in occupation and may have rights under the 1967 Act if she has not taken steps to protect her rights. Where title to land is registered a purchaser under s. 20 (1) of the Land Registration Act 1925 takes subject only to entries appearing on the register and to overriding interests.

Miller v. Cannon Hill Estates, Ltd., [1931] 2 K.B. 113 [270]
(Court of Appeal)

In a contract for the purchase of a house to be erected or in the course of construction there is an implied warranty by the vendor that the house shall be built in an efficient and workmanlike manner and of proper materials and be fit for human habitation. An oral representation by builders that all the houses on an estate are of the best materials and workmanship may amount to a warranty collateral to a subsequent formal contract. The plaintiff, who had been told by the manager of the defendant company that all their materials and workmanship were of the best, entered into a contract to purchase a site and a house to be built upon it. The contract provided that the interior of the house was "to be finished-off similar to the show-house . . . and the company will finish and complete the same to the purchaser's reasonable satisfaction." Some time after the conveyance was taken the house developed serious dampness and was unfit for habitation.

The plaintiff brought an action for breach of a collateral warranty founded on the manager's statements and was awarded damages.

Miller-Mead v. Minister of Housing and Local Government, [1963] 1 All E.R. 459 [271]

An enforcement notice may be served so long as prima facie case appears to exist but (*per* Lord UPJOHN) the notice must tell the person on whom it is served fairly what he has done and what he must do to remedy it. *Per* Lord DENNING, M.R.: "First it must appear to the planning authority that there has been a breach of the law in that either (a) there has been development without permission, or (b) there has been a failure to comply with a condition or limitation subject to which the permission was given. Second, the enforcement notice must specify which of those two breaches is 'alleged' to have taken place – note the word 'alleged' – and it must specify the steps to be taken to remedy it. Third, if it is shown that there was no such breach as alleged, the notice may be quashed. . . . Fourth, if the terms of the notice require more to be done than is necessary to remedy the breach, the notice can be cut down by making a variation in it." (See now Town and Country Planning Act 1968, s. 15 (6) and 16 (5).)

Miller and Pickersgill's Contract, Re, [1931] 1 Ch. 511; [1931] All E.R. Rep. 531 [272]

Since 1925 a grant of probate or letters of administration is a document of title to land. As a result of s. 36 (5) of the Administration of Estates Act 1925 (providing that a purchaser of land from personal representatives is not protected if there is a memorandum of a previous disposition endorsed on the grant) a purchaser must have the right to examine the original grant on the vendor's title. Therefore the purchaser has a right to have the grant included in the statutory acknowledgment for production of documents not being handed over to a purchaser of land.

Ministry of Housing and Local Government v. Sharp, [1970] 1 All E.R. 1009 (Court of Appeal) [273]

A purchaser of land was issued with a clear certificate of search in respect of local land charges. The local authority's employee had negligently failed to show a notice registered by the Minister in respect of payment of compensation for previous refusal of planning permission under s. 28 (5) of the Town and Country Planning Act 1954. Relying on the decision in *Stock* v. *Wanstead and South Woodford Corporation*, [1962] 2 Q.B. 479 the Minister had conceded that compensation could not be recovered from the purchaser and he sought to recover damages from the clerk to the local authority as registrar of local land charges and his employee who had issued the search certificate. It was held at first instance that the certificate of search was not conclusive against the purchaser except as provided by s. 17 (3) of the Land Charges Act 1925 and the Local Land Charges Rules 1934, r. 15, *i.e.* in respect of land charges proper not including matters registered in the local land charges register merely because the Town and Country Planning Acts provided they should be registered. The Court of Appeal held that s. 28 (5) of the 1954 Act, on its true construction, brought in the entire rule making power of s. 15 (6) of the Land Charges Act 1925. It entitled the Lord Chancellor to incorporate s. 17 (1) (2) (3) of the 1925 Act and apply them to local land charges. Section 17 (3) made the certificate conclusive in favour of purchasers. Hence the purchaser was not liable to pay the Minister. The register of local land charges was not liable to the Minister for breach of statutory duty as the courts were slow to find absolute statutory duty save where imposed by statute. (Lord DENNING dissented on this point and would have found the registrar in breach of statutory duty). However, the clerk who had made the search had been negligent and the local authority, as his employers, were vicariously liable to the Minister for his failure to exercise the duty of care.

Mitchell v. Beacon Estates (Finsbury Park), Ltd.   **[274]**
(1949), 1 P. & C.R. 32

The plaintiff purchased land with the intention of using it for car parking. He said that he had told a director of the vendor company that he wanted to use the land for the same purpose as it was then being used (car parking) and that the director replied: "That will be all right." The land was subject to a restriction to residential user which was registered in the Register of Planning Charges. The plaintiff took the conveyance and executed a mortgage. The London County Council stopped him from using the land as a car park. The plaintiff claimed rescission of the contract, the transfer and the mortgage or damages for fraudulent misrepresentation or breach of warranty. *Held*, there had been no express representation by the vendors; the plaintiff had failed to substantiate fraud and the action must fail. (But see *Sidney* v. *Buddery*.)

Moffatt v. Kazana, [1968] 3 All E.R. 271   **[275]**

The plaintiffs were executors of the estate of the deceased vendor of a house who had left in the roof-space of the house, after sale to the defendant, a biscuit tin containing money. Three years later the tin was discovered by a builder working for the defendant and by him handed to the Police. *Held*, the conveyance of the house, which did not mention chattels, did not pass title to the money nor does s. 62 of the Law of Property Act 1925 provide that a conveyance of real property shall include chattels. If the owner of chattels cannot be shown to have parted with his title to them he continues to be the owner and have a title superior to that of anyone else, including the finder or the owner of the property on which the chattels were found.

Molton Finance Co., Ltd., Re, [1968] Ch. 325; [1967] 3 All E.R. 843   **[276]**
(Court of Appeal)

A company received a loan of £15,000 secured by deposit of title deeds of land and a memorandum that the property was equitably charged with repayment of the loan. The equitable charge was void for want of registration. The lenders claimed a common law lien on the title deeds. *Held*, a lender's right to retention of title deeds depends on the validity of his charge so that, if the charge is not enforceable, the title deeds must be surrendered. (See also *Capital Finance Co., Ltd.* v. *Stokes*.)

Monnickendam v. Leanse (1923), 39 T.L.R. 445   **[277]**

When there is a binding contract for the sale of land, because all the essentials to make a valid contract exist, the purchaser will forfeit his deposit if he is in breach of contract even though the vendor may be unable to enforce the contract by action for lack of a sufficient memorandum to satisfy s. 4 of the Statute of Frauds (now s. 40 of the Law of Property Act 1925).

Morelle, Ltd. v. Wakeling, [1955] 1 All E.R. 708   **[278]**

The transfer of a registered title in land to a foreign company, which did not hold a licence in Mortmain and had not complied with the Companies Act 1948, s. 48, caused forfeiture to arise but having regard to s. 80 of the Land Registration Act 1925, this did not occur until completion of the transfer by registration. A registered proprietor of land with registered title, against whom rectification of the register can be ordered, can, until rectification, transfer a valid title to a *bona fide* purchaser. (Other points in this case were overruled by the judgment in *A.G.* v. *Parsons*, [1956] 1 All E.R. 65).

National Provincial Bank of England v. Jackson, [1886] 33 Ch.D. 1   **[279]**
(Court of Appeal)

The defendants executed two deeds, without reading them, in reliance on their solicitor brother. They knew the deeds dealt with their real property but did not know they were to be used to secure an advance for the brother. *Held,* a plea of *nou est factum* must fail; the deed was not void but only voidable for fraud. However, as the statements made by the borrower to the bank were such as to have put the bank upon enquiry, the bank's failure to make proper enquiries affected it with constructive notice of the borrower's fraud and therefore the bank's equity, by their negligence, was postponed to that of the defendants. (See also *Fuller* v. *De Ritter* and *Gallie* v. *Lee.*)

Neilson v. Poole (1969), 210 Estates Gazette 113   [280]

A large property, known as Brooklands, was divided into three parts. By a conveyance dated June 25th, 1952, the part known as Brooklands No. 2 was conveyed to the plaintiff. By a conveyance dated July 21st, 1952 Brooklands No. 3 was conveyed to M. By a conveyance dated September 1st, 1953 Brooklands No. 1 was conveyed to the predecessor in title of the defendant, who purchased subsequently by a conveyance dated December 19th, 1960. A boundary dispute arose. The parcels clause in the conveyance to the plaintiff contained the words "as the same are for the purposes of identification only more particularly delineated on the plan drawn herein". MEGARRY, J. held that this did not cause the plan to prevail over the description in the deed and found that such language seemed to negative any use of the plan as showing the precise boundaries of the land. An agreement as to the boundaries had been made by the defendant's vendor with the owners of the other two plots but had not been registered. There was no direct authority on whether a boundary agreement was registrable. If it involved an agreement to convey land then it could be registered as an estate contract, Class C. (IV) under the Land Charges Act 1925, but this agreement was to identify, not to convey. *Held,* where a boundary agreement did not contain an agreement to convey land or left it uncertain as to whether land was to be conveyed, it was not registrable. In this case the boundary on the agreement and in the conveyance to the defendant coincided so that there was clearly no intention to convey land for adjustment purposes in the agreement and so the agreement was not registrable. The plaintiff claimed that if he failed on the issue of the boundary, then he had acquired the disputed area of land by adverse possession, relying on acts of cultivation of the land. It was held that such acts were insufficient; one might frequently cut grass overlapping a neighbour's boundary. The defendant pleaded estoppel by failure of the plaintiff to assert all his rights but this plea failed as it was said that failure to dispute every possible point with a neighbour did not admit that what the neighbour did was of right. The plaintiff therefore succeeded.

Neushul v. Mellish and Harkavy (1967), 111 Sol. Jo. 399   [281]
(Court of Appeal)

A solicitor was held responsible for failure to advise a client on the business side as well as the legal side of a conveyancing transaction. The solicitor, when he acted for the mortgagee, had knowledge of the financial affairs of the mortgagor, who was also his client. He was in an impossible position and should have refused to act for the mortgagee.

Newton Abbot Co-operative Society, Ltd. v. Williams   [282]
and Treadgold, Ltd., [1952] 1 All E.R. 279

B.M. owned freehold premises on both sides of a street. She carried on an ironmongery business in one property ("the plaintiffs' premises") and in 1923 sold the other ("the defendants' premises") to G.M Ltd., a firm of grocers, who covenanted that neither they nor their successors in title would carry on a business competing with ironmongery. In 1947 the defendants acquired the premises subject to the covenant. In 1944 B.M. died and her executors assented to the vesting of the plaintiff's premises in L. but there was no mention in the assent of the benefit of the 1923 covenant. L. carried on the ironmongery business until 1948 when he assigned by deed the goodwill of the business and the benefit of the restrictive covenant to the B.T.C. Society and by a separate deed of even date granted them a lease of the premises for twenty-one years. In 1949 the Society amalgamated with the plaintiffs. The defendants exposed for sale articles of ironmongery and the plaintiffs claimed an injunction. *Held*, (i) the conveyance of 1923 failed to identify the land for the benefit of which the covenant was taken and therefore the benefit of the covenant could not be said to have passed with the assignment of the plaintiffs' premises without express mention; (ii) although the benefit of the covenant had not been assigned to L. by the executors of B.M., that benefit was held by the executors as bare trustee for L. who was therefore entitled in equity thereto and was entitled to assign it in equity on an assignment of the plaintiffs' premises; (iii) it could not be said that in 1923 B.M. took the covenant for the benefit of her business only and not for the benefit of the land, for the covenant enhanced the value of the land and there was nothing in the conveyance of 1923 to lead to the conclusion that the covenant was limited; (iv) it was not necessary that, for an assignee of the benefit of the covenant to maintain a suit based on the covenant, there should be something in the deed containing the covenant to define the land for the benefit of which the covenant was entered into, but the existence and situation of the land must be indicated in the deed or otherwise shown with reasonable certainty; bearing in mind the close juxtaposition of the plaintiffs' premises and the defendants' premises, the only reasonable inference to draw from the circumstances in 1923 was that B.M. took the covenant for the benefit of the plaintiffs' premises which were, therefore, sufficiently identified and the covenant was enforceable. (See also *Marten* v. *Flight Refuelling, Ltd.;* but see *Re Union of London and Smith's Bank, Ltd.'s Conveyance*.)

Nicholls and Von Joel's Contract, Re, [1910] 1 Ch. 43   [283]

An agreement was made for the sale of freehold ground rents, the title to which depended on the construction of a will. The purchaser objected to the title and the vendor took out a vendor and purchaser summons for the purpose of getting the question of construction determined. It was held that the matter of construction being one of real difficulty, the proper method of getting the question determined was not by vendor and purchaser summons but by way of originating summons. The judge offered to adjourn the case to enable the plaintiff to take out an originating summons. When the offer was refused, the judge held the title was too doubtful to force on a purchaser. The vendor appealed and the Court of Appeal made the same offer, which was accepted. On the originating summons the question of construction was decided in the vendor's favour and on the adjourned hearing of the appeal it was declared that the vendor had shown good title. *Held*, the vendor should pay the costs of the appeal and in the court below. (Applied in *Wilson* v. *Thomas,* [1958] 1 W.L.R. 422.)

Nisbet and Potts' Contract, Re, [1906] 1 Ch. 386   [284]
(Court of Appeal)

In 1872, K. entered into a restrictive covenant with a neighbour providing that no buildings other than private houses should be erected on K.'s land. H. obtained title to K.'s land by adverse possession and in 1878 sold the land to N. In 1903, N. agreed to sell the land to P. P. agreed not to require any evidence of N.'s title to the land beyond his conveyance from H. This conveyance did not disclose the existence of the covenant, but if P. had made enquiry as to title for the full statutory period (then 40 years) he would have discovered the existence of the covenant. P. wished to build shops on the land. The question arose whether the covenant could be enforced against him. *Held*, a restrictive covenant can be enforced against any subsequent owner of the land except a *bona fide* purchaser for value of the legal estate without notice. Such a covenant is enforceable against a squatter, both before and after he has acquired a statutory title by adverse possession. If a purchaser from a person who has acquired such a statutory title chooses to accept evidence of title for a shorter period than the statutory period he is fixed with constructive notice of all equitable interests which he would have discovered if he had made enquiries for the full period. P. was therefore bound by the covenant. (See also *Re Union of London and Smith's Bank, Ltd.'s Conveyance*.)

North v. Loomes, [1919] 1 Ch. 378; [1918–1919] All E.R. Rep. 936   **[285]**

If the memorandum of a contract for the sale of land omits a term which is solely for the benefit of the plaintiff, he may waive it and if the memorandum is then sufficient to satisfy the requirements of the Statute of Frauds, s. 4 (now Law of Property Act 1925, s. 40) he may enforce the contract by action.

Norton v. Knowles, [1967] 3 All E.R. 1061; [1968] 3 W.L.R. 183   **[286]**

Held, the occupier of a caravan was protected against harassment by the landowner under s. 30 (2) of the Rent Act 1965. It was immaterial that the caravan was not attached to the land; the caravan and the land together constituted "premises" for the purpose of protection of the "residential occupier" under the Act.

Norwich Union Life Insurance Society v. Preston,   **[287]**
  [1957] 2 All E.R. 428

On July 10th, 1956 a mortgagor was ordered within twenty-eight days of the service on him of the order to deliver to the mortgagees possession of the mortgaged premises. On September 14th the order was served on the mortgagor and on December 19th, possession not having been given, a writ of possession was issued. On January 9th, 1957 the sheriff's officer evicted the mortgagor. The mortgagor refused to remove his furniture from the premises, contending that the order for possession was spent. The mortgagees applied for an order that the mortgagor should remove his furniture within four days. *Held*, the mortgagees were entitled to the order they sought as the mortgagor had not given possession in compliance with the possession order since, by leaving his furniture on the premises, he was claiming a right to use the premises for his own purposes. *Cumberland Consolidated Holdings, Ltd.* v. *Ireland*, [1946] 1 All E.R. 284 applied.

Nye (C. L.), Ltd., Re, [1969] 2 All E.R. 587   **[288]**

On February 28th, 1964 a company mortgaged property to a bank, the transfers and charge being handed over undated. By an oversight the charge was not registered as required by s. 95 of the Companies Act 1948 within twenty-one days. This was noticed on June 18th, 1964, so the charge was dated that day and registered on July 3rd, 1964. On July 16th, 1964 the company went into liquidation. *Held*, (i) the charge was void against the liquidator since it had not been registered within twenty-one days of its creation; (ii) the bank was not entitled to rely on the certificate of registration under s. 98 (2) of the Companies Act 1948 as, although there was no suggestion that the registration had not been made *bona fide*, it was no function of registration to give protection to a mortgagee against his own misstatements.

Oak Co-operative Building Society v. Blackburn,   **[289]**
  [1968] 2 All E.R. 117 (Court of Appeal)

In 1958 a purchaser agreed to purchase property and entered into possession. She registered an estate contract in the Land Charges Register in 1959. The charge was registered against the name in which the vendor carried on business, Frank David Blackburn. The vendor's true name was Francis David Blackburn. Mortgagees who advanced money to Blackburn on the security of the property searched against him in the name of Francis Davis Blackburn. The official certificate of search did not disclose the estate contract but did refer to a registration against Francis David Blackburn against another address. Blackburn fell into arrears with mortgage repayments and the building society claimed possession. *Held*, the estate contract was valid against the building society: the purchaser's registration against the estate owner in a version of his proper name was not a nullity and was an effective registration against a person who applied for an official search against the wrong name. It was said that had a search been requested in the correct full names of the estate owner, a purchaser would have obtained a clear certificate and a clear title by virtue of s. 17 (3) of the Land Charges Act 1925.

Oliver v. Pitt and Zambra, [1953] C.P.L. 298   [290]

Particulars of sale described a house as being suitable for business purposes and almost centrally situated in an enclosed garden. The plaintiff purchased the property at an auction, intending to use it for his antique business and to employ the garden frontage for display of wrought-iron gates and garden decorations. After the sale it was discovered that the vendors, by an oversight, had omitted to disclose that a 10-feet strip of land along the entire frontage belonged to the highway authority and was held by the occupiers on a yearly tenancy at a rental of 1*s.* The plaintiff claimed rescission of the contract on the ground that he would not get substantially what he had contracted to purchase. The vendors claimed that they had not known that he required the land for any unusual purpose and that the matter could be dealt with by compensation. *Held*, the plaintiff was not getting in substance what he had contracted to buy. The 10-feet strip was held on a precarious tenancy which the plaintiff should not be forced to accept. It was a case in which it would be difficult to assess compensation. The plaintiff was entitled to rescind.

Owen v. Gadd, [1956] 2 All E.R. 28 (Court of Appeal)   [291]

A lease of a lock-up shop contained a covenant by the lessors that the lessee "shall and may peaceably and quietly hold and enjoy the . . . premises . . . without any lawful interruption or disturbance from or by the lessors." The lessors erected scaffold poles immediately in front of the shop in order to carry out necessary repairs to the upper part of the premises which they occupied: the poles remained in position for eleven days and interfered with the lessee's trade. *Held*, the lessee was entitled to damages for breach of the covenant for quiet enjoyment.

Page v. Midland Railway Company, [1894] 1 Ch. 11;   [292]
[1891–4] All E.R. Rep. 1005 (Court of Appeal)

A vendor of land is liable to a purchaser under his covenants for title for any defect which comes within the covenants although the defect is disclosed in the conveyance or is otherwise known to the purchaser. (See also *Butler* v. *Mountview Estates, Ltd.*)

Palmer v. Johnson, [1884] 13 Q.B.D. 351; [1881–5] All E.R. Rep. 719   [293]
(Court of Appeal)

The plaintiff purchased freehold property at an auction. The particulars of sale overstated the value of the rental so that the plaintiff paid more than he would otherwise have done. The conditions of sale provided that if an error were discovered in the particulars the purchaser should be entitled to compensation. The plaintiff did not discover the error until after he had taken the conveyance and paid the purchase money. *Held*, acceptance of the conveyance did not bar the purchaser's right to recover compensation. (But see *Joliffe* v. *Baker.*)

Parkash v. Irani Finance, Ltd., [1969] 1 All E.R. 930   [294]

The plaintiff purchased a property with registered title with the aid of a mortgage loan from the Abbey National Building Society (the second defendants).

The transfer to the plaintiff was dated August 10th, 1967. The first defendants, Irani Finance Ltd., had lodged a caution on July 10th, 1967 in respect of a charging order. On August 14th, 1967 the transfer to the plaintiff and the mortgage to the building society were lodged for registration. An official search at H.M. Land Registry failed to disclose the caution. *Held*, the purchaser and the building society took subject to the caution which, having been lodged, was effective. Any remedy lay against the compensation fund of the land Registry. (And see *Re White Rose Cottage*.)

Parker v. Clarke, [1960] 1 All E.R. 93   **[295]**

The defendants, Mr. and Mrs. C., an elderly couple, proposed that a niece and her husband, Mr. and Mrs. P., should share their home. This involved the younger couple selling their cottage. Mr. C. wrote to Mr. and Mrs. P. setting out the terms of the offer, including the shares to be paid of maintaining the home and that the house would be demised by will to Mrs. P. and her sister and daughter. The plaintiffs, Mr. and Mrs. P., agreed and sold their cottage. They used the proceeds partly to pay off a mortgage and lent part to their daughter to purchase a flat. The plaintiffs moved into the defendants' home with some of their own furniture. A will was made leaving the property as agreed. The plaintiffs did most of the housework, gardening and shopping and shared the household expenses. After some eighteen months the defendants told the plaintiffs they must leave the house and, after some unpleasantness they left rather then be evicted. The plaintiffs claimed damages for breach of contract. *Held*, (i) there was a legal contract between the parties. There had been intention to create legal relations and the defendant's letter was an offer which showed the duration of the term that the parties were to share the house was to be the duration of the defendants' lives; (ii) the defendant's letter was a sufficient note or memorandum for the purposes of s. 40 (1) of the Law of Property Act 1925; (iii) the plaintiffs were entitled to damages for breach of contract: (a) in respect of the value of living rent free in the defendants' house and sharing the amenities; (b) in favour of Mrs. P. in respect of the value to her of the prospect of inheriting the defendants' house at their deaths *i.e.* one-third of the present value of the house less certain deductions. (See also *Wakeham* v. *Mackenzie;* but see *Maddison* v. *Alderson*.)

Parker v. Judkin, [1931] 1 Ch. 475   **[296]**

Freehold property was conveyed by a company to J., free from incumbrances in 1925. The property had in 1914 been made subject to an annuity to his widow by a testator. The abstract of title included the will, the conveyance to the company in 1923 by the executors as beneficial owners free from incumbrances except specified mortgages and charges, a charge to a bank and reconveyance by the bank to the company. One of the executors was a director of the company at the date of the conveyance in 1923. The executors of the testator had assented to themselves before conveying to the company. The widow claimed that J. had purchased the property subject to her annuity. *Held*, that although the executors had been stated to convey to the company as beneficial owners the court could find that their status was as personal representatives and trustees and therefore the conveyance overreached the equities. J. was a purchaser for value without notice since reasonable enquiries would not have brought the incumbrance to his notice. None of the indicia on the face of the conveyance to the company was sufficient to put J. on enquiry as to whether the vendors were selling otherwise than as executors and he was entitled to assume they were so selling. The rule as to notice of a document being notice of its contents applies in general only to documents which form a chain and this did not include the articles of association of the company which might have been called for to prove the execution of the conveyance to the company.

Pascall v. Galinski, [1969] 3 All E.R. 1090 (Court of Appeal)   **[297]**

In 1880 a lease for 99 years from 1877 was granted at a ground rent of £9 per year. The freehold subsequently became vested in trustees and the leasehold in a Mrs. C. who had since died. The leasehold could be assigned without consent and the premises had been sublet. In March, 1967 the landlords served a notice under s. 146 of the Law of Property Act 1925 in respect of breach of covenant to repair. They did not know the name of the lessees and the notice was addressed to "the lessee" of the premises. The solicitors for the executors and trustees of the estate of Mrs. C. served a counter notice claiming the benefit of the Leasehold Property (Repairs) Act 1938 but refused to give the names of the lessees. The landlords served summonses on the defendants, including the sole partner in the firm of solicitors. The defendants appealed from an order granting leave under s. 1 (3) of the 1938 Act to the landlords to take action for forfeiture and damages, the county court judge having found that one or other of the defendants was the head lessee. *Held*, assuming the counter notice was valid, it was proper to give leave to the landlords to take action, even though the actual lessee had not been ascertained. The lessees' solicitors were not entitled to withhold the name of their clients. The appeal was dismissed.

Pennant's Will Trusts, Re. Pennant v. Ryland,   **[298]**
     [1969] 2 All E.R. 862

A testator, who died in 1958, devised land on trust for his widow during widow-hood with remainders over. Probate was granted to the widow and two other executors. No vesting assent was made to the widow. In 1960 the three executors sold and conveyed as personal representatives part of the land to the widow. The widow died in 1966. It was held that the land was settled land from the testator's death. Although the sale of part of the land to the widow appeared as a sale by the executors to one of themselves without the consent of the court, in fact it was a sale to the tenant for life by the trustees of the settlement. It there-fore fell within s. 68 of the Settled Land Act 1925. The court applied the principle that where the parties intended to effect a transaction which would only be lawful if made in the exercise of a statutory power, they must be deemed in law to have intended to exercise that power even if in fact they were unaware of its existence. Therefore the conveyance had been proper and the land now vested in the personal representatives of the widow who could give good title.

Perry v. Sharon Development Co., Ltd., [1937] 4 All E.R. 390   **[299]**
     (Court of Appeal)

On December 19th, 1935 the plaintiff agreed to purchase a house in the course of erection on a building estate. Completion was to be on January 7th, 1936 or "so soon thereafter as the premises shall be completed, finished and ready for occupation". At the date of the contract the plastering to the walls of the house was not complete and such things as a bath, water taps and grates had not been supplied. The plaintiff went into occupation on January 7th, 1936. In May he complained that there were defects. He relied on an implied warranty that the house should be of the same standard as the show house on the estate and that the construction should be carried out in an efficient and workmanlike manner. The defendants contended that the sale was of a completed house and there was no implied warranty. *Held*, this was a purchase of a house in the course of erection and the plaintiff was entitled to the implied warranty that the house would be completed in a workmanlike manner and on completion be fit for human habit-ation.

Petrofina (Gt. Britain), Ltd. v. Martin, [1966] 1 All E.R. 126   **[300]**

The respondent, having contracted to buy a filling station, entered into a "*solus* agreement" with the appellants whereby he undertook to buy all the petrol required at the filling station from the appellants for a minimum period of twelve years. *Held*, the "*solus* agreement" (an agreement in gross) was an agreement in restraint of trade and, as the appellants had failed to satisfy the court that it imposed a restraint that was no more than reasonable, it was invalid. "I am clearly of the opinion that where a public house is 'tied' to a brewery by any of the ordinary covenants in use in the trade, as between lessor and lessee, mortgagor and mortgagee, and vendor and purchaser, the 'tie' is enforceable at law" (*per* Lord DENNING, M.R.). (But see *Esso Petroleum Co., Ltd.* v. *Harper's Garage (Stourport), Ltd.*)

Pilkington v. Wood, [1953] 2 All E.R. 810   [301]

In 1950 the plaintiff purchased a freehold house for £6,000. He spent £400 to £500 on improvements and bought adjoining land for £334. In 1951 he contracted to sell the property for £7,500. The purchaser discovered a flaw in the title, there having been purchases of trust property by a trustee in 1937 and 1938. The purchaser refused to proceed. The plaintiff claimed against the defendant, the solicitor who had acted for him when he bought the property in 1950, for having advised that the title was good at the time when the plaintiff purchased. HARMAN, J. held that there was a serious blot on the title, not a mere technical defect, and said: "There is a real danger that anyone acquiring this property with notice may be dispossessed of it hereafter." It was held that the diminution in value of the property was £2,000; the plaintiff was not bound to resell the property in order to quantify the damages. Judgment was given for the plaintiff for £2,000 general damages with interest.

Pinewood Estate, Farnborough, Re, New Ideal Homesteads,   [302]
Ltd. v. Levack, [1958] Ch. 280; [1957] 2 All E.R. 517

A developer laid out land in lots and conveyed the lots to four purchasers, imposing restrictive covenants which were binding as a building scheme. In 1899 the purchasers entered into a deed to release and discharge each other from the covenants. In consideration of this release each of the parties covenanted for himself, his heirs and assigns, to observe the covenants so far as the covenants related to the land of the respective covenantors. The vendor was not a party to the deed of 1899. The applicant, a successor in title of purchasers who had bought as tenants in common and of another purchaser, applied for a declaration that the covenants were not enforceable against his land. The respondent, who was a successor in title of the purchasers who had bought as tenants in common, contended she was able to enforce the covenants in the deed of 1899. It was conceded that the deed contained no words annexing the benefit of the covenants to the land and there was not a complete chain of assignments for the benefit of the covenants from the respondent's predecessors in title to the respondent. *Held*, the covenants were not now enforceable against the applicant's land as (i) the deed of 1899 discharged the parties from the restrictive stipulations which were previously binding and brought the building scheme (as defined in *Elliston* v. *Reacher*, [1908] 2 Ch. 374) to an end; (ii) the benefit of the covenants in the deed of 1899 had not been annexed to the respondent's land and had not been assigned to her, the intention of the parties to the deed to be mutually bound not being sufficient of itself to annex the benefit of the covenants to the land. *Per Curiam:* the covenant in the deed of 1899 entered into by the two persons who purchased lots as tenants in common was a joint covenant, notwithstanding they held as tenants in common and therefore, following the reasoning of LUXMOORE, J. in *Ridley* v. *Lee*, [1935] Ch. at page 603, the deed of 1899 was void.

Plant v. Bourne (1897), 2 Ch. 281 (Court of Appeal)   [303]

"Twenty-four acres of land, freehold, at Totmonslow" was held to be sufficient description of property to be sold for the purpose of a memorandum in writing to satisfy s. 4 of the Statute of Frauds, as parol evidence was admissible to show what was the subject matter of the contract.

Plumrose, Ltd. v. Real and Leasehold Estates Investment [304]
Society, Ltd., [1970] 1 W.L.R. 52; [1969] 3 All E.R. 1441

A lease granted in 1957 and expiring in 1963 contained a covenant for renewal for a further seven years at the written request of the lessee. Assignees of the lease exercised the option but requested a grant of only a further term of four years. A new lease was granted in 1963 for four years in which it was recited that it was supplemental to the lease of 1957 and that the lessees had requested a term of four years in satisfaction of the right of renewal. There were covenants by the lessors and lessees that they would respectively "perform and observe the several covenants . . . in the lease . . . as fully as if the same . . . had been herein repeated in full with such modifications only as may be necessary to make them applicable to this demise." *Held*, the lessees' right of renewal had been fully exercised in 1963 although they had requested a shorter term than that to which they were entitled. The words in the covenant in the 1963 lease must be interpreted by looking at the 1957 lease and the correspondence between the parties.

Ponder v. Hillman, [1969] 3 All E.R. 694 [305]

Property described in a lease as "all that shop and premises" was being used by a subtenant as living accommodation. *Held*, that although the description in the lease was not sufficient to establish that the premises as a whole were not a dwelling-house within s. 1 (1) of the Rent Act 1968, yet, because the lease showed the intention of the parties at the time the lease was made was to let the property as a shop and not as a dwelling-house, the case did not fall within the Rent Acts.

Postill v. East Riding County Council, [1956] 2 All E.R. 685 [306]

Land used for a riding school and for grazing was used with planning permission for a circus, subject to a condition that the circus user should cease in September. It was held that the resumption ten months later of the circus user was not a continuance of the same user and did not amount to breach of the condition in the planning permission. It was also held that discontinuance does not necessarily mean permanent discontinuance. (But see *Fyson* v. *Buckingham County Council*.)

Prestbury Investments' Contract, Re. [1961], 179 [307]
Estates Gazette 557 (Court of Appeal)

Vendors contracted to sell vacant property which had outline planning permission for demolition and erection of 23 flats and 12 garages on the site. The purchasers failed to complete and the vendors served a twenty-one days' notice to complete under the terms of the contract on November 12th, 1959. As there was some doubt as to the effectiveness of the notice because of delay in service, a further notice was served on November 20th. The purchasers did not complete and on December 15th the vendors claimed the deposit was forfeited. On January 6th, 1960 the purchasers asked for more time and the vendors agreed and served another notice expiring on February 4th. It was held that the third notice waived the second. The purchasers failed to complete and a summons was issued by the vendors. Unknown to the purchasers the vendors had commenced demolition and sold the materials to the demolition contractors. *Held*, the vendors had not failed in their duty by being only able to offer something different from what they had contracted to sell. The purchasers were only buying to get the site for re-development and could not complain that work was done which they themselves knew would have to be done. The vendors had therefore not lost the right to specific performance and the purchasers, having failed to complete, should forfeit their deposit.

Priestley's Contract, Re, [1947] 1 All E.R. 716 [308]

P. and M. contracted to sell as trustees for sale under a trust deed and the purchaser was let into possession before completion. Completion was delayed by the discovery that P. and his wife were, in fact, the trustees for sale as the deed appointing M. a trustee had not been executed. *Held,* until the deed was executed M. had no title and the vendors were obliged to show title on their abstract and prove title by evidence before the date fixed for completion. Nevertheless the purchaser was required to pay interest on the purchase money from the date fixed for completion to the actual date of completion as the words "no interest shall become payable by the purchaser" in Clause 7 (3) of the Law Society's Conditions of Sale only applies to purchasers not in possession.

Property and Bloodstock, Ltd. v. Emerton, [1967]   [309]
3 All E.R. 321 (Court of Appeal, Civil Division)

Was a mortgagee's duly made contract for sale of mortgaged leasehold premises (the mortgagee's power of sale having arisen) prevented from terminating the mortgagor's right of redemption by a condition under its special conditions of sale that "the sale is subject to the vendor obtaining the consent of the" lessor to the assignment of the lease to the purchaser? *Held,* the obtaining of the landlord's consent was not a condition precedent to the formation of a contract of sale and creation of the relation of vendor and purchaser between the mortgagee and the purchaser (the landlord's consent had to be obtained by the date at which title had in fact to be established) and, as an unconditional contract for sale by a mortgagee precluded the mortgagor's right of redemption, the lessee had been precluded since the date of the contract from exercising the right of redemption. (But see *Chillingworth* v. *Esche*.)

Prothero v. Prothero, [1968] 1 All E.R. 1111   [310]

A husband held a long lease of the matrimonial home on trust for himself and his wife in equal shares. After the break-up of the marriage the husband purchased the reversion on the lease. *Held,* as the husband was a trustee of the lease he held the reversion on the same trusts and the wife was entitled to a half share of the reversion. It appeared that the court based its decision on *Keech* v. *Sandford* (1726), Sel. Cas. Ch. 61, which held that where a renewal of a lease was refused for the benefit of an infant a new lease granted to the infant's trustee personally must be held by him for the infant's benefit. It would seem more logical, however, to base the decision on the fact that the husband was enabled to purchase the freehold reversion at far less than the market value because of his position as one of the two joint lessees and hence it was the interest in the leasehold trust property which created this advantageous situation.

Puckett and Smith's Contract, Re, [1902] 2 Ch. 258   [311]

The purchaser, who was a builder, contracted to buy land. The vendor knew that the land was required for building purposes. Unknown to the vendor there was a culvert running under the land which made the land unsuitable for building. This was discovered by the purchaser before completion and he refused to complete unless there was abatement of the purchase price. The contract provided that there should be no compensation for errors. The vendor took out a summons for a declaration that he had shown good title in accordance with the contract. *Held,* good title had not been shown in accordance with the contract as the vendor could only offer something substantially different from that which the purchaser had contracted to buy. A latent defect, unknown to the parties at the time of the contract, would entitle the purchaser to rescind if it made the land substantially unfit for the purpose for which it was being sold. (But see *Shepherd* v. *Croft*.)

Purkiss' Application, Re, [1962] 2 All E.R. 690 (Court of Appeal)   [312]

A person wishing to develop land applied to the Lands Tribunal for discharge or modification of restrictive covenants imposed in 1870 by a deed poll. The Tribunal expressed its view that no building scheme had existed and that therefore objectors were not entitled to the benefit of the covenants. Nevertheless the

Tribunal found the proposed development would be incongruous and were not satisfied that discharge or modification of the covenants would not injure persons entitled to the benefit of the covenants. The developer appealed. *Held*, the appeal must be dismissed as the finding that the applicant had not discharged the burden of satisfying s. 84 (1) (c) of the Law of Property Act 1925 was a decision of fact and there was no question of law for the Court of Appeal to decide. The Tribunal did not have the jurisdiction to decide conclusively that there was no building scheme. The Tribunal should not undertake an investigation into the title of individual objectors but should either assume they are persons entitled to enforce the restriction or stand the matter over for the legal rights of the parties to be determined by the Court under s. 84 (2) of the Law of Property Act 1925.

Pyx Granite Co., Ltd. v. Ministry of Housing and   [313]
Local Government, [1959] 3 All E.R. 1
(House of Lords)

The question arose whether the jurisdiction of the court to adjudicate whether planning permission (in this case to develop land for quarrying purposes) was required had been excluded by s. 17 of the Town and Country Planning Act 1947 (now s. 43 of the Town and Country Planning Act 1962) which made provision for an application to the local planning authority for a determination. *Held*, the court's jurisdiction had not been excluded, and this was a case where it could properly be invoked. "There is nothing in the Act to suggest that, while a new remedy, perhaps cheap and expeditious, is given, the old and, as we like to call it, the inalienable remedy of Her Majesty's subjects to seek redress in her courts is taken away" (*per* VISCOUNT SIMONDS).

Quicke v. Chapman, [1903] 1 Ch. 659 (Court of Appeal)   [314]

By a building agreement between the Ecclesiastical Commissioners and the defendant, he was given right to erect houses on their land. As each house was completed the Commissioners were to grant a lease of it to the defendant for 99 years. The leases provided that the Commissioners could erect on adjoining land any buildings, whether or not they affected the light enjoyed by the lessees. It was also provided by the agreement that nothing therein should operate as an actual demise of the land to the defendant or create between him and the Commissioners the relation of landlord and tenant. The defendant erected a house (No. 28) and the Commissioners granted a lease. The defendant sold the house to the plaintiffs and transferred the lease to them. On an adjoining plot the defendant then erected a house (No. 30) which obstructed access of light to some of the plaintiffs' windows. They brought an action claiming damages and an injunction. *Held*, at the time the defendant transferred the lease of No. 28 to the plaintiffs he had no interest under the building agreement in the plot of No. 30 so as to enable him to make an express grant of an easement of light over it and therefore no such grant could be implied. The provisions of s. 6 (2) of the Conveyancing Act 1881 that a conveyance of land with houses on it shall operate to convey all rights appertaining to the land and enjoyed therewith applies only to such rights as the grantor could grant by express words and does not operate to convey an easement of light which he has no power to grant expressly.

Rawlinson v. Ames, [1925] Ch. 96   [315]

The parties entered into an oral contract with regard to the lease of a flat to which it was agreed certain alterations should be made by the plaintiff. The defendant visited the flat while this work was in hand and at her suggestion and request further alterations were carried out. The defendant subsequently repudiated the contract and the plaintiff brought an action for specific performance. *Held*, the plaintiff would succeed as the work carried out by the plaintiff at the defendant's request would not have been executed if the contract alleged had not been entered into, and for this reason these acts of part performance were sufficient to take the case out of s. 4 of the Statute of Frauds (now s. 40 (1) of the Law of Property Act 1925). (See also *Daniels* v. *Trefusis*.)

Rawlplug Co., Ltd. v. Kamvale Properties, Ltd. (1968),   **[316]**
208 Estates Gazette 147

The plaintiffs, Rawlplug, entered into a contract dated June 23rd, 1966 to sell land to the first defendants, Kamvale Properties, at £350,000 with completion on September 15th, 1966. The National Conditions of Sale were incorporated, Condition 22 providing that in appropriate circumstances either party might serve a 28-days' notice to complete. On September 20th, 1966 the plaintiffs served such notice requiring completion by October 19th. The notice was not complied with. There were further negotiations which resulted in a second contract dated January 17th, 1967 which recited the failure to complete and an agreement for sale at the price in the first contract plus a further £10,000. Completion was to be on March 15th, 1967 and time was of the essence. Interest on the balance of the purchase money was to be paid at 7% from 15th September, 1966 to March 15th, 1967. By a deed of the same date, executed by the second defendants, Mesco Properties Ltd., they agreed that in consideration of Rawlplug entering into this fresh contract for sale with Kamvale, Mesco guaranteed that in the event of Kamvale failing to complete on time, Mesco would purchase the property at the price and on the terms of the second contract within 14 days of receipt of notice requiring them to do so and would pay interest at 8% from March 15th, 1967 until completion. Kamvale did not complete and Rawlplug served a notice on Mesco to purchase but Mesco did not comply. There were further discussions. On July 8th, 1968 Kamvale registered at H.M. Land Registry a caution against dealings with the land on the ground that they were interested as purchasers under the contract dated January 17th, 1967. On July 18th, 1968 the plaintiffs contracted to sell the land to another purchaser and therefore sought to have the caution vacated. The defendants argued that the second contract was still in force, as by continuing to negotiate the plaintiffs had waived their rights to rely on the defendant's failure to complete, even though time was of the essence. *Held*, once the plaintiffs had treated the contract as at an end, negotiations could not revive it. Also delay in registering the caution for so long suggested that the defendants had not treated the interest as subsisting. An order was made that the caution be vacated. (See also *Re Engall's Agreement* and *Heywood* v. *B.D.C. Properties, Ltd.*)

Rayleigh Weir Stadium, Re, [1954] 2 All E.R. 283   **[317]**

M. and R. entered into partnership on October 11th, 1948. M. was fee simple owner of a greyhound racing stadium. The respondent claimed that on October 11th, 1948 M. and R. had agreed to sell to him a one-eighth share of the freehold in the premises and other property and he had paid the purchase price of £10,000, £5,000 to each of M. and R. On February 16th, 1949 the respondent had registered a Land Charge Class C (IV) and on 17 October he registered a Land Charge Class C (iii) under the Land Charges Act 1925. M. and R. were adjudicated bankrupt on December 14th, 1949. Their trustee in bankruptcy applied to have the land charges vacated so that he could sell the property. *Held*, from the time when M. took R. into partnership, M. held the freehold on trust for sale for himself and R., although he retained the legal estate. M. and R. each had an interest in half the proceeds of sale as, according to s. 1 (6) of the Law of Property Act 1925, a legal estate is not capable of subsisting or being created in an undivided share in land. Accordingly the contract they could each enter into would be to give the respondent an eighth share of half the proceeds of sale of the premises. That was not a contract to "convey or create a legal estate" and therefore the respondent's interest was not registrable as an estate contract under Class C (iv), nor was it registrable as a general equitable charge under Class C (iii), it being excluded from that class as affecting interests arising under a trust for sale. The respondent had no interest in the land which entitled him to register a charge against it and both registrations must be vacated. (See also *Irani Finance, Ltd.* v. *Singh;* but see *Cooper* v. *Critchley.*)

Regent Oil Co., Ltd. v. J. A. Gregory (Hatch End), Ltd.,   [318]
[1966] Ch. 402; [1965] 3 All E.R. 673 (Court of Appeal)

In 1956 a garage was leased to C. Ltd. for 21 years. Later C. Ltd. received a loan from the plaintiffs secured by charge by way of legal mortgage. C. Ltd. covenanted to purchase its total requirements of motor fuels from the plaintiffs. C. Ltd. attorned tenant to the plaintiffs at a peppercorn rent with a proviso that if the power of sale became exercisable under the mortgage, the plaintiffs might re-enter the property after giving seven days' notice to quit. In 1961 C. Ltd. surrendered the lease and took a new one which they charged to the plaintiffs on the same terms as the previous one. In 1962 C. Ltd. assigned the lease to the defendants. The assignment did not mention the charge but was admittedly subject to it. In 1964, when money was still owing on the charge, the defendants claimed to be free of the covenant to take supplies from the plaintiffs. *Held*, the covenants were binding on the defendants as (i) the attornment clause in the charge bound the assignee so that the relation of landlord and tenant subsisted between the plaintiffs and defendants and the burden of the covenants ran with the land as between tenant and landlord and bound the defendants; (ii) the effect of s. 87 (1) of the Law of Property Act 1925 was to put a chargee by way of legal mortgage in the same position as if the mortgage were by subdemise and the covenants related to the plaintiffs' security and were enforceable by the plaintiffs by virtue of s. 87 (1) which conferred the same protection and remedies as in a mortgage by subdemise. Section 87 (1) taken in conjunction with the attornment clause put the defendants in the position of tenant so that the burden of the covenant ran with the land to bind the defendants and the plaintiffs succeeded. (But see *Esso Petroleum Co., Ltd.* v. *Harper's Garage (Stourport), Ltd.*)

Regis Property Co., Ltd. v. Redman, [1956] 2 All E.R. 335   [319]
(Court of Appeal)

This was a dispute as to rent payable in respect of a rent-controlled flat. The landlords supplied hot water and central heating, although they did not covenant to do so. *Held*, the landlords were not at all times obliged to supply hot water and central heating by virtue of s. 62 of the Law of Property Act 1925. The obligation involved performance of services and was essentially a matter of personal contract as distinct from a right, easement or privilege capable of being granted by lease or conveyance so as to pass under the "general words" implied by s. 62. (See also *Le Strange* v. *Pettefar.*)

Reid v. Bickerstaff, [1909] 2 Ch. 305   [320]

This decision added to the essentials of a "scheme of development" for the purpose of mutual enforceability of restrictive covenants (as set out by PARKER, J. in *Elliston* v. *Reacher*, [1908] 2 Ch. 374) the requirement that the area of the scheme must be clearly defined. The court must be able to ascertain with reasonable certainty the geographical area within which the mutual obligations are intended to operate or the covenants will not be enforceable.

Richards (A) (Builders), Ltd. v. White (1963)   [321]
188 Estates Gazette 305 (Court of Appeal)

The appellants contracted to purchase a bungalow in course of erection. The contract provided that completion should be 14 days after notification that the Local Authority's building surveyor had inspected the property "and the purchaser shall accept such inspection as conclusive evidence that the property has been satisfactorily completed". After completion and possession of the property had been taken it was found to have substantial defects which were held to fall short of the implied warranty, as exemplified in *Miller* v. *Cannon Hill Estates*,

[1931] 2 K.B. 113. that the house should be completed in an efficient and work-manlike manner and proper materials used. *Held*, the builder was absolved from breach of such warranty by the term of the contract providing that the Local Authority's inspector's inspection should be conclusive. The appellants had put their name to a rashly drawn contract and could not complain.

Rich's Will Trusts, Re. (1962), 106 Sol. Jo. 75   **[322]**

A contract for the sale of land provided that the vendor's solicitors should be "instructed to obtain and fix a suitable mortgage advance". *Held*, the contract failed for uncertainty.

Ridley v. Lee, [1935] All E.R. Rep. 526   **[323]**

By conveyances dated February 20th, 1907 B., H. and S., tenants in common, conveyed to B. land subject to restrictive covenants. By a conveyance dated July 6th, 1907 B., H. and S. conveyed to the plaintiff land adjacent, the plaintiff covenanting with the vendors, their heirs and assigns, to observe certain stipulations, which were the same as those in the conveyances of February 20th. In 1933 B. conveyed to the defendant part of the land comprised in the conveyances of February 20th and the defendant started building in contravention of the stipulations. The plaintiff asked for a declaration that the defendant was bound by a building scheme and for an injunction to prevent his building. *Held*, (i) although the covenants entered into by B. in the conveyance of February 20th, 1907 were in form with B., H. and S. jointly and although each of the covenantors had at the time a separate interest in the land retained, the covenants were not joint and several, for a covenant with H. and S. alone would not create the necessary mutual obligation binding the whole interest in the land conveyed and that retained; a man could not contract with himself and so the covenants in the conveyances of February 29th, 1907 were void and unenforceable when entered into. Therefore there were no restrictive covenants relating to the land purchased by the plaintiff in 1907 and as no subsequent covenants were entered into, no building scheme came into existence; (ii) s. 82 of the Law of Property Act 1925 did not operate to render sufficient to constitute a building scheme that which was insufficient to create such a scheme in 1907. (See also *Re Pinewood Estate, Farnborough*.)

Riley v. Troll, [1953] 1 All E.R. 966   **[324]**

Correspondence stated "this agreement is subject to formal contract to be prepared by the vendors' solicitors if the vendors shall so require". *Held*, "if the vendors shall so require" merely related to who should prepare the formal contract and no such contract having been prepared there was no binding contract. (See also *Winn* v. *Bull*.)

Robertson's Application, Re, [1969] 1 All E.R. 257   **[325]**

This was the first application made to the court under s. 27 of the Leasehold Reform Act 1967. The tenant was unable to serve notice of his desire to acquire the freehold as the landlord could not be found. *Held*, the court could make an order vesting the property in the tenant and approving the conveyance. In this case the applicant's solicitor was approved as being able to execute the conveyance but it was suggested that in future a Master of the Court should execute the conveyance. The purchase money would be paid into court before the conveyance was executed.

Robson-Paul v. Farrugia (1969), 113 Sol. Jo. 346   **[326]**
    (Court of Appeal)

In 1956 the first defendant bigamously married the plaintiff and they became registered owners of a house. The plaintiff left the first defendant and he continued to live in the house. In 1965 the house was sold to the second defendant by the first defendant and a woman who held herself out to be his wife and joint registered proprietor of the house. The plaintiff brought an action against the defendants and obtained a declaration that the signature on the transfer was not her's and the transfer was a forgery and null and void. The second defendant remained in the house. The plaintiff brought a successful action in the county court for possession and damages for trespass, joining the first defendant as defendant since he could not be found to consent to be made a plaintiff. The second defendant appealed. *Held*, if a licence to the second defendant could be implied by the forged transfer by the first defendant, it was impossible to say that a licence given by one equitable tenant in common could not be terminated by the other tenant in common. If one could grant such a licence, the other could withdraw it. In view of the fact that the plaintiff and first defendant were the joint proprietors, the court had considered whether the order for possession should not have been made in favour of them both but in the circumstances the order was a proper one, and the appeal was dismissed.

Rodwell v. Gwynne Trusts, Ltd., [1970] 1 All E.R. 314 [327]
(House of Lords)

Section 1 of the Rent Act 1965 provides "The Rent Acts shall apply . . . to every tenancy . . . the rateable value of which on the appropriate day did not exceed, in Greater London £400. . . ." A tenant of a flat in London in November, 1965 obtained a reduction in the rateable value from £430 to £388 and obtained a refund of excess rates backdated to November, 1963. She was not held to have a protected tenancy under the Rent Acts 1965 and 1968 because the valuation list showed the reduced rateable value as taking effect from April 1st, 1965, whereas the appropriate date under the Act of 1965 for ascertaining the rateable value in the list was March 23rd, 1965 and on that date the value shown was £430. The principle of s. 43 of the 1965 Act was that the rateable value for Rent Act purposes was that shown in the valuation list on March 23rd, 1965. Section 43 (4) of the Rent Act 1965 had no application to a partial refund of rates under the Rating and Valuation Act 1961, s. 17.

Rooke's Will Trusts, Re, [1953] 2 All E.R. 110 [328]

Property including a farm was devised by a testator to trustees on trust for sale, with a direction to sell "as soon as possible after my death". The trustees, during the life of the testator's widow, were to have power to retain any investments. *Held*, power to postpone sale, implied in a trust for sale by s. 25 of the Law of Property Act 1925, was ousted by the contrary intention shown in the will. The widow had been given a life interest in the proceeds of sale but the trustees had no power to allow her to enjoy the property as specie. "Investment" means investment in the strict sense and did not include the farm which was subject to the direction to sell as soon as possible.

Rosemex Service Station, Re. Rosemex Service Station, Ltd. [329]
v. Shell-Mex and B.P., Ltd. (1968), 207 Estates Gazette 1229

In April, 1956 the defendants agreed to allow the plaintiffs to purchase petrol at a special rebate in consideration of a "tying agreement" to sell only the defendants' fuel oils. In November, 1956 the plaintiffs charged the premises by legal charge to the defendants to secure a loan, subject to a similar tie as in the sales agreement. *Held*, the sales agreement and the charge were two separate transactions. Hence the tie contained in the sales agreement did not form a clog on the equity of redemption of the mortgage. On redemption of the legal charge the sales agreement would still remain; that was a commercial transaction outside the ambit of the mortgage.

Rother v. Colchester Corporation, [1969] 2 All E.R. 600   **[330]**

Landlords let a shop on a housing estate for the trade of a general hardware merchant, ironmonger, grocer and greengrocer and covenanted in the lease not to let any other shop on the estate for the purpose of a general hardware merchant and ironmonger. Later another shop was let to a co-operative society which covenanted (a) to occupy the premises for the purpose of a food hall and not for any other purpose and (b) not to sell any other commodity or item which might cause the landlords to commit a breach of any of the covenants granted or to be granted in leases of adjacent shops. The tenant claimed that the co-operative society was selling items of general hardware and brought an action against the landlords for breach of covenant. *Held*, the landlords' covenant not to let other premises for the purpose of a general hardware merchant had not been broken. A covenant not to let premises for a particular purpose does not amount to a covenant not to permit the premises to be used for that purpose. The insertion of the covenants in the co-operative society's lease would amount to a sufficient discharge of the landlords' duty to the tenant. The tenant's restrictive covenant only protected him from the letting of adjacent property for the purpose of a general hardware merchant and ironmonger and the letting to the co-operative society for the express purpose of a food hall and not for any other purpose was a discharge of the landlords' obligation to the tenant. Sale of some articles of hardware in a food hall does not mean that the premises have been let for the purposes of a general hardware merchant.

Royal Victoria Pavilion, Ramsgate, Re, [1961] 3 All E.R. 83   **[331]**

A vendor company conveyed to the defendant company in 1952 two freehold and two leasehold properties, all used in the entertainment and catering business. The vendor company was entitled to a lease, with seventeen years' unexpired, of the Royal Pavilion. In the conveyance of 1952 the purchasers covenanted for themselves and their successors and assigns to observe certain covenants and indemnify the vendors against breaches. The vendors covenanted to "procure" that until March, 1969 (when the lease expired) the Royal Pavilion would be put only to certain limited use and to indemnify the purchasers against various business liabilities already accrued. The defendants still retained one of the four properties conveyed in 1952. The plaintiff had taken an assignment of the lease of the Royal Pavilion. The vendor company had been wound up in 1957. *Held*, the covenant to procure that the Royal Pavilion would be put to limited use was not binding on the plaintiff as assignee, as it was purely personal. The word "procure" was appropriate only to a personal relationship. Where the covenant was intended to run with the land "successors and assigns" had been included. Such words having been omitted from the covenant in question showed the draftsman had intended to create only a personal covenant. With regard to s. 79 of the Law of Property Act 1925, which provides that covenants are deemed to be made on behalf of successors in title "unless a contrary intention is expressed", this means unless a contrary indication is found in the instrument. Such an indication may be found in the wording and context even though the instrument contains no provision expressly excluding successors in title from its operation.

Russ and Brown's Contract, Re, [1934] Ch. 34; [1933]   **[332]**
    All E.R. Rep. 997 (Court of Appeal)

A contract for the sale of various houses described the property in the particulars of sale as "leasehold dwellinghouses". The conditions of sale referred to "the leases" under which the properties were held and provided that "the purchaser shall be deemed to purchase with full knowledge of their contents both with regard to the term, rent and otherwise, and no objection shall be raised to them of any nature whatsoever". The conditions further provided "where the property sold is held by underlease no objection or requisition shall be made on that account or on account of the covenants by the tenant not corresponding with the covenants by by the lessee in the superior lease or of any superior lease comprising other property than that sold. " The abstract of title showed the houses were held by underleases, not leases. The purchaser contended there had been misdescription in the particulars and refused to complete. *Held*, the purchaser was entitled to treat the offer as to sell houses held for terms of years from a freeholder, not houses held by underleases, and was not bound to accept the title.

Russell v. Archdale, [1962] 2 All E.R. 305   [333]

In 1938 the defendant acquired from a company certain land which was almost entirely surrounded by other land (the Hedgerley Park estate) owned by the company, and the company also owned other land in the neighbourhood. In the conveyance to her the defendant covenanted to observe and perform certain covenants "to the intent and so as to bind (so far as practicable) the land and premises hereby assured into whosoever hands the same may come and to benefit and protect the vendor's adjoining and neighbouring land". In 1958 the company conveyed part of the Hedgerley Park estate to the plaintiffs "together with the full benefit of the covenants and agreements entered into for the benefit of the Hedgerley Park estate so far as they affect the land hereby conveyed or any part thereof contained [*inter alia*, in the conveyance of 1938]". *Held*, although the annexation of the covenants was to the whole of the company's adjoining and neighbouring land and not to each and every part of it and the plaintiffs (the purchasers of part only) were not therefore entitled to the benefit of them, they were so entitled by virtue of the assignment of the benefit of the covenants contained in the conveyance of 1958. The fact that the defendant had obtained planning consent to use her premises in a way contrary to the covenants did not defeat the plaintiffs' claim.

Ryan v. Pilkington, [1959] 1 All E.R. 689 (Court of Appeal)   [334]

An estate agent was instructed to find a purchaser for property and introduced a prospective purchaser who agreed to buy "subject to contract". After visiting the premises he paid £100 deposit to the agent who signed a receipt as agent for the vendor. After a second visit to the property a further £100 deposit was paid to the agent who signed a receipt therefor as agent. On a third visit to the property the vendor told the prospective purchaser that the sale was off and advised that the £200 paid should be claimed from the agent. The prospective purchaser brought an action for the return of both deposits against the estate agent and the vendor. *Held*, an estate agent instructed to find a purchaser had ostensible authority to take a deposit as agent for the vendor. On the facts of this case it was within the scope of the agent's authority to take the deposits as agent for the vendor and he had done so. He could not have taken the deposits as stakeholder unless he had agreed to do so. The vendor was, therefore, liable to pay the £200 received by the estate agent as the vendor's agent. (See also *Goding v. Frazer*.)

Rycroft's Settlement, Re. Rycroft v. Rycroft, [1962]   [335]
Ch. 263; [1961] 3 All E.R. 581

A tenant for life of a compound settlement contracted to lease to a development company property which included both settled property and property which he owned beneficially. The rent was to be an aggregate figure for all the properties. In consideration of the development there were to be granted at future dates (which might not be for twelve years or so) separate leases of the property in three blocks. The proposed rent was more than one-fifth of the aggregate annual value of the land with the buildings thereon. *Held*, (i) the tenant for life could not grant a lease of settled land together with property of which he was absolute owner without providing for apportionment of the rent between the settled property and his own property; (ii) the tenant for life had power to contract to

G

grant under s. 90 (1) (iii) of the Settled Land Act 1925 future leases which, when granted, would be in conformity with the Act, notwithstanding the requirement of s. 42 (1) that a lease should take effect in possession not more than twelve months after its date and the definition of "lease" in s. 117 (1) (x) as including an agreement for a lease; (iii) the agreement provided for settled land to be leased in lots within s. 44 (3) of the Settled Land Act and since, whatever apportionment was made, the rent in the lease of at least one of the properties must exceed one-fifth of the annual value of the land, the tenant for life had no power to enter into that term of the agreement.

Ryder and Steadman's Contract, Re, [1927] 2 Ch. 62;　　　**[336]**
[1927] All E.R. Rep. 506 (Court of Appeal)

In 1924 land was conveyed to three persons in fee simple as tenants in common in undivided shares, subject to but with an indemnity against a jointure rent charge. In 1926 they contracted to sell "subject to" the rent charge, but with the benefit of the indemnity, and proposed to convey as joint tenants on the statutory trusts under the Law of Property Act 1925, Sched. I, Part IV, para. 1 (2). The purchaser objected that on January 1st, 1926 the land became settled land by reason of the jointure rent charge and the land was not vested in the vendors but in other persons specified in Sched. I, Part IV, para. 1 (3) of the Law of Property Act. *Held*, (i) Para. 1 (2) and 1 (3) of Part IV of Sched. I constituted alternative provisions, the former applying to land which was not, and the latter to land which was settled land under the law prior to January 1st, 1926. The land, not then being settled land, vested in the vendors as joint tenants under the statutory trusts and they could show a good title in accordance with the contract; (ii) s. 35 of the Law of Property Act 1925 did not apply where the sale was made subject to the incumbrance since the rights of the jointress were unaffected by the sale. Section 28 (1) did not apply for, as the equitable interest of the jointress would not attach to the proceeds of sale, the exercise of the powers in that sub-section would not operate to overreach the equitable interest of the jointress. Even were the land held from January 1st, 1926 on a compound settlement (which was doubtful) the vendors could convey subject to the rentcharge by virtue of s. 1 of the Law of Property (Amendment) Act 1926.

Saunders v. Cockrill (1902), 87 L.T. 30　　　**[337]**

S. agreed to purchase from C. a house in course of erection. C. agreed to complete the house in a proper and workmanlike manner. *Held*, that notwithstanding completion of the conveyance S. could maintain an action against C. for failing to supply and fix certain articles and for not completing the house in a proper and workmanlike manner.

Scott and Alvarez's Contract, Re, [1895] 2 Ch. 603　　　**[338]**
(Court of Appeal)

A purchaser entered into a contract for the purchase of land with a condition that he should not make any objection to the intermediate title between a certain lease and its assignment but should assume the assignment vested a good title in the assignees. He discovered there was a vital defect in the intermediate title and that the assignees had no title. *Held*, (i) the purchaser was bound in law by the condition and could not recover his deposit but (ii) that as the vendor could not give a holding title to the purchaser, the court would refuse a decree of specific performance to the vendor and would leave the parties to their remedies at law. (See now s. 49 (2) of the Law of Property Act 1925, as to return of the deposit.)

Sea View Gardens, Re. Claridge v. Tingey, [1966] 3 All E.R. 935　　　**[339]**
[1967] 1 W.L.R. 134

A company owned an estate which it sold off in plots. On October 6th, 1934 the company conveyed a plot ("the disputed plot") and the adjoining plot to H.

On October 24th, 1936 H. conveyed the disputed plot to the plaintiff. No memorandum of the sale was made on the company's title deeds. In 1964 the company transferred the disputed plot with other land to the defendant, who did not know of the previous conveyance of the disputed plot. In January, 1965 the defendant was registered as proprietor of the land and commenced building on it. In March, 1965 the plaintiff learned of the building operations and in August he issued a summons claiming relief under s. 82 of the Land Registration Act 1925, *i.e.* rectification of the Register. Rectification will not be granted against a proprietor in possession (except to give effect to overriding interests) unless the proprietor is party, privy or has contributed by act, neglect or default to the fraud, mistake or omission causing need for rectification, or it would be unjust to rectify against him. *Held,* (i) although the proprietor did not know of the error in the transfer, he had contributed to the Land Registry's mistake by presenting the transfer; (ii) insufficient evidence had been provided on which to decide whether rectification should be ordered and the matter was adjourned for further evidence. *Per Curiam :* If the owner learns of building by the registered proprietor and allows work to continue before intervening, it is not just to order rectification.

Selkirk v. Romar Investments Ltd., [1963] 3 All E.R. 994   [340]
   (Privy Council)

A contract for the sale of freehold land dated January 6th, 1959 contained a clause entitling the vendor to rescind if the purchaser should insist on any requisition with which the vendor was unable or unwilling to comply. The title contained a conveyance of March 16th, 1939 by M.E.K. as "the only son and heir-at-law" of K. The purchaser required proof of the death of K. and that the grantor was her only son and heir-at-law. It proved impossible to procure this evidence. The recitals in the 1939 conveyance would after twenty years, *i.e.* on March 16th, 1959, be sufficient evidence of the facts recited. The vendor gave notice to rescind but the purchaser sought a declaration that the vendor could not rescind. *Held,* the exercise of the power to rescind in the contract was not unreasonable, nor had the vendor entered into the contract recklessly. If the purchaser persisted in the requisition there was nothing the vendor could do but call off the contract and accordingly the power of rescission had been validly exercised.

Selwyn's Conveyance, Re, Hayman v. Soole, [1967]   [341]
   1 All E.R. 339

By a conveyance of 1924 No. 196 Kew Road was conveyed to a predecessor in title of the defendant. The conveyance contained a covenant "for the purchaser his heirs and assigns to the intent that this covenant shall bind the hereditaments purchased by him and the owner or owners for the time being and shall enure for the protection of the adjoining or neighbouring land part or lately part of the Selwyn Estate" to observe restrictive covenants (not to build more than one house). There had been sales of parts of the estate prior to the conveyance so that at the date of the conveyance so much of the neighbouring land as had been lately part of the estate was not all owned by the same person. The plaintiffs derived title from the same vendor as the defendant's predecessor but by conveyances later than his. The plaintiffs sought to prevent the defendant from erecting six houses on his land. *Held,* (i) the restrictive covenant of 1924 had been validly annexed to each of the plaintiff's lands so as to entitle him severally to the benefit. The covenant was not void for uncertainty as "neighbouring land part of or lately part of the Selwyn Estate" was a description from which the land could be ascertained and the word "lately" meant formerly and did not import uncertainty as to how long before; (ii) on its true construction the covenant showed by the words "lately part of" the estate an intention to confer protection on every part of such lands and a like intention to land then part of the estate.

The covenant was enforceable. *Per Curiam*, even if s. 56 of the Law of Property Act 1925 did not apply, it did not prevent valid annexation of the covenant so far as concerned land which the vendor did own and, if it did, this was a case where the covenant was severable. (See also *Russell* v. *Archdale*.)

Sheggia v. Gradwell, [1963] 3 All E.R. 114 (Court of Appeal)   [342]

S. instructed estate agents to find a purchaser for his business and leasehold premises. He signed an agreement appointing them sole agents for three months and containing the clause: "If within the said period of three months any person introduced by the agents enters into a legally binding agreement to purchase" commission would be payable to the agents. The agents found a purchaser who paid a deposit and a contract to purchase was entered into, providing that the purchaser should submit references to the landlord. The landlord was not satisfied with the financial position of the purchaser and required another reference or a guarantor before he would assent to the assignment of the lease. The purchaser withdrew. Under the contract the vendor had to return the deposit if the landlord did not consent to the assignment of the lease. The vendor and purchaser came to terms over the deposit. The agents claimed commission. *Held*, the agents were entitled to commission as the event in the agency agreement had occurred as the purchaser had entered into a legally binding contract, being an enforceable contract even though specific performance might not have been obtainable. (But see *Jaques* v. *Lloyd D. George and Partners*.)

Shepherd v. Croft, [1911] 1 Ch. 521   [343]

Particulars of sale of property being sold by private treaty described it as "very valuable and highly interesting freehold residential property" and stated: "Building advantages. The extensive road frontages which the property possesses considerably enhance its value as an investment. Reference to the annexed plan will show that several excellent building sites could be formed, which would find a ready sale at remunerative prices." There was a piped natural watercourse which crossed the property at an average depth of three feet from the surface of the land. This had not been disclosed by the vendor. The purchaser, on discovering the existence of the drain, refused to complete. *Held*, the drain was a latent defect which it was the vendor's duty to disclose. Nevertheless, the purchaser was getting substantially what he had contracted to purchase *i.e.* residential property with some building prospects. Hence specific performance would be ordered but with compensation for the cost of re-routing the drain and abatement of the purchase price for depreciation to the value of the land caused by the mere existence of the drain. (But see *Re Puckett and Smith's Contract*.)

Sidney v. Buddery (1949), 1 P. & C.R. 34   [344]

In 1947 the defendant contracted to sell a bungalow to the plaintiff by an agreement partly oral and partly in writing. The plaintiff went into possession without any deeds or receipt for the purchase money. She then found that the planning permission under which the bungalow had been erected was due to expire in 1949. The plaintiff claimed rescission. The bungalow had been erected on the cliff edge and moved to another site when threatened by sea coast erosion. Limited planning permission had been granted for the re-erection. The defendant had represented that the house "would last a lifetime". He pleaded that he merely meant that the construction was sound. The court held that whether it was the sea or the rural district council which would cause the plaintiff to have to move made no difference. These were matters which it was the defendant's duty to disclose. He had also failed to disclose restrictive covenants which also constituted a flaw in title. In fact the defendant, who had no title, had obtained the purchase money by means which the law regarded as fraudulent. The plaintiff was awarded return of the purchase price with interest and damages for the cost of investigation of title.

Sim v. Griffiths (1963), 107 Sol. Jo. 462   **[345]**

The vendor died after signing a contract for the sale of land and after the purchaser's part of the contract had been received but before the vendor's part had been posted. *Held*, contracts not having been exchanged, no binding contract had come into existence. As a defence to a claim for the return of the deposit, the vendor's personal representative could not raise the doctrine in *Central London Property Trust, Ltd.* v. *High Trees House, Ltd.*, [1947] K.B. 130 that the parties had treated the contract as binding and therefore were estopped from denying it was binding. That decision (as explained in *Coombe* v. *Coombe*, [1951] 2 K.B. 215) required that there be a pre-existing legal relationship. (See also *Eccles* v. *Bryant*.)

Simmons v. Midford, [1969] 2 All E.R. 1269   **[346]**

A conveyance of land in 1964 gave the purchaser a right to lay and maintain drains along a strip of land retained by the vendor and included a right to running of water and soil, together with rights to enter on the vendor's property for the purpose of maintaining the drains, the purchaser to make good any damage occasioned thereby. The purchaser erected a house and laid a drain under the vendor's land to the public sewer. In 1968 successors in title of the original vendor purported to grant a right to M. to connect a drain to that laid by the 1964 purchaser. *Held*, that S., successor in title to the 1964 purchaser, could restrain M. The ownership of the drain was appurtenant to S.'s land. The conveyance showed no intention that the drain should become annexed to the servient land.

Slough Estates, Ltd. v. Slough Borough Council, [1969]   **[347]**
    2 All E.R. 988 (Court of Appeal)

In 1945 planning permission was granted to a company in respect of an undeveloped part of an estate. By mistake the planning permission referred to the land "shown uncoloured on the plan", whereas the application had been in respect of land shown coloured on the plan. The company obtained fresh planning permission in respect of part of the land and received compensation for loss of development value in respect of the remainder. Not until 1966 did the company claim that the 1945 planning permission was still in force. It was held that the 1945 permission was valid outline permission to develop the undeveloped part of the land. The court rejected the word "uncoloured" as being erroneous and inapplicable. However, by accepting compensation for loss of development value, the company had abandoned the 1945 permission. (See now Town and Country Planning Act 1968, s. 66.) [An appeal was dismissed by the House of Lords (*Times,* May 11th, 1970) but LORD PEARSON reserved the question as to whether a planning permission could be abandoned.]

Smith v. Colbourne, [1914] 2 Ch. 533; [1914–15]   **[348]**
    All E.R. Rep. 800 (Court of Appeal)

By an agreement in a lease the defendant agreed to purchase the premises within one year of the death of the lessor (which occurred on October 7th, 1912). Part of the premises was a warehouse in the east and west walls of which were windows which were not ancient lights. In 1890 the lessor had entered into agreements with neighbours on both sides that his enjoyment of windows was by licence, that the windows should be glazed with opaque glass and should not open outwards and that within one month after determination of the licence he would block up the windows. The light through these windows was material to the premises. No notice of these agreements was given to the defendant. When he discovered them he objected to the title. The lessor's personal representatives brought an action for specific performance of the contract. *Held*, that the windows were not ancient lights would not be an objection to title in the absence of any express representation or warranty, which there was not. The agreements to enjoy light by licence were not binding on the purchaser and he could denounce them at any time. He could not be called upon to brick up the windows or reglaze them as that would be a positive act requiring expenditure of money which would not run with the land within the principle of *Tulk* v. *Moxhay* (1848) 2 Ph. 774. That the windows should not open outwards was a negative agreement but without an agreement there would be no right to open the windows to project over another's ground. Accordingly, the existence of the agreements did not create an incumbrance; there was no need to include them in the abstract and the plaintiffs were entitled to specific performance of the contract.

Smith v. East Elloe Rural District Council, [1956] A.C. 736 [349]

In 1940 the Council requisitioned a house for the purpose of housing evacuees. From March, 1945 the house stood empty. In 1946 the Council commenced negotiations with the plaintiff, the owner, to purchase the house for housing purposes. In 1948 no agreement having been reached, the Council made a compulsory purchase order which was confirmed by the Minister in December, 1948 after a public enquiry. In December, 1950 the Council served notice of entry but a few days before the notice expired they derequisitioned the house. The plaintiff brought an action for trespass on the ground that the purpose for which the requisitioning was continued had ceased to exist in 1948 and therefore the requisitioning after that date was unnecessary and in bad faith. It was held that the Clerk to the Council had exceeded his powers and should have distinguished between housing in a wartime emergency and housing as a long-term policy. The jury was directed that in order to find bad faith they must be satisfied that the Clerk knew he was acting wrongly, not that he was careless. The jury found for the plaintiff and assessed damages at £850, adding a rider that they held the Council responsible as a body.

Smith v. Hamilton, [1951] Ch. 174; [1950] 2 All E.R. 928 [350]

On February 26th, 1949 a purchaser signed a contract for the purchase of a house and paid 10% deposit to stakeholders. The contract incorporated the National Conditions of Sale 15th Edition, of which Condition 25 (1) provided that if the purchaser failed to complete, his deposit should be forfeited and the vendor could sell elsewhere. The date in the contract for completion was April 4th, 1949. The purchaser had difficulty in raising the balance of the purchase money and on March 29th her solicitors wrote that it would not be possible to complete on the date fixed by the contract. The vendor instructed the estate agents that if the purchaser did not complete by April 19th, they were to sell elsewhere. On April 5th, the vendor wrote the purchaser that he reserved his rights under the contract but was prepared, without prejudice, to delay exercising his rights until April 19th. On April 19th the purchaser was notified that the deposit was forfeited and the vendor proposed to resell. On April 21st the house was resold. On May 2nd the purchaser offered to complete, having the money available. She now claimed return of her deposit and damages. *Held*, (i) time not initially being of the essence of the contract, it was impossible for the vendor unilaterally to make it so in the absence of some impropriety by the purchaser; the letter of March 29th did not constitute such impropriety but, even if it did, it did not entitle the vendor to treat the contract as repudiated as early as two weeks after the original completion date; (ii) right to forfeit the deposit under Clause 25 did not arise until the purchaser had deprived himself of his equitable remedy of specific performance and the purchaser not having so deprived herself by April 5th, the purported forfeiture was bad and the resale wrongful; (iii) the purchaser was entitled to return of the deposit but as the stakeholder was not a party to the suit an order for return of the deposit could not be made. A declaration was therefore made that the purchaser could give a good receipt to the stakeholder for the deposit. The vendor was ordered to pay interest on the deposit until it was released. The purchaser was not entitled to claim as damages expenses incurred in respect of surveys by building societies who were potential mortgagees; one cannot recover as damages for breach of contract expenses incurred in trying to raise money to fulfil the contract.

Smith v. Land and House Property Corporation (1884),   [351]
28 Ch.D 7

The plaintiffs put an hotel up for sale stating it was let to a most desirable
tenant. Before completion of the purchase the tenant went into liquidation and
the purchasers refused to complete. The plaintiffs sued for specific performance.
It was found that the tenant had been badly in arrears with rent. *Held,* the
description of the tenant was an implied assertion that the vendors knew of no
facts that he was not a desirable tenant. This amounted to a misrepresentation
upon which the purchasers had relied in entering into the contract. Therefore the
vendors were not entitled to specific performance and the purchasers were entitled
to rescission.

Smith v. Mansi, [1962] 3 All E.R. 857; [1963] 1 W.L.R. 26   [352]
(Court of Appeal)

The plaintiff agreed to purchase the defendant's house, subject to contract.
Both instructed the same solicitor who noted that completion was to be at the end
of September. The solicitor prepared a contract incorporating the National
Conditions of Sale, 17th Edition, but without any date stated for the contract or
completion. This was sent to the purchaser with a covering letter stating that it
was understood that completion was to be at the end of September. In July the
purchaser signed the contract and took it to the vendor, who signed it and
returned it to the solicitor. The vendor told the solicitor not to "exchange"
contracts as he was uncertain about the date for completion. A few days later
the solicitor dated the contract and inserted September 30th for completion.
On August 11th the parties agreed that completion should be on October 16th
and so instructed the solicitor but on August 14th the vendor told the solicitor
to "hold the contract" as planning permission for his new house had been refused.
The vendor refused to complete claiming that the date in the contract, not being
the date finally agreed by the parties, there was no sufficient memorandum to
satisfy s. 40 of the Law of Property Act 1925 and also that there was no binding
contract as there had been no exchange of contracts. The purchaser sued for
specific performance. *Held,* (i) when one solicitor acts for both parties there is no
need for exchange of contracts; (ii) the parties were *ad idem* so there was a
contract when the vendor signed, and evidence of the vendor's mental intention
to vary the written contract was inadmissible; (iii) the date for completion of
September 30th was part of the contract, and had it not been, the date would have
been supplied by Condition 4 of the National Conditions of Sale; and (iv) the
original contract was varied by the new agreement on August 11th and letters
passing between the vendor and the solicitor constituted the necessary memorandum in writing. Hence there was an enforceable contract of which the purchaser was entitled to specific performance. (See also *Gavaghan* v. *Edwards.*)

Southend-on-Sea Corporation v. Hodgson (Wickford), Ltd.,   [353]
[1962] 1 Q.B. 416; [1961] 2 All E.R. 46

A builder who was considering purchasing a builder's yard wrote to the
Borough Engineer and Surveyor (an officer of the local planning authority)
enquiring whether the premises "can still be used for a builder's yard". He
received a reply that the land had an existing use as a builder's yard and no
planning permission was therefore necessary. Relying on this, the builder
purchased. Subsequently the local planning authority informed him that it had
decided that the premises did not have existing user as a builder's yard and
served an enforcement notice calling on the builder to cease the user as a builder's
yard. The builder appealed. *Held,* (i) estoppel could not be raised to hinder the
exercise of a statutory discretion conferred on a public authority; (ii) even if it
were assumed that the Borough Engineer's letter contained a representation
of fact (*i.e.* that the land had been used as a builder's yard long enough to attract
an existing user right), if the local planning authority were estopped from proving

facts that would show the enforcement notice was valid, it would be hindered in the exercise of its discretion under s. 23 of the Town and Country Planning Act 1947, and accordingly no estoppel was raised by the letter.

Spencer and Hauser's Contract, Re, [1928] Ch. 598; [1928]   **[354]**
    All E.R. Rep. 514

A contract for sale of land sold by auction, stated that the vendors were making title as trustees for sale under a will. They were, in fact, executors of the will. The purchaser contended that he did not have to accept title made as executors. *Held,* if it is stated in a contract for the sale of land that the vendor will make title in a specified capacity, it does not amount to a warranty that he will make title in a particular manner. The contract is no more than a warranty that a good title shall be made and the purchaser can be forced to accept a good title, even though made by the vendor in a capacity other than that specified. *Per Curiam:* The position of a legal personal representative when selling land is that, if he says there has been no assent, the purchaser need make no enquiry as to debts and funeral expenses. The mere fact that he had notice that debts had not been paid does not invalidate the title.

Stephen v. Prior and Taverner, [1952] C.P.L. 720   **[355]**

The plaintiff purchased in 1939 a house on a building estate. The defendants, who were developers, wrote to the plaintiff: "We enclose herewith contract . . . for the sum of £895 including all law costs, mortgages and road charges." Later they undertook, in consideration of completion of the sale, to pay "all charges in connection with the making up of the roads upon which the property abuts until . . . taken over by the local authority and to indemnify you in respect thereof." The sum of £40 was deposited in the joint names of the plaintiff and defendants pending making up of the roads. In 1950 the local authority resolved to make up the road and assessed the plaintiff's part of the cost as £173 19*s*. 2*d*. The plaintiff claimed a declaration that the defendants were liable to pay all the costs of the road charges in respect of his house. The defendants pleaded that their letter in 1939 was a written memorandum of an oral agreement that £40 should be set aside to meet all road charges leviable and that the plaintiff had agreed to accept £40 in full discharge; alternatively, that the agreement was not binding for lack of consideration. *Held,* there was a collateral contract that the defendants should be responsible for road charges and the contract had been completed on that footing. The £40 had merely been regarded as sufficient at that time. The defendants were ordered to indemnify the plaintiff for the road charges levied by the local authority.

Stilwell v. Blackman, [1967] 3 All E.R. 514   **[356]**

The plaintiff had purchased land from the original covenantee with benefit of a restrictive covenant annexed to the land as a whole but not to each and every part. The conveyance to the plaintiff contained an express assignment of the benefit of the covenant. The plaintiff sold a large part of the land and therefore could not rely on annexation of the covenant. The question was whether the fact that the covenant was originally annexed to the land would prevent the covenantee from expressly assigning the benefit of the covenant. *Held,* there can be an express assignment of the benefit of a covenant which is annexed to the land; any intention to forbid assignment must be expressly stated. Hence the benefit of the covenant was enforceable by him in respect of the land retained.

Stimson v. Gray, [1929] 1 Ch. 629   **[357]**

The plaintiff signed an agreement to purchase land and to take a conveyance "in the model form of conveyance specially prepared". The model form suppled was for a different property. The plaintiff went into possession before completion and wished to alter the property into a shop. The defendant objected, as had the correct form of conveyance been supplied it would have contained restrictions against user for trade purposes. The plaintiff refused to execute a conveyance containing such restrictions and sought to enforce the original agreement. *Held*, there was no enforceable contract as, owing to the non-existence of the appropriate form of model conveyance, a material term was missing which the court could not supply. As there was no contract, even though there had been an act of part performance by the plaintiff in entering into possession, there was no agreement of which the court could decree specific performance or for breach of which damages would be awarded.

Stirrup's Contract, Re, Stirrup v. Foel Agricultural   [358]
Co-operative Society Ltd., (1961) 1 All E.R. 805

A testator who died in 1908 devised his freehold house to his wife, Jane, for life and then to his daughter, Hannah, absolutely. Jane died in 1930, having appointed her son, Richard Stirrup, sole executor. Hannah had died in 1925, having appointed her brother, the said Richard Stirrup, and her husband, David Evans, to be her executors. In 1932 Richard Stirrup conveyed the house to himself and David Evans to hold on the trusts of Hannah's will. The administration of Hannah's estate was not complete and Richard Stirrup and David Evans held as personal representatives of Hannah. Richard Stirrup died in 1943. David Evans died in 1957, having appointed the National Provincial Bank his executors, so that the bank became executors of Hannah's estate by chain of representation. In 1958 the bank executed an assent under seal, in respect of the house, to the beneficiary next entitled, Ruth Jones. Jane Helen Stirrup, successor in title to Ruth Jones, entered into a contract to sell the house to the Foel Co-operative Society. The society objected to the title on the ground that the property should have vested in Ruth Jones by conveyance, not by assent. It was agreed that the property had devolved on the bank as personal representative but that the bank could not, under s. 36 (1) of the Administration of Estates Act 1925 use an assent, the property not having fallen into Hannah's estate until five years after death and that there should have been a conveyance by the bank to Jane Helen Stirrup. *Held*, (i) since the assent by the bank was under seal, it complied with s. 52 (1) of the Law of Property Act 1925, being a deed, and the court would not allow the manifest intention of the document to pass the fee simple to be defeated by the fact that a technically wrong method had been employed; (ii) that although the purchaser was entitled to be satisfied that the vendor was seised of the estate he purported to sell, it was immaterial to the purchaser whether a particular document had been used so long as it showed the vendor to be in possession and able to convey without possibility of litigation to the purchaser. (For criticisms of this decision see The Conveyancer Vol. 25 No. 6 at p. 490: Sir Lancelot Elphinstone on s. 36 of the Administration of Estates Act 1925; and *Contract and Conveyance* by J. T. Farrand at p. 366 on the use of a wrong document in conveyancing practice.)

Stock v. Meakin, [1900] 1 Ch. 683; [1900–3] All E.R. Rep. 826   [359]
(Court of Appeal)

A vendor sold freehold property as beneficial owner free from incumbrances. The contract was made on October 10th, 1898 and completion was on November 22nd, 1898. On July 27th, 1897 the local authority had passed a resolution authorising works under the Private Streets Works Act 1892. The works were completed on July 26th, 1898. The final apportionment of the costs of the works was made on December 29th, 1898. The purchaser paid the sum charged on the property by the local authority and brought an action to recover the sum from the vendor. *Held*, a claim by a local authority under the Act is a charge on the premises in respect of which an apportionment is made dating from the completion of the works and not from the date of final apportionment by the local authority. Hence the apportioned sum became a charge on the property from the date of completion of the works and was therefore an incumbrance existing at the date of the conveyance to the purchaser which the vendor, under his implied covenant as beneficial owner against incumbrances, was bound to discharge.

Stock v. Wanstead and South Woodford Corporation,   [360]
[1962] 2 Q.B. 479

The plaintiff who was about to purchase land for development obtained an official certificate of search in the Local Land Charges Register showing no entry in respect of planning charges registrable under the Town and Country Planning Acts 1947–54. In fact there was an entry in Part 3 (c) of the Register under s. 28 (and s. 46) of the Town and Country Planning Act 1954 of a notice that compensation was payable in respect of the land. In reliance on his "clear" certificate the plaintiff purchased the land and obtained planning permission for development. The Minister of Housing and Local Government claimed payment of £1,612 under s. 29 (1) of the 1954 Act. The plaintiff paid and then brought an action against the Council and the Town Clerk claiming damages for negligence and/or breach of statutory duty. *Held*, registration of the compensation notice placed the Minister within the class of "persons interested under or in respect of matters or documents whereof entries are required or allowed to be registered" in s. 17 (3) of the Land Charges Act 1925 and, by virtue of that section, the certificate was conclusive in favour of the plaintiff, so he had no liability to pay the Minister and accordingly was not entitled to recover anything from the Council. Followed in *Du Sautoy* v. *Symes* [1967] Ch. 1146. (But see *Ministry of Housing and Local Government* v. *Sharp*.)

Stone and Saville's Contract, Re, [1962] 2 All E.R. 114   [361]

An open contract for the sale of land did not disclose a restrictive covenant which appeared on the vendor's registered title. The vendor's solicitors did not deal with a requisition concerning the covenant but instead served notice to complete. The purchaser gave notice of rescission. The vendor forfeited the deposit. The purchaser issued a vendor and purchaser summons under s. 49 of the Law of Property Act 1925, asking for a declaration that good title had not been shown and for the return of his deposit. Before the hearing the vendor's solicitors produced evidence that the covenant had been released by a deed off the Register and contended it was open to the vendor to show good title at any time up to the hearing. They also contended that by taking out a vendor and purchaser summons the purchaser had affirmed the contract and could not rescind. *Held*, (i) the purchaser was entitled to rescind on receipt of the notice to complete as this made plain the vendor's refusal to answer the requisition; (ii) the purchaser had rescinded and the contract was determined. It was not revived by the issue of a vendor and purchaser summons. The purchaser was entitled to the return of his deposit.

Stoney v. Eastbourne Rural District Council, [1927] 1 Ch. 367   [362]

In 1927 the plaintiff purchased land from the Duke of Devonshire who conveyed as beneficial owner in fee simple. In 1924 a public right of footway, the existence of which was unknown to the Duke and the plaintiff at the time of the sale, was established in an action by the plaintiff against the defendant Council who proved acts of public user back to 1850. The plaintiff sued the Duke for damages for breach of his implied covenants for title and sought to prove dedication by him or his predecessors in title subsequent to 1782, back to which date it was admitted there had been no purchaser for value in the Duke's chain of title. *Held*, the onus was on the plaintiff to prove that the dedication was made by some person through whom the Duke claimed otherwise than by purchase for value and as the plaintiff had not produced sufficient evidence to discharge the onus of proving dedication subsequent to 1782 her action failed.

Stourcliffe Estates Co. v. Bournemouth Corporation,   **[363]**
[1910] 2 Ch. 12; [1908–10] All E.R. Rep. 785 (Court of Appeal)

The corporation purchased land on the sea cliffs for use as a public garden and the conveyance contained a covenant by the corporation not to erect any buildings "except such structures as summer-houses or bandstand or shelters not exceeding 12 feet in height for the accommodation and convenience of the public". The corporation proposed to build a structure with covered space as a shelter and a public lavatory at each end. *Held*, the vendors were entitled to an injunction to restrain the corporation from erecting the shelter. The covenant was binding on the corporation since the corporation had freely entered into it. It did not prevent their using the land as a public park or exercising their statutory power of providing public lavatories in appropriate cases. It is not necessary that with every piece of land a corporation acquires it should have a right to put a urinal there. The proposed structure was not a "shelter" within the meaning of the covenant. The word "convenience" in the covenant was not descriptive of a building and did not import a public lavatory.

Strand Securities, Ltd. v. Caswell, [1965] 1 All E.R. 820   **[364]**
(Court of Appeal)

The plaintiffs' predecessor in title who held a registered lease sublet a flat to the first defendant. The sublease was dated May 29th, 1952 and was for a term of 39¼ years. No application was made to register or protect the sublease at the Land Registry. The first defendant allowed his stepdaughter and her family to occupy the flat rent free from September, 1961. On March 21st, 1962 the registered lease was transferred to the plaintiffs, who knew of the sublease and the occupation of the flat. The first defendant applied to register the sublease on April 5th, 1962. It was the Land Registry's practice to require registration of the lessor's land certificate on first registration and they refused to accept the application until the land certificate of the registered lease was produced. On April 24th, 1962 the plaintiffs applied for registration of the transfer to them of the registered lease, together with the land certificate. The Registry treated the production of the land certificate as serving also the purpose of the first defendant's application and both applications as taking place on April 24th. The Registry accorded precedence to the plaintiffs' application and no notice of the sublease was entered on the charges register of the lease pending determination of the action. The plaintiffs asked for a declaration that the sublease was void against them. *Held*, (i) the first defendant's application to register the sublease was complete without the land certificate for the lease. The registration of the sublease should have been on April 5th and taken priority to the plaintiffs' transfer. The register must be rectified to show the sublease as an incumbrance binding on the plaintiffs; (ii) the first defendant was not in actual occupation of the flat for the purposes of s. 70 (1) (g) of the Land Registration Act 1925 to constitute an overriding interest, since he received no rent, did not share the accommodation and his stepdaughter was not an employee. *Per* RUSSELL, L.J., HARMAN, L.J. concurring: Where there are simulanteous applications to register a transfer of a leasehold and to register a subleasehold interest, effect should be given to the sublease. *Per* Lord DENNING, M.R.: Weight should not be given to Land Registry practice where to do so would be to make bad law.

Stride v. Hayter, [1953] C.P.L. 28   **[365]**

In 1928 land adjoining the plaintiff's house was conveyed to his brother. For more than twelve years the plaintiff enjoyed uninterrupted possession of the land. The brother purported to sell the land to the defendant who entered and commenced building a house. The plaintiff claimed an injunction restraining the defendant from entering on the land and damages for trespass. He alleged his brother's title had been extinguished under the Limitation Act 1939, or, alternatively he had been given the land by his brother under an oral agreement, in exchange for interests in other land given by him to his brother. The defendant contended that he had purchased the land without notice of any adverse interest, that there had not been possession by the plaintiff for the purpose of the Limitation Act and, if the plaintiff's possession relied on a contract, it required registration under the Land Charges Act 1925. It was held that although there had been no formal agreement between the plaintiff and his brother, there had been an understanding and the plaintiff had therefore been in possession under a claim of right for more than the statutory period and had acquired a possessory title. The brother had no title to convey and the defendant was therefore a trespasser.

Stromdale and Ball, Ltd. v. Burden, [1952] 1 All E.R. 59   [366]

The defendant was tenant of a house. She let the ground floor to D. and R. for three years by a tenancy agreement dated October 25th, 1946. By a deed dated March 16th, 1948 between the defendant (1), D. and R. (2) and the directors of the plaintiff company, as sureties (3), the defendant granted D. and R. licence to assign their interest to the plaintiff company. By Clause 4 of the deed the defendant granted an option to the plaintiff company to purchase her leasehold interest in the whole house on giving fourteen days' notice at any time during the term granted by the agreement. On August 19th, 1948 the plaintiff company gave notice of its intention to exercise the option but the defendant refused to proceed. The company applied for specific performance. *Held*, (i) an option to purchase land was an "agreement . . . respecting land" within s. 56 (1) of the Law of Property Act 1925 and Clause 4 of the deed gave the plaintiffs an interest in land within s. 56 (1). Therefore the subsection enabled the company to enforce the option notwithstanding it was not a party to the deed; (ii) the option was an offer made to the company which the company had accepted and there was a complete contract which the company could enforce. The defendant had claimed that the document of March 16th, 1948 was not effectively executed as a deed as she had not sealed it. The evidence was that the document had borne a wafer seal which had subsequently become detached. *Per* DANCKWERTS, J.: ". . . if a party signs a document bearing wax or wafer or other indication of a seal with the intention of executing the document as a deed, that is sufficient adoption or recognition of the seal to amount to due execution as a deed."

Sykes v. Midland Bank Executor and Trustee Co., Ltd.,   [367]
   [1969] 2 All E.R. 1238

The plaintiffs had a London office and in 1963 entered into negotiations for an underlease for ten years for extra accommodation. The immediate lessors held the lease from superior landlords and the underlease contained a clause (2(xi)) under which the plaintiffs covenanted not to use the premises other than as offices and showrooms for any other business "for which the permission in writing of the lessor and superior lessors had first been obtained, such permission by the lessor not to be unreasonably withheld". A later clause contained a covenant against assigning or subletting without the prior consent of the lessors and superior lessors and by virtue of s. 19 (1) (a) of the Landlord and Tenant Act 1927 this covenant was subject to a proviso that consent was not to be unreasonably withheld. In 1965 the plaintiffs sought to sublet or assign the remainder of their term but the superior landlord for nearly three years refused consent to change of user to other than professional offices. The plaintiffs brought an action for damages against the estate of their solicitor (who had died) for professional negligence in failing to advise them of the legal effect of Clause 2 (xi). *Held*, (i) the solicitor had been negligent. The plaintiffs did not understand the effect of the two clauses together and the solicitor should have realised this. The wording of Clause 2 (xi) was unusual; (ii) the damage crystallised at the time the plaintiffs became liable for rent. The measure of damages was the capitalised value of the excess of the rent actually reserved under the lease over the current market rent;

(iii) no allowance for tax liability should be made. *Per Curiam:* The test for negligence is whether the court is prepared to hold that in the particular case the solicitor ought to have realised that the consequences in law of any particular words used in the lease might well not be fully realised by his client. [The Court of Appeal (*The Times*, March 13th, 1970) reduced the damages awarded from £9,000 to £2. It was held there is no duty on a solicitor acting for a firm to communicate advice to other than the partner dealing with the matter. A solicitor acting for a client in negotiations for a lease is under a duty to draw his client's attention to any unusual clause which may affect the client's interest even though the client is a professional man with experience of property but the client cannot recover more than nominal damages for breach of contract if he would probably have entered into the lease anyhow and would have ignored his solicitor's advice had it been given.]

Taylor v. Eton Rural District Council (1958), 9 P. & C.R. 430   **[368]**

On "the appointed day" under the Town and Country Planning Act 1947 there were three caravans on a site. The number was increased to twenty without planning permission being obtained. The local authority served an enforcement notice requiring removal of all the caravans. *Held*, the notice must be varied to permit three caravans. The statute would allow the owner to use the land exactly as he had used it before 1948.

Taylor v. Taylor, [1968] 1 All E.R. 843 (Court of Appeal)   **[369]**

It was held that a summons by a wife under s. 17 of the Married Women's Property Act 1882 for a declaration that she is entitled to an interest in the matrimonial home is not registrable as a pending action under the Land Charges Act 1925, as any beneficial interest of the wife would be an interest not in the legal estate but in the proceeds of sale. (See also *Re Rayleigh Weir Stadium.*)

Terrene, Ltd. v. Nelson, [1937] 3 All E.R. 739   **[370]**

The particulars of property supplied to an intending purchaser of an estate said that an inn and a farm on the estate were let at a rent of £193. The vendor said that he had had an offer of £250 per annum but had been unwilling to disturb the tenant. The electricity was generated from turbines and an estimate of the income produced had been made by calculation at a flat rate. In fact electricity was supplied at varying rates. It was stated that there was a small revenue from water supplied to houses on the estate. It was not revealed that water was supplied by the local authority and had to be paid for. The purchaser brought an action for damages for breach of warranty after completion of the sale, contending that the offer of £250 rent had not been made at all recently; that there was not so much electricity generated as had been estimated and that there had been no mention of the outgoings in respect of water. *Held*, apart from special arrangement or special evidence of intention, which was not here shown, a vendor does not guarantee or warrant the correctness of information given. The court would not allow damages for breach of an innocent misrepresentation under the guise of a breach of warranty. (But see now Misrepresentation Act 1967.)

Tew v. Tew's Trustee (1968), 207 Estates Gazette 1111   **[371]**

The plaintiff's husband took an assignment in August, 1951 of a lease for 75 years dated October 18th, 1909. The purchase price of £1,700 was paid by the plaintiff entirely out of her own resources. It was intended that the property should be used for a market garden as a joint venture. In 1967 the plaintiff's husband was adjudicated bankrupt. It was claimed for the trustee in bankruptcy that the beneficial ownership of the property was vested in the husband and wife in equal shares and therefore half of that interest now vested in the husband's trustee. *Held*, there was a strong presumption of a resulting trust in favour of the wife and that the trustee in bankruptcy must show that the wife had a positive intention of making a gift to the husband of either the whole or part of the property. Because a joint venture or partnership was to be run on land it did not follow that the person who paid for the land was putting his beneficial interest into the partnership and hence the joint venture point was not strong enough to discharge the presumption of a trust for the wife.

Thomas v. Kensington, [1942] 2 All E.R. 263 [372]

The plaintiff lent the defendant £300 and took a promissory note for £330 and an agreement that if the £330 were not paid on the date in the note the plaintiff should have the option of accepting in lieu one acre of land, to be selected by the defendant, and to have a suitable frontage of not less than 90 feet. The defendant defaulted in payment on the due date and the plaintiff claimed to exercise his option. The defendant contended that the plaintiff had no right of action until the defendant tendered an acre of land on default in payment. He could not tender the land as it was mortgaged to a bank. The plaintiff demanded damages in lieu but the defendant maintained that this was a contract for the sale of land to which the rule in *Flureau* v. *Thornhill* ((1776), 2 Wm. Bl. 1078) applied *i.e.* there should be no damages where the reason the vendor could not complete was because of a flaw in title. *Held*, the plaintiff had a contractual right to demand an acre of land selected by the defendant and in default was entitled to recover damages. The fact that there was an existing mortgage on the land, even if known to the purchaser, did not put the case within the principle of *Flureau* v. *Thornhill*. (See also *Bain* v. *Fothergill*; but see *Re Daniel, Daniel* v. *Vassall*.)

Thomas v. Rose, [1968] 3 All E.R. 765 [373]

A contract appointed an agent to make a contract for the sale of land and it was agreed that the proceeds of sale were to be divided between the agent and the vendor. The agent registered the agreement as an estate contract under the Land Charges Act 1925 s. 10 (1), Class C (iv). *Held*, the registration must be vacated as the contract was not registrable as an estate contract as it merely provided the machinery for the making of a further contract by the vendor to sell the land, nor would the agreement to divide the proceeds of sale create an equitable charge on the land.

Tickner v. Buzzacott, [1965] 1 All E.R. 131 [374]

From 1941 until her death in 1960 Mrs. S. was in possession, adverse to her leaseholder, of property demised by the defendant's predecessor in title for a term of 75 years from March 25th, 1930. Mrs. S. paid the rent to the defendant's predecessor in title or to the defendant, who did not know that Mrs. S. was a squatter. In 1962, when the property was unoccupied, the defendant forfeited the lease for non-payment of rent and re-entered. The plaintiff, as personal representative of Mrs. S., brought an action for possession of the property and relief against forfeiture, it being agreed that the true lessee's title was extinguished as against Mrs. S. *Held*, (i) Mrs. S. did not hold under the lease and the defendant was not estopped from denying this by reason of having accepted rent from her. Nor did Mrs. S. hold under a yearly tenancy by reason of payment of rent, for while the lease was on foot, only a reversionary tenancy could have been granted and, from the circumstances, no intention to create the landlord-tenant relationship could be inferred; (ii) Mrs. S. was only a squatter. A squatter who has acquired title by adverse possession against the leaseholder, but not against the freeholder, cannot, if the lease is forfeited, apply for relief against forfeiture. Hence the plaintiff's claim failed. The reader may also wish to refer to *Fairweather* v. *St. Marylebone Property Co., Ltd.*, [1962] 2 All E.R. 288; [1963] A.C. 510 (House of Lords).

Timmins v. Moreland Street Property Co., Ltd., [1957] [375]
3 All E.R. 265 (Court of Appeal)

The plaintiff and a Mr. Chait, a director and authorised agent of the defendant company, orally agreed that the plaintiff should sell and the defendant company should buy certain freehold property at an agreed price. Chait gave the plaintiff a cheque, which he signed on behalf of the defendant company and drew in favour of the plaintiff's solicitors, and the plaintiff gave him a receipt in the following terms: "Received of Moreland Street Property Co., Ltd., the sum of £3,900 as a deposit for the purchase of 6, 8 and 41 Boundary Street, Shoreditch (freehold), which I agree to sell at £39,000. Dated this 20th day of July, 1955. W. H. Timmins". *Held*, the contract could not be enforced as there was no sufficient memorandum or note in writing signed on behalf of the party to be charged, the defendant company, to satisfy the requirements of s. 40 of the Law of Property Act 1925. The cheque could not be read with the receipt as it contained no reference to it.

Torrance v. Bolton (1872), 8 Ch.App. 118   [376]

A property was being sold by auction. In the particulars of sale it was described as being an absolute reversion in a freehold estate falling into possession on the death of a person then aged seventy. The conditions of sale were produced and read at the auction and these stated that the property was subject to two mortgages. The property was knocked down to a purchaser who later said that he was deaf and did not hear what was read at the auction and that he did not know that he was buying only the equity of redemption. Although the purchaser's solicitor had paid the deposit after reading the conditions, the purchaser was held able to rescind and have his deposit returned with interest. It was stated that the court looked with disfavour on the practice of not producing the conditions of sale until the time of the auction.

Trigg v. C. and A. Land Developments, Ltd. (1968),   [377]
205 Estates Gazette 995

By a contract dated June 24th, 1966 and incorporating the Law Society's Conditions of Sale, 1953 Edition, the plaintiff agreed to purchase from the defendants a plot of land with the house to be erected thereon. A clause in the contract provided "the conveyance shall be completed within 14 days of the vendor giving notice to the purchaser or his solicitors that the said dwellinghouse is complete to the reasonable satisfaction of the purchaser or his surveyor when the full amount of the purchase money due under the agreement plus the cost of any extra work shall be paid". The plaintiff paid £550 deposit. On September 30th, 1966 the plaintiff's solicitors wrote to the vendors' solicitors that the plaintiff's financial arrangements had broken down and he would be unable to complete. On October 5th the defendants' solicitors served notice that they were ready to complete. On October 20th the plaintiff's solicitors repeated the plaintiff could not complete. On October 24th the vendors' solicitors served notice to complete in conformity with Condition 36 of the Law Society's Conditions of Sale which provided that if the purchaser failed to remedy his default within 21 days the deposit should be forfeited to the vendor. The plaintiff claimed that Condition 36 was varied by Clause 17 of the agreement which read: "In the event of the purchaser failing to carry out the terms of this agreement or if the purchaser commits an act of bankruptcy . . . or if the whole of the work is delayed for three months . . . the vendors may, without prejudice to any right or remedies hereunder . . . give notice to the purchaser to determine this agreement and in such event the deposit paid . . . shall forthwith be repaid to the purchaser." *Held*, there was no inconsistency between Clause 17 and Condition 36. Where the two overlapped the vendor could choose whether to rescind immediately under Clause 17 or to serve notice under Condition 36. A stronger case would be required for Condition 36 to be found to be modified by implication by Clause 17. The plaintiff therefore was unable to require repayment of his deposit.

Tulk v. Moxhay (1848), 2 Ph. 774   [378]

The plaintiff, who owned several houses in Leicester Square, sold the garden in the centre of the square to one Elms who covenanted, for himself, his heirs, and assigns, that he would keep the gardens and railings around them in their present condition and continue to allow the inhabitants of the square to have the use and enjoyment of the gardens. The land in question was sold to the defendant and the conveyance to him did not contain a covenant in similar terms although he knew of the restriction contained in the deed to which the plaintiff and Elms were parties. The defendant announced that he intended to build on the land and the plaintiff, who still remained the owner of several adjacent houses, sought an injunction to restrain him from doing so. *Held*, the injunction would be granted as the covenant would be enforced in equity against all subsequent purchasers with notice. (See also *Re Nisbet and Potts' Contract*.)

Turner v. Moon, [1901] 2 Ch. 825   [379]

When land was conveyed to the purchaser the vendor omitted to disclose that it was subject to a right of way. The purchaser did not know of the incumbrance until the right of way was asserted against him. *Held*, the purchaser was entitled to damages for breach of implied covenants for title for quiet enjoyment and freedom from incumbrances under s. 7 of the Conveyancing Act 1881. Right of action on a covenant for title is barred by twelve years' lapse of time but time does not begin to run until the incumbrancer seeks to enforce his rights, but Joyce, J. held that in respect of the covenant for full power to convey and the covenant for freedom from incumbrances, the breach is at the time of the conveyance.

Twort v. Webb, [1952] C.P.L. 547   [380]

The plaintiffs, as executors, contracted to sell to the defendant a cottage. A plan on the contract defined the area of the land. The defendant found that a small part of the garden had been conveyed by the testator to the electricity authority and a sub-station erected thereon. The plaintiffs offered compensation but the defendant refused to complete. The plaintiffs claimed specific performance with abatement of the purchase money and damages. The defendant counter-claimed for rescission and return of the deposit on the ground that the sub-station was a potential danger which would prevent the improvement of the property and reduce its value. It was held (*per* Vaisey, J.) that the plaintiffs had made an innocent error as to the area of the land which could be compensated for by abatement of the purchase price and specific performance was decreed with £175 reduction in the price and no order as to costs. (See also *Shepherd* v. *Croft*.)

Union of London and Smith's Bank Limited's   [381]
Conveyance, Re, Miles v. Easter, [1933]
1 Ch. 611 (Court of Appeal)

A question arose as to whether the defendants were entitled to the benefit of certain restrictive covenants—they were not the original covenantees. *Held*, apart from building scheme cases, "a purchaser from the original covenantee of land retained by him when he executed the conveyance containing the covenant will be entitled to the benefit of the covenant if the conveyance shows that the covenant was intended to enure for the benefit of that particular land ... if what is being acquired by the purchaser was only part of the land shown by the conveyance as being intended to be benefited, it must also be shown that the benefit was intended to enure to each portion of that land. In such cases the benefit of the restrictive covenant will pass to the purchaser without being mentioned. It runs with the land. In all other cases the purchaser will not acquire the benefit of the covenant unless that benefit be expressly assigned to him" (*per* Romer, L.J.). (See also *Stilwell* v. *Blackman*.)

Vartoukian v. Daejan Properties Ltd. (1969), 113 Sol. Jo. 640   [382]

Auction particulars described property as being subject to existing leases including a 99 years' lease at a ground rent of £30 per annum. In fact the lease had not been executed and there was a short lease at a rack rent. Between contract and completion the vendors granted a new lease which was a long lease at a ground rent. The purchasers contended that the property was not now of the same value, a new long lease having been granted, and that it was not an "existing lease" under the contract. *Held*, that the lease was binding on the purchasers. They were not entitled to damages as that would put them in a better position than they would have been under the contract. They had got what they were entitled to had it been possible to carry out the contract according to its terms.

Vincent v. Premo Enterprises (Voucher Sales), Ltd.,   [383]
   [1969] 2 All E.R. 941 (Court of Appeal)

V. agreed to grant a lease to the P. company which was already in occupation of two other rooms under a sub-tenancy. The lease was expressed to commence on March 25th but possession of the rooms not already in the company's occupation was not given until May 1st. The lease was executed by V. on June 14th and the counterpart was signed by the directors of the company and sealed on June 27th. One of the directors of the company had said that he would only sign provided the date for possession and an adjustment of the rent had been agreed before the lease and counterpart were exchanged. Before exchange took place there was a dispute as to the date from which rent was payable and the company purported to repudiate the lease. The counterpart was returned to V. but the company's seal had been torn off and the directors' signatures obliterated. *Held*, the counterpart lease had been delivered in escrow subject to the condition that the date on which possession was given be ascertained and the rent adjusted accordingly. The date of possession had been ascertained at a hearing in the county court and V. having then agreed to adjust the rent, the condition had been fulfilled and the document had become a deed. Hence there had come into existence a lease binding upon the parties. (See also *Beesly* v. *Hallwood Estates, Ltd.*)

V.T. Engineering Ltd. v. Richard Barland & Co., Ltd.   [384]
   (1968), 19 P & C.R. 890

The plaintiffs had an unrestricted grant to a right of way for access to their factory. The defendants started to build over the roadway but planned to leave a tunnel to give the plaintiffs access to the dominant tenement. The plaintiffs contended they were entitled to sufficient width of road to swing and manœuvre loading and unloading and this would be restricted by the tunnel. It was held that a right to "lateral swing space" would give the dominant owner a right to a strip of indefinite dimensions on either side of the road which would be unreasonable. However, the grantor was liable to allow sufficient tolerance for wide loads. In the case of "vertical swing space" it was held that the way must be unobstructed to a reasonable height. It made no difference that the user claimed was not in contemplation at the time the grant was made. (See also *Bulstrode* v. *Lambert; Cordell* v. *Second Clanfield Properties, Ltd.*, and *Jelbert* v. *Davis*.)

Wakeham v. Mackenzie, [1968] 1 W.L.R. 1175   [385]

This was an action for specific performance of an agreement that the plaintiff should have the legal title to a house and its contents. The plaintiff gave up her home to live with and take care of a neighbour who was too old and ill to live alone, in return for his promise that she should have the house and contents on his death. There was nothing in writing. In an action for specific performance the executors pleaded s. 40 of the Law of Property Act 1925. *Held*, the plaintiff's act had been in part performance of an existing contract and the executors must perform the contract and convey the property to the plaintiff. This may be distinguished from *Maddison* v. *Alderson* ((1883), 8 App. Cas. 467) where the plaintiff had originally been paid a wage which she could have continued to claim and she had not given up a home of her own. (See also *Parker* v. *Clarke*.)

Walker v. Ware Railway Co. (1865), 35 L. J. Ch. 94   [386]

The remedies given to vendors by the Lands Clauses Consolidation Act 1845 do not exclude the ordinary lien of a vendor for unpaid purchase money. A vendor has a lien on lands contracted to be sold to a body having compulsory purchase powers, as well as for compensation money as for purchase money, where the amounts of such purchase and compensation money are settled by the same award.

Want v. Stallibrass (1873), L.R. 8 Ex. 175   [387]

The defendant contracted to sell land to the plaintiff under conditions of sale which provided "all objections and requisitions not stated in writing and delivered to the vendors' solicitor within 14 days of the delivery of the abstract shall be considered as waived and in this respect time shall be of the essence of the contract" and "if the purchaser shall fail to comply with these conditions, his or her deposit shall be thereon actually forfeited to the vendors". The abstract showed a defect in title but objection was not taken until after 14 days of the delivery of the abstract. The plaintiff brought an action to recover the deposit. *Held*, he was entitled to succeed (*per* KELLY, C.B.) on the ground that no complete abstract had been delivered and therefore the time limited for taking objections had never commenced running; (*per* MARTIN and POLLOCK, B.B.) on the ground that the condition as to forfeiture of deposit did not apply where the vendor was unable to give a good title, but only to objections and requisitions which might properly have been enforced against a vendor who had a valid title.

Watkins v. Standley, [1952] C.P.L. 118   [388]

The defendant inserted an advertisement in a newspaper offering for sale sixty acres of land "noted for its ability for feeding and summer grazing". This description had been used in a catalogue when the defendant had purchased the land some years earlier. The plaintiff entered into negotiations and paid 10% deposit to the defendant's solicitors as stakeholders. Subsequently he alleged the land was unsuitable for grazing and claimed return of the deposit contending misrepresentation and that the consideration for the payment of the deposit had wholly failed. The court found that the land was suitable for grazing but not for feeding cattle for slaughter. Although the advertisement had been made in good faith the representation was untrue in part and had induced the plaintiff to enter into the transaction. *Held*, the plaintiff was entitled to return of the deposit because there had been no concluded contract and, if there had been, he would have been entitled to rescission on the ground of misrepresentation.

Watson v. Burton, [1956] 3 All E.R. 929; [1957] 1 W.L.R. 19   [389]

Industrial land sold by auction was mistakenly stated in the particulars of sale to be approximately 3,920 square yards but was only approximately 2,360 square yards. The purchaser inspected the property before purchase. A condition in the contract provided that any error or misstatement should not annul the contract and that there should be no claim for compensation, provided that the purchaser should not be compelled to accept property which differed substantially from the property agreed to be sold. Before completion the purchaser discovered the property was substantially less in area than stated. He nevertheless paid the deposit, showed prospective sub-purchasers and tenants over the property and did some repairs. *Held*, the purchaser was entitled to rescind as the statement of the site area was a term of the contract and the difference of nearly 40% in the area was substantial so that the purchaser could not be given what he bargained for and also it fell within the provision in the contract. The purchaser had not waived his right to rescind, since his conduct was consistent with his intention to try initially to obtain an abatement of the purchase price. The vendor could not, by offering to waive the condition as to compensation, be entitled to specific performance if the purchaser was unwilling to accept compensation.

Webb v. Pollmount, Ltd., [1966] 1 All E.R. 481 **[390]**

In 1961 premises were demised by a lease to the plaintiff for seven years. Clause 6 of the lease provided that the plaintiff should have an option "during the first three years of the term of the lease to purchase the freehold of the property at the price of £3,500 and during the next four years at the price of £4,000". In 1962 the freehold reversion of the premises was conveyed to the defendant company subject to the lease and the company registered as absolute proprietor. In 1963 the plaintiff gave notice in writing of the exercise of the option. The defendant company refused to sell the freehold and the plaintiff commenced proceedings for specific performance of the contract for the sale of the reversion. *Held,* s. 70 (1) (g) of the Land Registration Act 1925 applied to the rights of the person in actual occupation of the land; the option over the physical land itself was an interest which was capable of enduring through different ownerships of the land and was accordingly an overriding interest. Hence the defendants were bound by the option as registered land is purchased subject to overriding interests.

Weg Motors Ltd. v. Hales, [1961] 3 All E.R. 181 **[391]**
(Court of Appeal)

By a lease certain land with garages thereon was demised to the plaintiff company for a term of twenty-one years from December 25th, 1938 and by an agreement made on the same date and between the same parties, but signed before the execution of the lease, it was provided: "In consideration of the lessees taking a lease of even date with but executed after these presents . . . the lessees shall have the option of taking a further lease of the premises demised by the . . . lease for a term of twenty-one years." *Held,* the lease and the option agreement were contemporaneous and intimately related and their execution formed a single transaction: it followed that the right and obligation of the option agreement were properly incidents of the demise, were for the renewal of the lease and, as such, were excepted from the scope of the rule against perpetuities. Further, the option agreement was not, when it was entered into, a contract to create a term of years and it was not, therefore, rendered void by s. 149 (3) of the Law of Property Act 1925: it was not until the option was exercised (30th April, 1959) that the option agreement could be said to create a term of years. (See also *Gartside* v. *Silkstone and Dodworth Coal and Iron Co.*)

Wembley Park Estate Co.'s Transfer, Re, [1968] 1 All E.R. 457 **[392]**

In 1929 a company had sold a plot of land and the purchaser entered into restrictive covenants. The benefit of the covenants was not expressly assigned or annexed. Other plots in the area were sold by the company subject to like covenants. The plaintiffs had an option to purchase the plot and sought a declaration under s. 84 (2) (a) of the Law of Property Act 1925 that the land was not affected by the restrictive covenants. *Held,* the land was not bound by the covenants. No building scheme had been established which would have caused the covenants to bind the land. For a building scheme to have come into existence the conditions in *Elliston* v. *Reacher* and *Reid* v. *Bickerstaff* must be complied with.

West (Richard) and Partners (Inverness) Ltd. and **[393]**
Another v. Dick [1969] 1 All E.R. 943 (Court of Appeal)

An agreement to purchase land in Scotland was conditional on planning consent being granted for use as an hotel. Planning consent was granted subject to conditions (i) that before alterations were commenced approval of the local authority as building authority should be obtained and (ii) that private access to a trunk road be improved, together with provision of adequate visibility splay to the satisfaction of the county surveyor. The purchaser sought to resile on the ground that the conditional consent granted was not the planning consent required by the contract. The vendors brought an action for specific performance. The vendors had a registered office in England and the purchaser lived in England. It was held that the English courts have jurisdiction to decree specific performance of a contract for the sale of land outside the jurisdiction against a defendant within the jurisdiction, as the courts of equity are courts of conscience operating *in personam* and not *in rem*. Affirming MEGARRY, J., the Court of Appeal held: to satisfy condition (i) would involve considerable expense but the conditions imposed by the local authority as building authority were no part of the planning scheme in itself and had nothing to do with the vendor; to sastify condition (ii) would not entail great expense or bother the purchaser. Hence the condition in the contract as to grant of planning consent had been satisfied and the vendors were entitled to specific performance. (But see *Hargreaves Transport Ltd.* v. *Lynch*.)

Westminster Bank, Ltd. v. Minister of Housing and   **[394]** Local Government, [1970] 1 All E.R. 734

The bank applied for planning permission for a proposed extension and was refused. An appeal to the Minister was also refused. The ground for both refusals was that the local planning authority proposed to widen the road behind the bank. No improvement line had been prescribed under s. 72 of the Highways Act 1959 but any development which would have interfered with the road widening had been refused. The bank appealed to the Queen's Bench Division under s. 179 of the Town and Country Planning Act 1962. The court quashed the Minister's decision (sub nom. *Westminster Bank* v. *Beverley Corporation*, [1968] 2 All E.R. 104) firstly on the ground that as discretion to decide a planning application was a general one, it must be exercised within the planning context. Highway controls were specialised and where the two overlapped, the specialised control must be used in preference to the general control. As the road widening could have been effected by prescribing an improvement line under the Highways Act, this was specialised control of planning powers. Hence the reason given for refusal of planning permission was legally unsound and the refusal must be quashed. The second ground was that under planning control the landowner would have no right to compensation but a person whose property is injuriously affected as a result of a line being prescribed under the Highways Act has a right to compensation for the injury sustained. The general maxim being that property may not be taken without compensation, it did not appear that Parliament had intended under planning legislation to take away the right to compensation under the Highways Act. The court also held that, in the circumstances, the use of planning powers was unreasonable and the Minister had misdirected himself. The decision was reversed by the Court of Appeal ((1969) 1 Q.B. 499). The bank appealed to the House of Lords. It was held that where Parliament has enacted two different ways of preventing development, one of which provides for payment of compensation and the other does not, a local authority is acting within its powers if it chooses to refuse planning permission by a method which does not involve payment of compensation. The planning authority had to choose whether to leave the bank without compensation or impose a burden on ratepayers. One would think it would be equitable if the burden were shared but the Minister of Transport in a circular to local authorities in 1954 had made it clear that there would be no grant if a local authority proceeded in such a way that compensation would be payable. There was nothing to indicate any disapproval of that policy by Parliament. Some importance had been attached to the fact that the road widening scheme did not appear in the area development plan but the court did not have to consider how far the Minister was entitled to have regard to schemes still inchoate. The Minister must have regard to public interest and exercise his discretion and it could not be said in the present case that his decision was unjustifiable. The bank's appeal was dismissed.

Weston v. Henshaw, [1950] Ch. 510 **[395]**

In 1921 a father sold freehold property to his son who, in 1927, sold it back to his father. The father died, having settled the property by will on his son for life and then on the grandson. In 1940 the executors of the father's will vested the property in the son by vesting assent under the Settled Land Act 1925. In 1944 the son charged the property by way of legal mortgage, the charge reciting that he was the fee simple owner under the conveyance of 1921. In 1945 and 1946 he charged the property to secure further advances. In 1946 he died. In 1947 the grandson obtained letters of administration to the son's estate and the charges were then discovered. The grandson brought an action for a declaration that the charges were void against him and for delivery up of the charges for cancellation and of the title deeds of the property. *Held,* (i) the son had committed fraud but not forgery; (ii) that s. 18 of the Settled Land Act 1925, which invalidates transactions not in accordance with the Act, was not to be read subject to s. 112 (2) and accordingly was not subject to the limitation that it should apply only to transaction by, or purporting to be by, the tenant for life; (iii) that s. 110 (i), which protects a person dealing in good faith with a tenant for life, applied only a person dealing with a tenant for life as such and who knew him to be a limited owner; (iv) that by virtue of s. 18 (1) (a) and (b) the charges were void as against the plaintiff; (v) the court would not order the defendant to deliver up the charges for cancellation since they gave no security as against the property and, as against the executors, were evidence of the advance of money in respect of which the defendant could claim and (vi) for the protection of the property there should be indorsed on the charge the declaration that it and further charges were void as against the plaintiff.

Westripp v. Baldock, [1939] 1 All E.R. 279 (Court of Appeal) **[396]**

The plaintiff and defendant occupied adjoining houses included within a building scheme with restrictions imposed in 1874, enforceable against each other. One covenant was that on no lot should there be erected a shop, warehouse or factory or any trade carried on or operative machinery fixed. The defendant was a jobbing builder. He leaned ladders, planks, etc., against the side wall of the plaintiff's house and erected a shed and a lean-to store for builder's fittings. The plaintiff brought an action for trespass, damage caused by damp to the brickwork of his wall and breach of covenant. The defendant contended that owing to change in the character of the locality the covenant was no longer binding. *Held,* (i) the defendant was carrying on a trade in breach of covenant and the plaintiff was entitled to an injunction; (ii) the neighbourhood, being still mainly residential, had not suffered such a change as would release the covenant. The Court of Appeal found that the court below was entitled to take into account that there had been submitted to the Minister a scheme zoning the street as residential. (See also *Chatsworth Estates Co.* v. *Fewell.*)

Wheeldon v. Burrows (1879), 12 Ch.D. 31 **[397]**
(Court of Appeal)

A workshop and an adjacent piece of land belonging to the same owner were put up for sale by auction. The piece of land only was sold and conveyed to Wheeldon and some five weeks later Burrows contracted to buy the workshop, and it was conveyed to him in due course. The workshop had windows overlooking and receiving their light from the piece of land first sold. *Held,* as the vendor had not when he conveyed the piece of land reserved the right of access of light to the windows, no such right passed to the purchaser of the workshop, and Wheeldon could build so as to obstruct the windows of the workshop. "In the case of a grant you may imply a grant of such continuous and apparent easements or such easements as are necessary to the reasonable enjoyment of the property conveyed, and have in fact been enjoyed during the unity of ownership, but ... with the exception ... of easements of necessity, you cannot imply a similar reservation in favour of the grantor of land" (*per* THESIGER, L.J.).

White Rose Cottage, Re, [1965] 1 All E.R. 11 (Court of Appeal)   [398]

A company, which was the registered proprietor of White Rose Cottage with absolute freehold title under the Land Registration Act 1925, created an equitable mortgage to a bank by a memorandum under seal and deposit of the land certificate. The memorandum contained an undertaking to execute a legal mortgage, a declaration of trusteeship and power to the bank to appoint a new trustee, and a power of attorney enabling the bank to transfer the legal estate to a purchaser in the exercise of the statutory power of sale. A notice of deposit of the land certificate was entered on the Register on May 7th, 1962. Judgment creditors registered cautions to protect charging orders (creating equitable charges) in respect of judgment debts against the company on June 22nd and August 14th, 1962. In August the bank sought to register notice of its equitable mortgage under s. 49 of the Land Registration Act but the chargees objected unless their charges were given priority. On October 26th the bank, under the power of attorney, transferred the property to a purchaser who charged it on the same day by registered charge to a building society. The chargees objected to registration of the transfer unless they were given priority. *Held*, notice of deposit of the land certificate was valid either as a notice of charge under s. 49 or s. 52 of the Land Registration Act or as a caution under r. 239 of the Land Registration Rules, which would make the bank first in time; (ii) the transfer purported to be a sale by the mortgagor, although by its attorney, and a release by the mortgagees. Hence the transferee took what the mortgagor had to give *i.e.* the legal estate subject to the charges protected by the cautions.

White and Smith's Contract, Re, [1896] 1 Ch. 637   [399]

On a sale of leaseholds by auction the particulars and conditions of sale contained no statement as to the nature of the covenants in the lease nor any notice that the lease might be inspected prior to the auction. The covenants were onerous. The rule laid down by the Court of Appeal in *Reeve* v. *Berridge* (1888), (20 Q.B.D. 523) that it is prima facie the duty of a vendor to disclose all that is necessary to protect himself and not the duty of the purchaser to demand inspection of the vendor's title deeds before entering into a contract, is not confined to sales by private treaty but also applies to sales by auction. *Held*, the purchaser was not affected with constructive notice of the covenants. Having not been given an opportunity of inspecting the lease he was not bound to complete the contract.

Wicks v. Gregg, [1952] C.P.L. 558 (Court of Appeal)   [400]

The plaintiff was negotiating to purchase a house from the defendant. He informed the estate agent that he would have to obtain a mortgage. The house was subject to restrictive covenants which were not disclosed to the plaintiff. At an interview with the estate agent, the plaintiff's son was persuaded to sign a document, as agent for his father, agreeing to purchase the property. The document stated the purchase was subject to restrictive covenants. The document had not been drawn by a solicitor and there was no counterpart. The plaintiff paid a deposit but later decided not to proceed with the purchase owing to the restrictive covenants. The defendant claimed there was a binding contract and refused to return the deposit. *Held*, there was no concluded agreement. The document signed by the son had not been treated as a binding contract. As it stated the purchase was subject to restrictive covenants, explanation was required before signature. The plaintiff was entitled to return of his deposit.

Wilkes v. Spooner, [1911] 2 K.B. 473 (Court of Appeal)   **[401]**

A purchaser of land from one who has purchased for value without notice, either actual or constructive, of a restrictive covenant, is not bound by the covenant, although he himself has notice of it.

Wilkinson (A.L.), Ltd. v. Brown, [1966] 1 All E.R. 509   **[402]**
    (Court of Appeal)

The vendor of leasehold property agreed to pay estate agents' commission "'in the event of your introducing . . . a person prepared to purchase" at an acceptable price and agreed "should I withdraw from any proposed sale negotiated by you or revoke these instructions at any time before a binding contract is signed by me I will pay you commission". The vendor's lease could not be assigned without the landlord's consent. The estate agents introduced N. who was prepared to purchase at a price the vendor agreed to accept. N's purchase was subject to his being able to sell his own property and arrange a mortgage. The landlord refused consent to the assignment as N's references were unsatisfactory but later offered to consent. Meanwhile N.'s sale of his own property went off but his solicitors wrote that N. was willing to purchase if he could find a purchaser for his own property. The vendor sold to another purchaser, not introduced by the agents, at a higher price. *Held*, the estate agents were not entitled to commission. There was never more than an expectancy that N. would enter into a contract. He was never ready, willing and able to enter into a contract and therefore not a person "prepared to purchase".

Williams v. Ministry of Housing and Local Government (1967),   **[403]**
    18 P & C.R. 514; 203 Estates Gazette 688

A building in a nursery garden was used for the sale of the nursery produce. *Held*, this was a use ancillary to the agricultural user of the whole premises. Hence, if the building were used to sell produce not grown in the nursery this could change the use of the building to a shop which would constitute development requiring planning permission.

Williams and Newcastle's (Duchess) Contract, Re, [1897]   **[404]**
    2 Ch. 144

Rule 5 in s. 2 of the Vendor and Purchaser Act 1874 that "where the vendor retains any part of an estate to which any documents of title relate, he shall be entitled to retain such documents" was held to apply only to land, including leaseholds. A mortgage security comprised land and policies of assurance on the life of the mortgagor. The land was sold by the mortgagee who retained the insurance policies. *Held*, the purchaser was entitled to have the mortgage deed delivered to him as the mortgagee retained no land.

Wilson v. Wilson, [1969] 3 All E.R. 945   **[405]**

In 1961 the plaintiff and defendant applied to a building society for a loan on the security of a freehold property which the defendant wished to purchase. The plaintiff was joined because the defendant's income was insufficient to qualify him for a loan. The property was transferred to the plaintiff and defendant as beneficial joint tenants and the title and building society charge were registered in the joint names. The plaintiff contributed no part of the purchase price or costs. In 1967 the plaintiff served notice to sever the joint tenancy in equity and in April, 1967 commenced an action claiming half of the property. The defendant counterclaimed for a declaration that the property was held in trust for him absolutely and sought leave at the trial to amend his defence and claim rectification. *Held*, the defendant would be given leave to amend as the deed ought to be rectified to give effect to the true intention of the parties. Where a deed was rectifiable, the doctrine of estoppel by deed would not bind the parties to it. It made no difference that one party to the deed, *i.e.* the vendor, was not before the court as he was not concerned or affected by the rectification.

Wimbush v. Cibulia, Same v. Levinski, [1949] 2 All E.R. 432   **[406]**
    (Court of Appeal)

In 1925 C. took a weekly tenancy of two first-floor rooms as a separate dwelling.
In 1933 he took a tenancy of two rooms on the ground floor and two rooms in the
basement. The two tenancies were distinct with separate rent books. C. used the
two first-floor rooms as bedrooms, the two ground-floor rooms as a living-room
and kitchen, and a workroom, and one basement room as a larder. In 1948 the
landlord claimed possession of the ground floor and basement rooms on the
footing that they were not let as a "separate dwelling" within the Increase of
Rent and Mortgage Interest (Restrictions) Act 1920, s. 12 (2). In 1916 L. became
tenant of the ground floor and basement of a house. In 1946 by a separate agreement he became tenant of two rooms on the first floor. He used one first-floor
room as a kitchen and the other as a living-room, one ground-floor room as a
bedroom and the other as a workshop and the basement rooms as a scullery and
coal store. The landlord claimed possession of the ground floor and basement
rooms on the ground that they were not let as a "separate dwelling" within
s. 12 (2) of the 1920 Act. *Held*, it was impossible to hold that the rooms comprised
in the second tenancy in the first case and in the first tenancy in the second case
constituted the separate dwelling of the tenant since essential operations of living
were carried on in premises other than those claimed but the circumstances in
which and the purposes for which the second tenancy in each case was granted
indicated, although the second tenancy was in the form of a separate transaction,
that the intention was to treat both tenancies as one letting and so interdependent
that neither could be determined without the other. The cases must be remitted
to the county court to determine whether the second letting was separate or
whether the real agreement to be imputed to the parties involved such a consolidation as to make a single tenancy. (But see *Metropolitan Properties Co.
(F. G. C.), Ltd.* v. *Barder.*)

Wimpey (George) & Co., Ltd. v. Sohn, [1966] 1 All E.R. 232   **[407]**
    (Court of Appeal)

The plaintiffs agreed to purchase from the defendants an hotel property.
Included in the contract was an adjoining strip of garden land, "the blue land".
The conditions of sale provided that the title to the blue land was to be by
statutory declaration that the land had been in the undisputed possession of the
defendants or their predecessors in title for 20 years and upwards. When the
defendants purchased the property in 1952 they had acquired only rights of user
over the land at the back of the hotel, which included the blue land. Prior to 1942
the public had had access to the blue land from a road but from then access was
only through hotel property, by reason of fencing constructed around the blue
land. The defendants were unable to show undisputed possession of the blue land
for 20 years but sought to force on the plaintiffs a possessory title based on 12
years' adverse possession and s. 4 (3) and s. 10 of the Limitation Act 1939. *Held*,
the plaintiffs were entitled to rescind. (i) Where the vendors offered 20 years'
undisputed possession they did not perform their contract by offering 12 years'
adverse possession. (*Re Atkinson and Horsell's Contract* distinguished); (ii)
although fencing of land belonging to another could be an act of exclusion of the
owner, yet in the present case fencing may have been erected to protect the
garden rights. The act was equivocal and evidence did not establish the intention
to exclude the freeholder so that the defendants failed to show title to the blue
land by adverse possession. (But see *Re Spencer and Hauser's Contract.*)

Windsor Refrigerator Co., Ltd. v. Branch Nominees, Ltd.,   **[408]**
    [1961] Ch. 88 (Court of Appeal)

At first instance it was held that a document appointing a Receiver to be
effective on certain conditions was not validly delivered as a deed, although it
was executed under seal, as the conditions made it revocable. On appeal it was

held that, assuming the document was invalid as a deed on the ground that it could not be delivered in escrow subject to an overriding power to recall it, it could nevertheless be valid as an appointment in writing. (See also *Foundling Hospital* v. *Crane* and *Beesly* v. *Hallwood Estates, Ltd.*)

Winn v. Bull (1877), 7 Ch.D. 29   **[409]**

Correspondence in connection with sale of land used the words "subject to the preparation and approval of a formal contract". *Held*, an offer "subject to contract" means the matter is subject to negotiation and there is no binding contract at that stage. (See *Chillingworth* v. *Esche*.)

Wyse v. Leahy (1875), I.R. 9 C.L. 384   **[410]**

The plaintiff had acquired property the extent of which was in dispute under a Landed Estate Court conveyance in which no map was referred to. The defendants sought to rely on a copy of the ordnance map attached to the conveyance. The trial judge refused to look at the map which did not form part of the conveyance, not being referred to therein, but merely attached. The report does not show whether the wording of the parcels clause in the conveyance was ambiguous or gave rise to particular difficulty. (But see *Leachman* v. *L. & K. Richardson, Ltd.*)

Yandle & Sons v. Sutton, Young v. Sutton, [1922] Ch. 199;   **[411]**
        [1922] All E.R. Rep. 425

A purchaser agreed to buy land but refused to complete on the ground that there was a public right of way across the land. *Held*, the existence of a right of way is not a defect in itself; it may be a defect only as indicating the existence of rights in other persons. If the right of way is patent, then a purchaser takes subject to it as he takes what he sees, but he is not subjected to all the rights which he might have discovered if he had pursued enquiries. If the condition of the land indicated a private right of way but in fact there was a public right of way which was more onerous than the private right, a purchaser might be entitled to rescind or to resist a demand for specific performance. A purchaser is only liable to take property subject to those defects which are patent to the eye, including those which are a necessary consequence of something which is patent to the eye. In the circumstances of the case the judge found that the purchaser's attention had been drawn by the vendors to the right of way. The circumstances could have been compatible with a public right of way, a private right of way or an accommodation track for the use of shooting parties or gamekeepers; hence it was not a patent, but a latent, right of way and the purchaser was entitled to rescind.

Young v. Ashley Gardens Properties, Ltd., [1903] 2 Ch. 112   **[412]**

A lease contained a covenant not to assign without the written licence of the lessor, "such licence not to be unreasonably withheld". *Held*, that the lessor does not have to give reasons for refusing a licence but if he grants a licence containing an unreasonable condition the court may make a declaration that the lessee can assign without consent.

STATUTES

SETTLED LAND ACT 1925
(15 & 16 Geo., 5c. 18; 23 Halsbury's Statutes (2nd Edn.) 12)

1. What constitutes a settlement. [413]

(1) Any deed, will, agreement for a settlement or other agreement, Act of Parliament, or other instrument, or any number of instruments, whether made or passed before or after, or partly before and partly after, the commencement of this Act, under or by virtue of which instrument or instruments any land, after the commencement of this Act, stands for the time being:
  (i) limited in trust for any persons by way of succession; or
  (ii) limited in trust for any person in possession:
    (a) for an entailed interest whether or not capable of being barred or defeated;
    (b) for an estate in fee simple or for a term of years absolute subject to an executory limitation, gift, or disposition over on failure of his issue or in any other event;
    (c) for a base or determinable fee or any corresponding interest in leasehold land;
    (d) being an infant, for an estate in fee simple or for a term of years absolute; or
  (iii) limited in trust for any person for an estate in fee simple or for a term of years absolute contingently on the happening of any event; or
  (iv) . . .
  (v) charged, whether voluntarily or in consideration of marriage or by way of family arrangement, and whether immediately or after an interval, with the payment of any rentcharge for the life of any person, or any less period, or of any capital, annual, or periodical sums for the portions, advancement, maintenance, or otherwise for the benefit of any persons, with or without any term of years for securing or raising the same;
creates or is for the purposes of this Act a settlement and is in this Act referred to as a settlement, or as the settlement, as the case requires:

Provided that, where land is the subject of a compound settlement, references in this Act to the settlement shall be construed as meaning such compound settlement, unless the context otherwise requires.

13. Dispositions not to take effect until vesting instrument is made. [414]

Where a tenant for life or statutory owner has become entitled to have a principal vesting deed or a vesting assent executed in his favour, then until a vesting instrument is executed or made pursuant to this Act in respect of the settled land, any purported disposition thereof *inter vivos* by any person, other than a personal representative (not being a disposition which he has power to make in right of his equitable interests or powers under a trust instrument), shall not take effect except in favour of a purchaser of a legal estate [without notice of such tenant for life or statutory owner having become so entitled as aforesaid] but, save as aforesaid, shall operate only as a contract for valuable consideration to carry out the transaction after the requisite vesting instrument has been executed or made, and a purchaser of a legal estate shall not be concerned with such disposition unless the contract is registered as a land charge.

[Nothing in this section affects the creation or transfer of a legal estate by virtue of an order of the court or the Minister or other competent authority.]

114

18. Restrictions on dispositions of settled land where   **[415]**
trustees have not been discharged.

(1) Where land is the subject of a vesting instrument and the trustees of the settlement have not been discharged under this Act, then:

(*a*) any disposition by the tenant for life or statutory owner of the land, other than a disposition authorised by this Act or any other statute, or made in pursuance of any additional or larger powers mentioned in the vesting instrument, shall be void, except for the purpose of conveying or creating such equitable interests as he has power, in right of his equitable interests and powers under the trust instrument, to convey or create; and

(*b*) if any capital money is payable in respect of a transaction, a conveyance to a purchaser of the land shall only take effect under this Act if the capital money is paid to or by the direction of the trustees of the settlement or into court; and

(*c*) notwithstanding anything to the contrary in the vesting instrument, or the trust instrument, capital money shall not, except where the trustee is a trust corporation, be paid to or by the direction of fewer persons than two as trustees of the settlement.

20. Other limited owners having powers of tenant for life.   **[416]**

(1) Each of the following persons being of full age shall, when his estate or interest is in possession, have the powers of a tenant for life under this Act, (namely):

(i) A tenant in tail, including a tenant in tail after possibility of issue extinct, and a tenant in tail who is by Act of Parliament restrained from barring or defeating his estate tail, and although the reversion is in the Crown, but not including such a tenant in tail where the land in respect whereof he is so restrained was purchased with money provided by Parliament in consideration of public services;

(ii) A person entitled to land for an estate in fee simple or for a term of years absolute with or subject to, in any of such cases, an executory limitation, gift, or disposition over on failure of his issue or in any other event;

(iii) A person entitled to a base or determinable fee, although the reversion or right of reverter is in the Crown, or to any corresponding interest in leasehold land;

(iv) A tenant for years determinable on life, not holding merely under a lease at a rent;

(v) A tenant for the life of another, not holding merely under a lease at a rent;

(vi) A tenant for his own or any other life, or for years determinable on life, whose estate is liable to cease in any event during that life, whether by expiration of the estate, or by conditional limitation, or otherwise, or to be defeated by an executory limitation, gift, or disposition over, or is subject to a trust for accumulation of income for any purpose;

(vii) A tenant by the curtesy;

(viii) A person entitled to the income of land under a trust or direction for payment thereof to him during his own or any other life, whether or not subject to expenses of management or to a trust for accumulation of income for any purpose, or until sale of the land, or until forfeiture, cesser or determination by any means of his interest therein, unless the land is subject to an immediate binding trust for sale;

(ix) A person beneficially entitled to land for an estate in fee simple or for a term of years absolute subject to any estates, interests, charges, or powers of charging, subsisting or capable of being exercised under a settlement;

(x) ...

72. Completion of transactions by conveyance.   [417]

(1) On a sale, exchange, lease, mortgage, charge, or other disposition, the tenant for life may, as regards land sold, given in exchange, leased, mortgaged, charged, or otherwise disposed of, or intended so to be, or as regards easements or other rights or privileges sold, given in exchange, leased, mortgaged, or otherwise disposed of, or intended so to be, effect the transaction by deed to the extent of the estate or interest vested or declared to be vested in him by the last or only vesting instrument affecting the settled land or any less estate or interest, in the manner requisite for giving effect to the sale, exchange, lease, mortgage, charge, or other disposition, but so that a mortgage shall be effected by the creation of a term of years absolute in the settled land or by charge by way of legal mortgage, and not otherwise.

(2) Such a deed, to the extent and in the manner to and in which it is expressed or intended to operate and can operate under this Act, is effectual to pass the land conveyed, or the easements, rights, privileges or other interests created, discharged from all the limitations, powers, and provisions of the settlement, and from all estates, interests, and charges subsisting or to arise thereunder, but subject to and with the exception of—

  (i) all legal estates and charges by way of legal mortgage having priority to the settlement; and

 (ii) all legal estates and charges by way of legal mortgage which have been conveyed or created for securing money actually raised at the date of the deed; and

(iii) all leases and grants at fee-farm rents or otherwise, and all grants of easements, rights of common, or other rights or privileges which—

> (a) were before the date of the deed granted or made for value in money or money's worth, or agreed so to be, by the tenant for life or statutory owner, or by any of his predecessors in title, or any trustees for them, under the settlement, or under any statutory power, or are at that date otherwise binding on the successors in title of the tenant for life or statutory owner; and

> (b) are at the date of the deed protected by registration under the Land Charges Act, 1925, if capable of registration thereunder.

(3) Notwithstanding registration under the Land Charges Act 1925 of:

> (a) an annuity within the meaning of Part II of that Act;

> (b) a limited owner's charge or a general equitable charge within the meaning of that Act;

a disposition under this Act operates to overreach such annuity or charge which shall, according to its priority, take effect as if limited by the settlement.

(4) Where a lease is by this Act authorised to be made by writing under hand only, such writing shall have the same operation under this section as if it had been a deed.

110. Protection of Purchasers, etc.   [418]

(1) On a sale, exchange, lease, mortgage, charge, or other disposition, a purchaser dealing in good faith with a tenant for life or statutory owner shall, as against all parties entitled under the settlement, be conclusively taken to have given the best price, consideration, or rent, as the case may require, that could reasonably be obtained by the tenant for life or statutory owner, and to have complied with all the requisitions of this Act.

TRUSTEE ACT 1925

(15 & 16 Geo. 5c. 20; 20 Halsbury's Statutes (2nd Edn) 427)

40. Vesting of trust property in new or continuing trustees.   [419]

(1) Where by a deed a new trustee is appointed to perform any trust, then:

> (a) if the deed contains a declaration by the appointor to the effect that any estate or interest in any land subject to the trust, or in any

chattel so subject, or the right to recover or receive any debt or other thing in action so subject, shall vest in the persons who by virtue of the deed become or are the trustees for performing the trust, the deed shall operate, without any conveyance or assignment, to vest in those persons as joint tenants and for the purposes of the trust the estate interest or right to which the declaration relates; and

(b) if the deed is made after the commencement of this Act and does not contain such a declaration, the deed shall, subject to any express provision to the contrary therein contained, operate as if it had contained such a declaration by the appointor extending to all the estates interests and rights with respect to which a declaration could have been made.

(2) Where by a deed a retiring trustee is discharged under the statutory power without a new trustee being appointed, then:

(a) if the deed contains such a declaration as aforesaid by the retiring and continuing trustees, and by the other person, if any, empowered to appoint trustees, the deed shall, without any conveyance or assignment, operate to vest in the continuing trustees alone, as joint tenants, and for the purposes of the trust, the estate, interest, or right to which the declaration relates; and

(b) if the deed is made after the commencement of this Act and does not contain such a declaration, the deed shall, subject to any express provision to the contrary therein contained, operate as if it had contained such a declaration by such persons as aforesaid extending to all the estates, interests and rights with respect to which a declaration could have been made.

(3) An express vesting declaration, whether made before or after the commencement of this Act, shall, notwithstanding that the estate, interest or right to be vested is not expressly referred to, and provided that the other statutory requirements were or are complied with, operate and be deemed always to have operated (but without prejudice to any express provision to the contrary contained in the deed of appointment or discharge) to vest in the persons respectively referred to in subsections (1) and (2) of this section, as the case may require, such estates, interests and rights as are capable of being and ought to be vested in those persons.

(4) This section does not extend:

(a) to land conveyed by way of mortgage for securing money subject to the trust, except land conveyed on trust for securing debentures or debenture stock;

(b) to land held under a lease which contains any covenant, condition or agreement against assignment or disposing of the land without licence or consent, unless, prior to the execution of the deed containing expressly or impliedly the vesting declaration, the requisite licence or consent has been obtained, or unless, by virtue of any statute or rule of law, the vesting declaration, express or implied, would not operate as a breach of covenant or give rise to a forfeiture;

(c) to any share, stock, annuity or property which is only transferable in books kept by a company or other body, or in manner directed by or under an Act of Parliament.

In this subsection "lease" includes an underlease and an agreement for a lease or underlease.

(5) For purposes of registration of the deed in any registry, the person or persons making the declaration expressly or impliedly, shall be deemed the conveying party or parties, and the conveyance shall be deemed to be made by him or them under a power conferred by this Act.

(6) This section applies to deeds of appointment or discharge executed on or after the first day of January, eighteen hundred and eighty-two.

LAND CHARGES ACT 1925

(15 & 16 Geo. 5c. 22; 20 Halsbury's Statutes (2nd Edn.) 1063)

10. Register of land charges.   **[420]**

(1) The following classes of charges on, or obligations affecting, land may be registered as land charges in the register of land charges, namely:

Class A: A rent, or annuity, or principal money payable by instalments or otherwise, with or without interest, being a charge (otherwise than by deed) upon land created pursuant to the application of some person either before or after the commencement of this Act:

   (i) under the provisions of any Act of Parliament, for securing to any person either the money spent by him or the costs, charges, and expenses incurred by him for repaying the money spent, or the costs, charges, and expenses incurred by another person under the authority of an Act of Parliament; or

  (ii) under section thirty-five of the Land Drainage Act 1861; or

[(iii) under section seventy-two, seventy-three, seventy-four or eighty-two of the Agricultural Holdings Act 1948, or any previous similar enactment]; or

  (iv) under section four or section six of the Tithe Act 1918; or

  (v) under section one of the Tithe Annuities Apportionment Act 1921; or

  (vi) under paragraph (6) of the Twelfth Schedule to the Law of Property Act 1922

but not including a rate or scot.

Class B: A charge on land (not being a local land charge) of any of the kinds described in Class A, created otherwise than pursuant to the application of any person, either before or after the commencement of this Act, but if created before such commencement only if acquired under a conveyance made after such commencement.

Class C: A mortgage charge or obligation affecting land of any of the following kinds, created either before or after the commencement of this Act, but if created before such commencement only if acquired under a conveyance made after such commencement, namely:

   (i) Any legal mortgage not being a mortgage protected by a deposit of documents relating to the legal estate affected, and (where the whole of the land affected is within the jurisdiction of a local deeds registry) not being registered in the local deeds register (in this Act called a "puisne mortgage"); and

  (ii) Any equitable charge acquired by a tenant for life or statutory owner under the Finance Act 1894, or any other statute, by reason of the discharge by him of any death duties or other liabilities, and to which special priority is given by the statute (in this Act called "a limited owner's charge"); and

 (iii) Any other equitable charge, which is not secured by a deposit of documents relating to the legal estate affected and does not arise or affect an interest arising under a trust for sale or a settlement and is not included in any other class of land charge (in this Act called "a general equitable charge"):

    [Provided that a charge given by way of indemnity against rents equitably apportioned or charged exclusively on land in exoneration of other land and against the breach or non-observance of covenants or conditions, shall not be deemed to be a general equitable charge and shall not be registrable as a land charge under this Act]; and

  (iv) Any contract by an estate owner or by a person entitled at the date of the contract to have a legal estate conveyed to him to convey or create a legal estate, including a contract conferring either expressly or by statutory implication a valid option of purchase, a right of pre-emption or any other like right (in this Act referred to as "an estate contract").

Class D: A charge or obligation affecting land of any of the following kinds, namely:

(i) Any charge acquired by the Commissioners of Inland Revenue under any statute passed or hereafter to be passed for death duties leviable or payable on any death which occurs after the commencement of this Act; and

(ii) A covenant or agreement (not being a covenant or agreement made between a lessor and lessee) restrictive of the user of land entered into after the commencement of this Act (in this Act referred to as "restrictive covenant"); and

(iii) Any easement right or privilege over or affecting land created or arising after the commencement of this Act, and being merely an equitable interest (in this Act referred to as an "equitable easement").

Class E: An annuity within the meaning of Part II of this Act created before the commencement of this Act and not registered in the register of annuities.

(2) A land charge shall be registered in the name of the estate owner whose estate is intended to be affected except that, in the case of a land charge registered before the commencement of this Act, under any enactment replaced by this Act, in the name of a person not being the estate owner, it may remain so registered until it is registered in the name of the estate owner in the prescribed manner.

(3) Where a land charge is not created by an instrument, short particulars of the effect of the charge shall be furnished with the application to register the charge.

(4) Nothing in this section shall be deemed to authorise the Commissioners of Inland Revenue to register a land charge in respect of any claim for death duties unless the duty has become a charge on the land, and the application to register any such charge shall state the duties in respect of which the charge is claimed, and, so far as possible, shall define the land affected, and such particulars shall be entered or referred to in the register.

(5) In the case of a land charge for securing money, created by a company, registration under section ninety-three of the Companies (Consolidation) Act, 1908, shall be sufficient in place of registration under this Act, and shall have effect as if the land charge had been registered under this Act.

[(6) In the case of a general equitable charge, restrictive covenant equitable easement or estate contract affecting land within any of the three ridings, and in the case of any other land charge (not being a local land charge) created by a document which shows on the face of it that the charge affects land within any of those ridings, registration shall be effected in the prescribed manner in the appropriate local deeds registry in place of the registry.]

(7) A puisne mortgage created before the commencement of this Act may be registered as a land charge before any transfer of the mortgage is made.

13. Protection of purchasers against land charges created **[421]** after certain dates.

(1) A land charge of Class A created after the thirty-first day of December, eighteen hundred and eighty-eight, shall be void as against a purchaser of the land charged therewith or of any interest in such land, unless the land charge is registered in the register of land charges before the completion of the purchase.

(2) A land charge of Class B, C or Class D, created or arising after the commencement of this Act, shall (except as hereinafter provided) be void as against a purchaser of the land charged therewith, or of any interest in such land; unless the land charge is registered in the appropriate register before the completion of the purchase:

Provided that, as respects a land charge of Class D and an estate contract created or entered into after the commencement of this Act, this subsection only applies in favour of a purchaser of a legal estate for money or money's worth.

119

15. Registration of local land charges. [422]

(1) Any charge (hereinafter called "a local land charge") acquired either before or after the commencement of this Act by the council of any administrative county, metropolitan borough, or urban or rural district, or by the corporation of any municipal borough, or by any other local authority under the Public Health Acts, 1875 to 1907, the Metropolis Management Acts, 1855 to 1893, or the Private Street Works Act 1892, or under any similar statute (public general or local or private) passed or hereafter to be passed, which takes effect by virtue of the statute, shall be registered in the prescribed manner by the proper officer of the local authority, and shall (except as hereinafter mentioned in regard to charges created or arising before the commencement of this Act) be void as against a purchaser for money or money's worth of a legal estate in the land affected thereby, unless registered in the appropriate register before the completion of the purchase.

[For the purposes of this section any sum which is recoverable by a local authority under any of the Acts aforesaid from successive owners or occupiers of the property in respect of which the sum recoverable shall, whether such sum is expressed to be a charge on the property or not, be deemed to be a charge.]

(2) Except as expressly provided by this section, the provisions of this Act relating to a land charge of Class B shall apply to a local land charge.

(3) As regards a local land charge, the registration by the proper officer shall (without prejudice to the right of the registrar also to register the charge if and when the prescribed application and information is made and furnished to him) take the place of registration by the registrar, and, in reference thereto, the proper officer of the local authority shall have all the powers and be subject to the same obligations as the registrar has or is subject to in regard to a land charge.

(4) Where a local authority has expended money for any purpose which, when the work is completed and any requisite resolution is passed or order is made, will confer a charge upon land, the proper officer of the local authority may in the meantime register a local charge in his register against the land generally, without specifying the amount, but the registration of any such general charge shall be cancelled within the prescribed time not being less than one year after the charge is ascertained and allotted, and thereupon the specific local land charges shall, unless previously discharged, be registered as of the date on which the general charge was registered.

(5) Nothing in this section operates to impose any obligation to register any local land charge created or arising before the commencement of this Act except after the expiration of one year from such commencement or to discharge a purchaser from liability in respect of any local land charge which is not for the time being required to be registered.

(6) Separate rules may be made under this Act in reference to local land charges for giving effect to the provisions of this section and in particular:

(a) for prescribing the mode of registration of a general or specific charge whether by reference to the estate owner or to the land affected or otherwise].

(b) . . .

(c) for prescribing the proper officer to act as local registrar, and making provision as to official certificates of search to be given by him in reference to subsisting entries in his register;

(d) for determining the effect of an official certificate of search in regard to the protection of a purchaser, solicitor, trustee or other person in a fiduciary position, and for prescribing the fees to be paid for any such certificate or for a search;

(e) for prescribing the fees, if any, to be paid for the cancellation of an entry in the register.

[(7) The foregoing provisions of this section shall apply to:

(a) . . .

(*b*) any prohibition of or restriction on the user or mode of user of land or buildings imposed by a local authority after the commencement of this Act by order, instrument, or resolution, or enforceable by a local authority under any covenant or agreement made with them after the commencement of this Act, or by virtue of any conditions attached to a consent, approval, or licence granted by a local authority after that date, being a prohibition or restriction binding on successive owners of the land or buildings, and not being:

(i) a prohibition or restriction operating over the whole of the district of the authority or over the whole of any contributory place thereof; or

(ii) . . .

(iii) a prohibition or restriction imposed by a covenant or agreement made between a lessor and lessee;

as if the . . . resolution, authority, prohibition, or restriction were a local land charge, and the same shall be registered by the proper officer as a local land charge accordingly.]

(8) This section applies to local land charges affecting registered as well as unregistered land.

ADMINISTRATION OF ESTATES ACT 1925
(15 & 16 Geo. 5c. 23; 9 Halsbury's Statutes (2nd Edn.) 718)

1. Devolution of real estate on personal representative.   [423]

(1) Real estate to which a deceased person was entitled for an interest not ceasing on his death shall on his death, and notwithstanding any testamentary disposition thereof, devolve from time to time on the personal representative of the deceased, in like manner as before the commencement of this Act chattels real developed on the personal representative from time to time of a deceased person.

(2) The personal representatives for the time being of a deceased person are deemed in law his heirs and assigns within the meaning of all trusts and powers.

(3) The personal representatives shall be the representative of the deceased in regard to his real estate to which he was entitled for an interest not ceasing on his death as well as in regard to his personal estate.

2. Application to real estate of law affecting chattels real.   [424]

(1) Subject to the provisions of this Act, all enactments and rules of law, and all jurisdiction of any court with respect to the appointment of administrators or to probate or letters of administration, or to dealings before probate in the case of chattels real, and with respect to costs and other matters in the administration of personal estate, in force before the commencement of this Act, and all powers, duties, rights, equities, obligations, and liabilities of a personal representative in force at the commencement of this Act with respect to chattels real, shall apply and attach to the personal representative and shall have effect with respect to real estate vested in him, and in particular all such powers of disposition and dealing as were before the commencement of this Act exercisable as respects chattels real by the survivor or survivors of two or more personal representatives, as well as by a single personal representative, or by all the personal representatives together, shall be exercisable by the personal representatives or representative of the deceased with respect to his real estate.

(2) Where as respects real estate there are two or more personal representatives, a conveyance of real estate devolving under this Part of this Act shall not, save as otherwise provided as respects trust estates including settled land, be made without the concurrence therein of all such representatives or an order of the court, but where probate is granted to one or some of two or more persons named as executors, whether or not power is reserved to the other or others to prove, any conveyance of the real estate may be made by the proving executor or executors

I   121

for the time being, without an order of the court, and shall be as effectual as if all the persons named as executors had concurred therein.

(3) Without prejudice to the rights and powers of a personal representative, the appointment of a personal representative in regard to real estate shall not, save as hereinafter provided, affect—

(a) any rule as to marshalling or as to administration of assets;

(b) the beneficial interest in real estate under any testamentary disposition;

(c) any mode of dealing with any beneficial interest in real estate, or the proceeds of sale thereof;

(d) the right of any person claiming to be interested in the real estate to take proceedings for the protection or recovery thereof against any person other than the personal representative.

3. Interpretation of Part I.   [425]

(1) In this Part of this Act "real estate" includes:

(i) Chattels real, and land in possession, remainder, or reversion, and every interest in or over land to which a deceased person was entitled at the time of his death; and

(ii) Real estate held on trust (including settled land) or by way of mortgage or security, but not money to arise under a trust for sale of land, nor money secured or charged on land.

(2) A testator shall be deemed to have been entitled at his death to any interest in real estate passing under any gift contained in his will which operates as an appointment under a general power to appoint by will, or operates under the testamentary power conferred by statute to dispose of an entailed interest.

(3) An entailed interest of a deceased person shall (unless disposed of under the testamentary power conferred by statute) be deemed an interest ceasing on his death, but any further or other interest of the deceased in the same property in remainder or reversion which is capable of being disposed of by his will shall not be deemed to be an interest so ceasing.

(4) The interest of a deceased person under a joint tenancy where another tenant survives the deceased is an interest ceasing on his death.

(5) On the death of a corporator sole his interest in the corporation's real and personal estate shall be deemed to be an interest ceasing on his death and shall devolve to his successor.

This subsection applies on the demise of the Crown as respects all property, real and personal, vested in the Crown as a corporation sole.

7. Executor of executor represents original testator.   [426]

(1) An executor of a sole or last surviving executor of a testator is the executor of that testator.

This provision shall not apply to an executor who does not prove the will of his testator, and, in the case of an executor who on his death leaves surviving him some other executor of his testator who afterwards proves the will of that testator, it shall cease to apply on such probate being granted.

(2) So long as the chain of such representation is unbroken, the last executor in the chain is the executor of every preceding testator.

(3) The chain of such representation is broken by:

(a) an intestacy; or

(b) the failure of a testator to appoint an executor; or

(c) the failure to obtain probate of a will;

but is not broken by a temporary grant of administration if probate is subsequently granted.

(4) Every person in the chain of representation to a testator:

(a) has the same rights in respect of the real and personal estate of that testator as the original executor would have had if living; and

(b) is, to the extent to which the estate whether real or personal of that testator has come to his hands, answerable as if he were an original executor.

9. Vesting of estate of intestate between death and grant   [427] of administration.

Where a person dies intestate, his real and personal estate, until administration is granted in respect thereof, shall vest in the Probate Judge in the same manner and to the same extent as formerly in the case of personal estate if vested in the ordinary.

36. Effect of assent or conveyance by personal representative.   [428]

(1) A personal representative may assent to the vesting, in any person who (whether by devise, bequest, devolution, appropriation or otherwise) may be entitled thereto, either beneficially or as a trustee or personal representative, of any estate or interest in real estate to which the testator or intestate was entitled or over which he exercised a general power of appointment by his will, including the statutory power to dispose of entailed interests, and which devolved upon the personal representative.

(2) The assent shall operate to vest in that person the estate or interest to which the assent relates, and, unless a contrary intention appears, the assent shall relate back to the death of the deceased.

(3) The statutory covenants implied by a person being expressed to convey as personal representative, may be implied in an assent in like manner as in a conveyance by deed.

(4) An assent to the vesting of a legal estate shall be in writing, signed by the personal representative, and shall name the person in whose favour it is given and shall operate to vest in that person the legal estate to which it relates; and an assent not in writing or not in favour of a named person shall not be effectual to pass a legal estate.

(5) Any person in whose favour an assent or conveyance of a legal estate is made by a personal representative may require that notice of the assent or conveyance be written or endorsed on or permanently annexed to the probate or letters of administration, at the cost of the estate of the deceased, and that the probate or letters of administration be produced, at the like cost, to prove that the notice has been placed thereon or annexed thereto.

(6) A statement in writing by a personal representative that he has not given or made an assent or conveyance in respect of a legal estate, shall, in favour of a purchaser, but without prejudice to any previous disposition made in favour of another purchaser deriving title mediately or immediately under the personal representative, be sufficient evidence that an assent or conveyance has not been given or made in respect of the legal estate to which the statement relates, unless notice of a previous assent or conveyance affecting that estate has been placed on or annexed to the probate or administration.

A conveyance by a personal representative of a legal estate to a purchaser accepted on the faith of such a statement shall (without prejudice as aforesaid and unless notice of a previous assent or conveyance affecting that estate has been placed on or annexed to the probate or administration) operate to transfer or create the legal estate expressed to be conveyed in like manner as if no previous assent or conveyance had been made by the personal representative.

A personal representative making a false statement, in regard to any such matter, shall be liable in like manner as if the statement had been contained in a statutory declaration.

(7) An assent or conveyance by a personal representative in respect of a legal estate shall, in favour of a purchaser, unless notice of a previous assent or conveyance affecting that legal estate has been placed on or annexed to the probate or administration, be taken as sufficient evidence that the person in whose favour the assent or conveyance is given or made is the person entitled to have the legal estate conveyed to him, and upon the proper trusts, if any, but shall not

otherwise prejudicially affect the claim of any person rightfully entitled to the estate vested or conveyed or any charge thereon.

(8) A conveyance of a legal estate by a personal representative to a purchaser shall not be invalidated by reason only that the purchaser may have notice that all the debts, liabilities, funeral, and testamentary or administration expenses, duties, and legacies of the deceased have been discharged or provided for.

(9) An assent or conveyance given or made by a personal representative shall not, except in favour of a purchaser of a legal estate, prejudice the right of the personal representative or any other person to recover the estate or interest to which the assent or conveyance relates, or to be indemnified out of such estate or interest against any duties, debts, or liability to which such estate or interest would have been subject if there had not been any assent or conveyance.

(10) A personal representative may, as a condition of giving an assent or making a conveyance, require security for the discharge of any such duties, debt, or liability, but shall not be entitled to postpone the giving of an assent merely by reason of the subsistence of any such duties, debt or liability if reasonable arrangements have been made for discharging the same; and an assent may be given subject to any legal estate or charge by way of legal mortgage.

(11) This section shall not operate to impose any stamp duty in respect of an assent, and in this section "purchaser" means a purchaser for money or money's worth.

(12) This section applies to assents and conveyances made after the commencement of this Act, whether the testator or intestate died before or after such commencement.

39. Powers of management.   [429]

(1) In dealing with the real and personal estate of the deceased his personal representatives shall, for purposes of administration, or during a minority of any beneficiary or the subsistence of any life interest, or until the period of distribution arrives, have:

 (i) the same powers and discretions, including power to raise money by mortgage or charge (whether or not by deposit of documents) as a personal representative had before the commencement of this Act, with respect to personal estate vested in him, and such power of raising money by mortgage may in the case of land be exercised by way of legal mortgage; and

 (ii) all the powers, discretions and duties conferred or imposed by law on trustees holding land upon an effectual trust for sale (including power to overreach equitable interests and powers as if the same affected the proceeds of sale); and

 (iii) all the powers conferred by statute on trustees for sale, and so that every contract entered into by a personal representative shall be binding on and be enforceable against and by the personal representative for the time being of the deceased, and may be carried into effect, or be varied or rescinded by him, and, in the case of a contract entered into by a predecessor, as if it had been entered into by himself.

(2) Nothing in this section shall affect the right of any person to require an assent or conveyance to be made.

(3) This section applies whether the testator or intestate died before or after the commencement of this Act.

42. Power to appoint trustees of infants' property.   [430]

Where an infant is absolutely entitled under the will or on the intestacy of a person dying before or after the commencement of this Act (in this subsection called "the deceased") to a devise or legacy, or to the residue of the estate of the deceased, or any share therein, and such devise, legacy, residue or share is not under the will, if any, of the deceased, devised or bequeathed to trustees for the infant, the personal representatives of the deceased may appoint a trust corporation of two or more individuals not exceeding four (whether or not including the personal representatives or one or more of the personal representatives), to be the trustee or trustees of such devise, legacy, residue or share for the infant, and to be trustees of any land devised or any land being or forming part of such residue or share for the purposes of the Settled Land Act 1925, and of the statutory provisions relating to the management of land during a minority, and may execute or do any assurance or thing requisite for vesting such devise, legacy, residue or share in the trustee or trustees so appointed.

On such appointment the personal representatives, as such, shall be discharged from all further liability in respect of such devise, legacy, residue, or share, and the same may be retained in its existing condition or state of investment, or may be converted into money, and such money may be invested in any authorised investment.

(2) Where a personal representative has before the commencement of this Act retained or sold any such devise, legacy, residue or share, and invested the same or the proceeds thereof in any investments in which he was authorised to invest money subject to the trust, then, subject to any order of the court made before such commencement, he shall not be deemed to have incurred any liability on that account, or by reason of not having paid or transferred the money or property into court.

LANDLORD AND TENANT ACT 1927
(17 & 18 Geo. 5c. 36; 13 Halsbury's Statutes (2nd Edn.) 883)

19. Provisions as to covenants not to assign, etc., without   **[431]**
licence or consent.

(1) In all leases whether made before or after the commencement of this Act containing a covenant or agreement against assigning, underletting, charging or parting with the possession of demised premises or any part thereof without licence or consent, such covenant condition or agreement shall, notwithstanding any express provision to the contrary, be deemed to be subject:

(a) to a proviso to the effect that such licence or consent is not to be unreasonably withheld, but this proviso does not preclude the right of the landlord to require payment of a reasonable sum in respect of any legal or other expenses incurred in connection with such licence or consent; and

(b) (if the lease is for more than forty years, and is made in consideration wholly or partially of the erection, or the substantial improvement, addition or alteration of buildings, and the lessor is not a Government department or local or public authority, or a statutory or public utility company) to a proviso to the effect that in the case of any assignment, under-letting, charging or parting with the possession (whether by the holders of the lease or any under-tenant whether immediate or not) effected more than seven years before the end of the term no consent or licence shall be required, if notice in writing of the transaction is given to the lessor within six months after the transaction is effected.

COMPANIES ACT 1948
(11 & 12 Geo. 6 c. 38; 3 Halsbury's Statutes (2nd Edn.) 452)

95. Registration of charges created by companies registered   **[432]**
in England.

(1) Subject to the provisions of this Part of this Act, every charge created after the fixed date by a company registered in England and being a charge to which this section applies shall, so far as any security on the company's property or undertaking is conferred thereby, be void against the liquidator and any creditor of the company, unless the prescribed particulars of the charge together with the instrument, if any, by which the charge is created or evidenced, are delivered to or received by the registrar of companies for registration in manner required by

this Act within twenty-one days after the date of its creation, but without prejudice to any contract or obligation for repayment of the money thereby secured, and when a charge becomes void under this section the money secured thereby shall immediately become payable.

(7) The holding of debentures entitling the holder to a charge on land shall not for the purposes of this section be deemed to be an interest in land.

96. Duty of company to register charges created by company.   **[433]**

(1) It shall be the duty of a company to send to the registrar of companies for registration the particulars of every charge created by the company and of the issues of debentures of a series requiring registration under the last foregoing section, but registration of any such charge may be effected on the application of any person interested therein.

(2) Where registration is effected on the application of some person other than the company, that person shall be entitled to recover from the company the amount of any fees properly paid by him to the registrar on the registration.

(3) If any company makes default in sending to the registrar for registration the particulars of any charge created by the company or of the issues of debentures of a series requiring registration as aforesaid, then, unless the registration has been effected on the application of some other person, the company and every officer of the company who is in default shall be liable to a default fine of fifty pounds.

97. Duty of company to register charges existing on   **[434]**
    property acquired.

(1) Where a company registered in England acquires any property which is subject to a charge of any such kind as would, if it had been created by the company after the acquisition of the property, have been required to be registered under this Part of this Act, the company shall cause the prescribed particulars of the charge, together with a copy (certified in the prescribed manner to be a correct copy) of the instrument, if any, by which the charge was created or is evidenced, to be delivered to the registrar of companies for registration in manner required by this Act within twenty-one days after the date on which the acquisition is completed:

Provided that, if the property is situate and the charge was created outside Great Britain, twenty-one days after the date on which the copy of the instrument could in due course of post, and if despatched with due diligence, have been received in the United Kingdom shall be substituted for twenty-one days after the completion of the acquisition as the time within which the particulars and the copy of the instrument are to be delivered to the registrar.

(2) If default is made in complying with this section, the company and every officer of the company who is in default shall be liable to a default fine of fifty pounds.

AGRICULTURAL HOLDINGS ACT 1948
(12 & 13 Geo. 6c. 63; 28 Halsbury's Statutes (2nd Edn.) 25)

24. Restrictions on operation of notices to quit.   **[435]**

(1) Where notice to quit an agricultural holding or part of an agricultural holding is given to the tenant thereof, and not later than one month from the giving of the notice to quit the tenant serves on the landlord a counter-notice in writing requiring that this subsection shall apply to the notice to quit, then, subject to the provisions of the next following subsection, the notice to quit shall not have effect unless the Minister consents to the operation thereof.

(2) The foregoing subsection shall not apply where:
    (a) the Minister has consented under this section to the operation of the notice to quit before the giving thereof and that fact is stated in the notice;

(*b*) the notice to quit is given on the ground that the land is required for a use, other than for agriculture, for which permission has been granted on an application made under the enactments relating to town and country planning, or for which (otherwise than by virtue of any provision of those enactments) such permission is not required, and that fact is stated in the notice;

(*c*) the Minister, in pursuance of an application in that behalf made to him in accordance with the following provisions of this Act not more than six months before the giving of the notice to quit, was satisfied in relation to the holding that the tenant was not fulfilling his responsibilities to farm in accordance with the rules of good husbandry, and certified that he was so satisfied, and that fact is stated in the notice;

(*d*) at the date of the giving of the notice to quit the tenant had failed to comply with a notice in writing served on him by the landlord requiring him within two months from the service of the notice to pay any rent due in respect of the agricultural holding to which the notice to quit relates, or within a reasonable time or within such reasonable period as was specified in the notice to remedy any breach by the tenant that was capable of being remedied of any term or condition of his tenancy which was not inconsistent with the fulfilment of his responsibilities to farm in accordance with the rules of good husbandry, and it is stated in the notice to quit that it is given by reason of the matter aforesaid;

(*e*) at the date of the giving of the notice to quit the interest of the landlord in the agricultural holding to which the notice relates had been materially prejudiced by the commission by the tenant of a breach, which was not capable of being remedied, of any term or condition of the tenancy that was not inconsistent with the fulfilment by the tenant of his responsibilities to farm in accordance with the rules of good husbandry, and it is stated in the notice that it is given by reason of the matter aforesaid;

(*f*) at the date of the giving of the notice to quit the tenant was a person who had become bankrupt or compounded with his creditors, and it is stated in the notice that it is given by reason of the matter aforesaid;

(*g*) the tenant with whom the contract of tenancy was made had died within three months before the date of the giving of the notice to quit, and it is stated in the notice that it is given by reason of the matter aforesaid.

(3) Nothing in this section shall apply to a notice to terminate a tenancy of an agricultural holding subsisting under a written contract entered into before the twenty-fifth day of March, nineteen hundred and forty-seven—

(*a*) where, immediately before the creation of the tenancy, the holding had been for a period of not less than twelve months in the occupation of the landlord;

(*b*) the holding is let upon the express terms that, if the landlord desires to resume that occupation before the expiration of a specified period not exceeding seven years, the landlord shall be entitled to give notice to quit without becoming liable to pay to the tenant any compensation for disturbance; and

(*c*) the notice to terminate the tenancy is given so as to enable the landlord to resume occupation of the holding within the specified period.

35. Application of sections 36 to 45. **[436]**

(1) The provisions of the ten next following sections shall have effect with respect to the rights of the tenant of an agricultural holding with respect to compensation for improvements specified in the Second Schedule to this Act carried out on the holding, being improvements begun before the first day of March, nineteen hundred and forty-eight.

(2) Improvements falling within the foregoing subsection are in this Act referred to as "old improvements".

36. Tenant's right to compensation for old improvements.   [437]

(1) The tenant shall, subject to the provisions of this Act, be entitled on the termination of the tenancy, on quitting the holding, to obtain from his landlord compensation for an old improvement carried out by the tenant:

Provided that where the contract of tenancy was made before the first day of January, nineteen hundred and twenty-one, the tenant shall not be entitled to compensation under this section for an improvement which he was required to carry out by the terms of his tenancy.

(2) Nothing in this section shall prejudice the right of a tenant to claim any compensation to which he may be entitled under custom or agreement, or otherwise, in lieu of any compensation provided by this section.

37. Measure of compensation for old improvements.   [438]

The amount of any compensation under this Act for an old improvement shall be such sum as fairly represents the value of the improvement to an incoming tenant.

38. Compensation for certain old improvements conditional   [439] on consent of landlord to execution thereof.

(1) Compensation under this Act shall not be payable for an old improvement specified in Part I of the Second Schedule to this Act unless, before the execution thereof, the landlord consented in writing (whether unconditionally or upon terms as to compensation or otherwise agreed between him and the tenant) to the execution thereof.

(2) Where the consent was given upon agreed terms as to compensation, compensation payable under the agreement shall be substituted for compensation under this Act.

39. Conditions attaching to right to compensation for   [440] drainage.

(1) Compensation under this Act shall not be payable for an old improvement consisting of that specified in Part II of the Second Schedule to this Act unless the tenant gave to the landlord, not more than three nor less than two months before beginning to execute the improvement, notice in writing under section three of the Agricultural Holdings Act 1923, of his intention to execute the improvement and of the manner in which he proposed to execute it, and:

(a) the landlord and tenant agreed on the terms on which the improvement was to be executed; or

(b) in a case where no agreement was reached and the tenant did not withdraw the notice, the landlord failed to exercise the right conferred on him by that section to execute the improvement himself within a reasonable time:

Provided that this subsection shall not have effect:

(i) if the landlord and tenant agreed, by the contract of tenancy or otherwise, to dispense with notice under the said section three; or

(ii) where the improvement consists of mole drainage works executed by the tenant in pursuance of a direction given to him under or by virtue of Defence Regulations.

(2) If the landlord and tenant agreed (whether after notice was given under the said section three or by an agreement to dispense with notice under that section) upon terms as to compensation upon which the improvement was to be executed, compensation payable under the agreement shall be submitted for compensation, under this Act.

40. Conditions attaching to right to compensation for [441] repairs to buildings.

Compensation under this Act shall not be payable in respect of any such repairs as are mentioned in paragraph 29 of the Second Schedule to this Act unless, before beginning to execute the repairs, the tenant gave to the landlord notice in writing under paragraph 29 of the First Schedule to the Agricultural Holdings Act, 1923, of his intention to execute the repairs, together with particulars thereof, and the landlord failed to exercise the right conferred on him by that paragraph to execute the repairs himself within a reasonable time after receiving the notice.

41. Agreements as to compensation for old improvements [442] specified in Part III of Second Schedule.

Where an agreement in writing entered into before the first day of January, nineteen hundred and twenty-one, secures to the tenant for an old improvement specified in Part III of the Second Schedule to this Act fair and reasonable compensation, having regard to the circumstances existing when the agreement was made.

42. Exclusion of right to compensation for old improvements [443] begun in last year of tenancy.

(1) The tenant shall not be entitled to compensation under this Act in respect of an old improvement (other than manuring) begun by him within one year before he quits the holding:
Provided that this subsection shall not apply—

(a) where the tenant, before beginning the improvement, served notice on his landlord of his intention to begin it, and the landlord either assented to the making of the improvement or failed for a month after the receipt of the notice to object to the making of the improvement; or

(b) in a case where the tenant is a tenant from year to year, where he began the improvement before the receipt of a notice to quit given by the landlord; or

(c) where the improvement consists of mole drainage works executed by the tenant in pursuance of a direction given to him under or by virtue of Defence Regulations.

(2) In this section the expression "manuring" means any of the improvements specified in paragraphs 25 to 27 of the Second Schedule to this Act.

43. Reduction in amount of, and exclusion of right to, [444] compensation for old improvements in certain cases.

(1) In the ascertainment of the amount of the compensation payable under this Act to the tenant in respect of an old improvement, there shall be taken into account:

(a) any benefit which the landlord has given or allowed to the tenant in consideration of the tenant's executing the improvement, whether expressly stated in the contract of tenancy to be so given or allowed or not; and

(b) as respects manuring, the value of the manure required by the contract of tenancy or by custom to be returned to the holding in respect of any crops grown on and sold off or removed from the holding within the last two years of the tenancy or other less time for which the tenancy has endured, not exceeding the value of the manure which would have been produced by consumption on the holding of the crops so sold off or removed.

(2) In assessing the amount of any compensation payable to the tenant, whether under this Act or under custom or agreement, by reason of the improvement of the holding by:

(a) the addition thereto of lime in respect of which a contribution has been made under Part I of the Agriculture Act, 1937; or

(b) mole drainage works in respect of which a grant has been made under section fifteen of the Agriculture (Miscellaneous War Provisions) Act 1940;

the contribution shall be taken into account as if it had been a benefit allowed to the tenant in consideration of his executing the improvement, and the compensation shall be reduced accordingly.

(3) Notwithstanding anything in the foregoing provisions of this Act, the tenant shall not be entitled to compensation thereunder for an old improvement made on land which, at the time when the improvement was begun, was not a holding within the meaning of the Agricultural Holdings Act 1923, as originally enacted, and would not have fallen to be treated as such a holding by virtue of section thirty-three of that Act.

(4) In this section the expression "manuring" means any of the improvements specified in paragraphs 25 to 27 of the Second Schedule to this Act.

44. Old improvements made during any tenancy of a series to qualify for compensation.   [445]

Where the tenant has remained in the holding during two or more tenancies, he shall not be deprived of his right to compensation under this Act in respect of old improvements by reason only that the improvements were made during a tenancy other than the one at the termination of which he quits the holding.

45. Right to compensation for old improvements of tenant who has paid compensation therefor to outgoing tenant.   [446]

Where, on entering into occupation of the holding, the tenant, with the consent in writing of his landlord, paid to an outgoing tenant any compensation payable under or in pursuance of this Act or the Agricultural Holdings Act 1923, in respect of the whole or part of an old improvement, he shall be entitled, on quitting the holding, to claim compensation for the improvement or part in like manner, if at all, as the outgoing tenant would have been entitled if the outgoing tenant had remained tenant of the holding and quitted it at the time at which the tenant quits it.

HIGHWAYS ACT 1959
(7 & 8 Eliz. 2c. 25; 39 Halsbury's Statutes (2nd Edn.) 402)

72. Power to prescribe improvement line for widening street.   [447]

(1) Where in the opinion of a highway authority:

(a) a street, being a highway maintainable at the public expense by them, is narrow or inconvenient, or without any sufficiently regular boundary line, or

(b) it is necessary or desirable that such a street should be widened,

the authority may prescribe in relation to either one side or both sides of the street, or at or within a distance of fifteen yards from any street corner, a line to which the street is to be widened (in this section referred to as an "improvement line").

(2) Where an improvement line prescribed under this section in relation to any street is in force, then, subject to the next following subsection, no new building shall be erected, and no permanent excavation below the level of the street shall be made, nearer to the centre line of the street than the improvement line, except with the consent of the authority who prescribed the line, and the authority may give a consent for such period and subject to such conditions as they may deem expedient:

Provided that the prohibition imposed by this subsection shall not affect any right of statutory undertakers to make an excavation for the purpose of laying, altering, maintaining or renewing any main, pipe, electric line, cable, duct or other work or apparatus.

(3) Where an authority have prescribed an improvement line under this section, a person aggrieved by the decision to prescribe the line or by the refusal of consent under the last foregoing subsection or by the period for which the consent is given or any conditions attached thereto may appeal to a court of quarter sessions.

(4) Subject to the provisions of section fifteen of the Land Charges Act, 1925 (which provided that a local land charge shall be void as against a purchaser for money or money's worth unless registered under that section), a condition imposed in connection with the giving of a consent under subsection (2) of this section shall be binding on the successor in title to every owner, and on every lessee and every occupier, of any land to which it relates.

(5) If a person contravenes the provisions of this section, or any condition imposed in connection with the giving of a consent thereunder, he shall, without prejudice to any other proceedings which may be available against him, be guilty of an offence and shall be liable in respect thereof to a fine not exceeding five pounds, and, if the offence in respect of which he was convicted is continued after the conviction, he shall be guilty of a further offence and shall be liable in respect thereof to a fine not exceeding forty shillings for each day on which the offence is so continued.

(6) Where in the opinion of a highway authority an improvement line prescribed by them under this section, or any part of such a line, is no longer necessary or desirable and should be revoked, they may revoke the line or that part thereof.

(8) Any person whose property is injuriously affected by the prescribing of an improvement line under this section shall, subject to the following provisions thereof, be entitled to recover from the authority who prescribed the line compensation for the injury sustained.

(9) A person shall not be entitled to compensation on account of any building erected, contract made, or other thing done, after the date on which a plan showing the improvement line was deposited in accordance with the provisions of paragraph 4 of the Ninth Schedule to this Act, not being work done for the purpose of finishing a building the erection of which had begun before that date, or of carrying out a contract made before that date.

(10) Nothing in this section shall, without the consent of the undertakers concerned, apply to or affect:

(a) any property occupied or used by railway undertakers for the purposes of a railway comprised in the railway undertaking; or

(b) any property belonging to any of the following undertakers and used by them for the following purposes respectively, that is to say, by canal undertakers for those of a canal comprised in the canal undertaking, by inland navigation undertakers for those of a navigation comprised in the inland navigation undertaking, by dock undertakers for those of a dock comprised in the dock undertaking, or by harbour undertakers for those of a harbour comprised in the harbour undertaking; or

(c) any land used by gas undertakers for the manufacture or storage of gas, by electricity undertakers for the generation of electricity or by water undertakers as a pumping station or reservoir for water.

A consent required by this subsection shall not be unreasonably withheld, and any question arising under this subsection whether the withholding of a consent is unreasonable shall, except where the street in question is one for which the Minister is the highway authority, be determined by the Minister of Housing and Local Government.

(11) The provisions of the Land Charges Act 1925, with respect to the registration of local land charges shall apply to any prohibition or restriction on the use of land or buildings imposed by the Minister by the prescription of an improvement line under this section or by virtue of any condition imposed by him in connection

with the giving of a consent under subsection (2) of this section as if the prescription or condition were a local land charge, and any such prohibition or
restriction shall be registered accordingly by the proper officer of the local
authority within whose area the land to which it relates is situated.

(12) In this section "building" includes any erection of whatsoever material
and in whatsoever manner constructed and any part of a building, and "new
building" includes any addition to an existing building.

81. Prevention of obstruction to view at corners.   [448]

(1) Where, in the case of a highway maintainable at the public expense, the
highway authority for the highway deem it necessary for the prevention of danger
arising from obstruction to the view of persons using the highway to impose
restrictions with respect to any land at or near any corner or bend in the highway
at any junction of the highway with a road to which the public has access, the
authority may, subject to the provisions of this section, serve a notice, together
with a plan showing the land to which the notice relates,—

    (a) on the owner or occupier of the land, directing him to alter any wall (not
        being a wall forming part of the structure of a permanent edifice), fence,
        hoarding, paling, tree, shrub or other vegetation thereon so as to cause it
        to conform with any requirements specified in the notice; or

    (b) on every owner, lessee and occupier of the land, restraining them either
        absolutely or subject to such conditions as may be specified in the notice
        from causing or permitting any building, wall, fence, hoarding, paling,
        tree, shrub or other vegetation to be erected or planted on the land.

A notice under this subsection may at any time be withdrawn by the authority
by whom it was given.

(2) A notice restraining the erection of any building on land shall not be served
by a highway authority who are not the local authority for the area in which the
land is situated, except with the consent of that authority.

(3) A copy of a notice under paragraph (a) of subsection (1) of this section
shall be served on the owner or on the occupier of any land according as the
notice was served on the occupier or on the owner thereof.

(4) A notice under paragraph (b) of subsection (1) of this section shall not
prevent any owner, lessee or occupier of any land from executing or permitting
the reconstruction or repair, in such manner as not to create any new obstruction
to the view of persons using the adjacent highways, of any building which was on
the land before the service of the notice.

(5) A restriction imposed by a notice under subsection (1) of this section shall
come into force on the service of the notice and, while in force but subject to the
provisions of section fifteen of the Land Charges Act, 1925 (which provides that a
local land charge shall be void as against a purchaser for money or money's worth
unless registered under that section), shall be binding on the successor in title to
every owner, and on every lessee and every occupier, of the land to which it
relates.

(6) A person on whom a notice has been served under subsection (1) of this
section may, within fourteen days from the date of the receipt thereof by him,
give notice to the authority by whom the notice was given objecting to any
requirement specified therein, or to any restriction imposed thereby, and stating
reasons for his objections, and thereupon the question whether the notice is to
be withdrawn as respects any requirement or restriction objected to shall be
determined, if the parties so agree, by single arbitrator appointed by them and,
in default of agreement, it shall be determined by a county court.

In determining a question under this subsection the arbitrator or court shall
have power to order that the requirement or restriction objected to shall have
effect subject to such modifications, if any, as the arbitrator or court may direct.

(8) Subject to the provisions of this section, if a person on whom a notice has
been served under subsection (1) thereof contravenes the provisions of the notice,
he shall, without prejudice to any other proceedings which may be available

against him, be guilty of an offence and shall be liable in respect thereof to a fine not exceeding five pounds, and, if the offence in respect of which he was convicted is continued after the conviction, he shall be guilty of a further offence and shall be liable in respect thereof to a fine not exceeding forty shillings for each day on which the offence is so continued.

(10) A person on whom a notice is served under subsection (1) of this section shall be entitled to recover from the authority by whom the notice was served any expenses reasonably incurred by him in carrying out any directions contained in the notice.

If any question arises whether any expenses were reasonably incurred by any person in carrying out any directions contained in a notice served under the said subsection (1), it shall be determined, if the parties so agree, by a single arbitrator appointed by them and, in default of agreement, it shall be determined by a county court.

(11) Any two or more authorities on whom powers are conferred by this section may by agreement exercise those powers jointly, and the agreement may provide for the apportionment of any expenses incurred thereunder.

(12) Nothing in this section shall:

(a) authorise the service of a notice under this section with respect to any wall forming part of an ancient monument or other object of archæological interest, except with the consent of the Minister of Works; or

(b) apply with respect to a wall belonging to any of the following undertakers, that is to say, railway undertakers, canal undertakers, inland navigation undertakers, dock undertakers, or harbour undertakers, where the wall forms part of or is necessary for the maintenance of a railway comprised in the railway undertaking, a canal comprised in the canal undertaking, a navigation comprised in the inland navigation undertaking, a dock comprised in the dock undertaking, or a harbour comprised in the harbour undertaking.

(13) The provisions of the Land Charges Act, 1925, with respect to the registration of local land charges shall apply to any prohibition or restriction on the use of land or buildings imposed by the Minister by a notice served by him under this section as if the notice were a local land charge, and any such prohibition or restriction shall be registered accordingly by the proper officer of the local authority within whose area the land to which it relates is situated.

(14) In this section:

"building" includes any erection of whatsoever material and in whatsoever manner constructed, and any part of a building;

"wall" includes any partition of whatsoever material constructed and any bank.

CHARITIES ACT 1960
(8 & 9 Eliz. 2c. 58; 40 Halsbury's Statutes (2nd Edn.) 121)

38. Repeal of law of mortmain. **[449]**

(1) The Mortmain and Charitable Uses Act, 1888, the Mortmain and Charitable Uses Act, 1891, and the Mortmain and Charitable Uses Act Amendment Act, 1892, together with any enactments amending those Acts (and in particular section eighty-seven of the Education Act, 1944, and sections fourteen and four hundred and eight of the Companies Act, 1948) shall cease to have effect.

(2) No right or title to any property shall be defeated or impugned, and no assurance or disposition of property shall be treated as void or voidable, by virtue of any of the enactments mentioned in the foregoing subsection, or of any other enactment relating to mortmain, if at the passing of this Act the possession is in accordance with that right or title or with that assurance or disposition, and no step has been taken to assert a claim by virtue of any such enactment:

Provided that this subsection shall not validate any assurance or disposition so as to defeat a right or title acquired by adverse possession before the passing of this Act.

(3) The repeal by this Act of the Mortmain and Charitable Uses Act, 1891, shall have effect in relation to the wills of persons dying before the passing of this Act so as to abrogate any requirement to sell land then unsold, but not so as to enable effect to be given to a direction to lay out personal estate in land without an order under section eight of that Act or so as to affect the power to make such an order.

(4) Any reference in any enactment or document to a charity within the meaning, purview and interpretation of the Charitable Uses Act, 1601, or of the preamble to it, shall be construed as a reference to a charity within the meaning which the word bears as a legal term according to the law of England and Wales.

(5) No repeal made by this Act shall affect any power to hold land in Northern Ireland without licence in mortmain; but (without prejudice to the general provision made later in this Act about the powers of the Parliament of Northern Ireland) if that Parliament repeals any of the Acts relating to mortmain in Northern Ireland, then notwithstanding any enactment limiting the powers of that Parliament the repeal may extend to sections fourteen and four hundred and eight of the Companies Act 1948, as they affect land in Northern Ireland, and to any corresponding enactments of that Parliament as those enactments affect land in Great Britain, and may also extend to any other enactment of the Parliament of the United Kingdom so far as it relates to holding land in mortmain in Northern Ireland.

TOWN AND COUNTRY PLANNING ACT 1962
(10 & 11 Eliz. 2c. 38; 42 Halsbury's Statutes (2nd Edn.) 955)

13. Development requiring planning permission. [450]

(1) Subject to the provisions of this section, planning permission is required for the carrying out of any development of land.

(2) Where on the first day of July, nineteen hundred and forty-eight (in this Act referred to as "the appointed day"), land was being used temporarily for a purpose other than the purpose for which it was normally used, planning permission is not required for the resumption of the use of the land for the last-mentioned purpose.

(3) Where on the appointed day land was normally used for one purpose and was also used on occasions, whether at regular intervals or not, for another purpose, planning permission is not required in respect of the use of the land for that other purpose on similar occasions.

(4) Where land was unoccupied on the appointed day, but had before that day been occupied at some time on or after the seventh day of January, nineteen hundred and thirty-seven, planning permission is not required in respect of the use of the land for the purpose for which it was last used before the appointed day.

(5) Where planning permission to develop land has been granted for a limited period, planning permission is not required for the resumption, at the end of that period, of the use of the land for the purpose for which it was normally used before the permission was granted.

(7) Notwithstanding anything in subsections (2) to (4) of this section, the use of land as a caravan site shall not, by virtue of any of those subsections, be treated as a use for which planning permission is not required, unless the land was so used on one occasion at least during the period of two years ending with the ninth day of March, nineteen hundred and sixty.

(8) Where by a development order planning permission to develop land has been granted subject to limitations, planning permission is not required for the use of that land which (apart from its use in accordance with that permission) is the normal use of that land, unless the last-mentioned use was begun in contra-

vention of the provisions of this Part of this Act or in contravention of previous planning control.

(9) Where an enforcement notice has been served in respect of any development of land, planning permission is not required for the use of that land for the purpose for which (in accordance with the provisions of this Part of this Act) it could lawfully have been used if that development had not been carried out.

23. Appeals against planning decisions.   [451]

(1) Where an application is made to a local planning authority for planning permission to develop land, or for any approval of that authority required under a development order, and that permission or approval is refused by that authority or is granted by them subject to conditions, the applicant, if he is aggrieved by their decision, may by notice under this section appeal to the Minister.

28. Orders requiring discontinuance of use or alteration   [452]
   or removal of buildings or works.

(1) If it appears to a local planning authority that it is expedient in the interests of the proper planning of their area (including the interests of amenity) regard being had to the development plan and to any other material considerations—

(a) that any use of land should be discontinued, or that any conditions should be imposed on the continuance of a use of land, or

(b) that any buildings or works should be altered or removed,

the local planning authority may by order require the discontinuance of that use, or impose such conditions as may be specified in the order on the continuance thereof, or require such steps as may be so specified to be taken for the alteration or removal of the buildings or works, as the case may be.

LAW OF PROPERTY (JOINT TENANTS) ACT 1964
(1964 c. 63; 44 Halsbury's Statutes (2nd Edn.) 992)

1. Assumption on sale of land by survivor of joint tenants.   [453]

(1) For the purposes of section 36 (2) of the Law of Property Act 1925, as amended by section 7 of and the Schedule to the Law of Property (Amendment) Act 1926, the survivor of two or more joint tenants shall in favour of a purchaser of the legal estate, be deemed to be solely and beneficially interested if he conveys as beneficial owner or the conveyance includes a statement that he is so interested.

Provided that the foregoing provisions of this subsection shall not apply if, at any time before the date of the conveyance by the survivor:

(a) a memorandum of severance (that is to say a note or memorandum signed by the joint tenants or one of them and recording that the joint tenancy was severed in equity on a date therein specified) had been endorsed on or annexed to the conveyance by virtue of which the legal estate was vested in the joint tenants; or

(b) a receiving order in bankruptcy made against any of the joint tenants, or a petition for such an order, had been registered under the Land Charges Act 1925, being an order or petition of which the purchaser has notice, by virtue of the registration, on the date of the conveyance by the survivor.

(2) The foregoing provisions of this section shall apply with the necessary modifications in relation to a conveyance by the personal representatives of the survivor of joint tenants as they apply in relation to a conveyance by such a survivor.

2. Retrospective and transitional provisions.   [454]

Section I of this Act shall be deemed to have come into force on 1st January, 1926, and for the purposes of that section in its application to a conveyance executed before the passing of this Act a statement signed by the vendor or by his personal representatives that he was solely and beneficially interested shall be treated as if it had been included in the conveyance.

LAND REGISTRATION ACT 1966
(1966 c. 39; 46 Halsbury's Statutes (2nd Edn.) 597)

1. Amendments of Land Registration Act 1925.　　　　　　**[455]**

(1) In Part XI of the Land Registration Act 1925 (power to make Orders in Council making registration compulsory in countries and other areas)—

a) section 120 (2) and sections 121 and 122 (requirements to be complied with before making of an Order), and

(*b*) section 120 (3) (utilisation of existing land registries),

shall cease to have effect.

(2) Applications under sections 4 and 8 of the said Act (first registration of title) as respects land outside an area of compulsory registration shall not be entertained except in such classes of cases as the registrar may, by notice published in such way as appears to him appropriate, from time to time specify and in those cases the registrar may require the applicant under either of those sections to show that there are special considerations which make it expedient to grant the application.

In this subsection "area of compulsory registration" means an area as respects which an Order in Council made or having effect under the said section 120 is in force.

(3) The registrar may under section 83 (8) of the Land Registration Act 1925 grant any indemnity on account of costs or expenses taken into account under that subsection notwithstanding that no other indemnity money is payable (but subject to subsection (5) (c) of that section under which no indemnity is payable on account of costs incurred in taking or defending proceedings without the consent of the registrar).

(4) Subsection (5) (*a*) of the said section 83 (losses wholly or partly due to fraud by the applicant for indemnity or, in certain cases, fraud by his predecessor in title) shall apply to any loss incurred after the commencement of this Act as if references in that paragraph to fraud included references to any act, neglect or default.

LAND COMMISSION ACT 1967
(1967 c1.)

6. General powers of acquisition.　　　　　　**[456]**

(1) Subject to the following provisions of this Part of this Act, on and after the first appointed day the Commission shall have power to acquire by agreement, or, on being authorised to do so in accordance with the following provisions of this Part of this Act, shall have power to acquire compulsorily, any land which in their opinion is land suitable for material development.

(2) Where the Commission exercise their powers under the preceding subsection in relation to any land, the Commission shall have power to acquire by agreement, or, on being authorised to do so in accordance with the following provisions of this Part of this Act, shall have power to acquire compulsorily, any land contiguous or adjacent to that land which in their opinion is required for the purpose of executing works for facilitating the development or use of the first-mentioned land.

(3) The Commission shall not have power by virtue of subsection (1) of this section to acquire any land compulsorily unless, on the date on which the compulsory purchase order authorising the acquisition is made, one or more of the following conditions is fulfilled in relation to that land, that is to say:

(*a*) planning permission for the carrying out of material development of the land is for the time being in force and the whole or part of the development authorised by that planning permission has not been carried out;

(b) in the current development plan, or in any proposals submitted to the planning Minister by a local planning authority for altering or adding to that plan, the land is defined or otherwise indicated in any such manner, or is allocated for purposes of any such description, as may be prescribed for the purposes of this subsection;

(c) the land is designated by the current development plan as subject to compulsory acquisition;

(d) the land forms part of an area designated as the site of a new town by an order made, or having effect as if made, under the New Towns Act 1965, or, as respects Scotland, under the New Towns Act 1946;

(e) the land is, or forms part of, an area which has been declared to be a clearance area by a resolution under section 42 of the Housing Act 1957, or under section 34 of the Housing (Scotland) Act 1966, which is for the time being in force.

(4) Without prejudice to the last preceding subsection, the Commission shall not have power by virtue of subsection (1) of this section, in pursuance of a compulsory purchase order made before such day as the Ministers may by order appoint for the purposes of this subsection (in this Act referred to as "the second appointed day"), to acquire any land compulsorily except for one of the following purposes, that is to say:

(a) securing the carrying out at an early date of material development which, in the opinion of the Commission, ought to be so carried out;

(b) securing that the land is developed as a whole, or as part of an area which, in the opinion of the Commission, ought to be developed as a whole;

(c) making the land available for development or use by, or for the purposes of, a person or body of persons who could be authorised to acquire it compulsorily for that development or use;

(d) disposing of the land in accordance with the provisions of section 18 of this Act.

(5) Where the last preceding subsection applies to a compulsory acquisition, and the purpose of the acquisition is that which is specified in paragraph (c) of that subsection, the power of the Commission mentioned in that subsection shall not be exercisable except:

(a) with the approval of the Minister concerned, if the purpose is to make the land available for development or use by, or for the purposes of, a Minister, or

(b) in any other case, with the approval of the person or body of persons who could be authorised to acquire the land compulsorily as mentioned in that paragraph, or, in default of such approval, with the approval of the Minister who could authorise that person or body so to acquire the land.

(6) No order shall be made appointing a day for the purposes of subsection (4) of this section unless a draft of the order has been laid before Parliament and approved by a resolution of each House of Parliament.

(7) In relation to planning permission granted on an outline application (that is to say, an application for planning permission subject to subsequent approval on any matters) the reference in subsection (3) (a) of this section to the development authorised by the planning permission shall be construed as including all development for which planning permission was granted on that application either with or without any requirement as to subsequent approval.

LEASEHOLD REFORM ACT 1967
(1967 c.88)

1. Tenants entitled to enfranchisement or extension. [457]

(1) This Part of this Act shall have effect to confer on a tenant of a leasehold house, occupying the house as his residence, a right to acquire on fair terms the freehold or an extended lease of the house and premises where:

(a) his tenancy is a long tenancy at a low rent and the rateable value of the house and premises on the appropriate day is not (or was not) more than £200 or, if it is in Greater London, than £400; and

(b) at the relevant time (that is to say, at the time when he gives notice in accordance with this Act of his desire to have the freehold or to have an extended lease, as the case may be) he has been tenant of the house under a long tenancy at a low rent, and occupying it as his residence, for the last five years or for periods amounting to five years in the last ten years;

and to confer the like right in the other cases for which provision is made in this part of this Act.

(2) In this Part of this Act references, in relation to any tenancy, to the tenant occupying a house as his residence shall be construed as applying where, but only where, the tenant is, in right of the tenancy, occupying it as his only or main residence (whether or not he uses it also for other purposes); but:

(a) references to a person occupying a house shall apply where he occupies it in part only; and

(b) in determining in what right the tenant occupies, there shall be disregarded any mortgage term and any interest arising in favour of any person by his attorning tenant to a mortgagee or chargee.

(3) This Part of this Act shall not confer on the tenant of a house any right by reference to his occupation of it as his residence (but shall apply as if he were not so occupying it) at any time when:

(a) it is let to and occupied by him with other land or premises to which it is ancillary; or

(b) it is comprised in an agricultural holding within the meaning of the Agricultural Holdings Act 1948.

(4) In subsection (1) (a) above, "the appropriate day", in relation to any house and premises, means March 23rd, 1965 or such later day as by virtue of section 43 (3) of the Rent Act 1965 would be the appropriate day for purposes of that Act in relation to a dwelling house consisting of that house.

6. Rights of trustees. [458]

(1) Where a tenant of a house is occupying it as his residence, his occupation of it at any earlier time shall for purposes of this Part of this Act be treated as having been an occupation in right of the tenancy if at that time:

(a) the tenancy was settled land for purposes of the Settled Land Act 1925, and he was sole tenant for life within the meaning of that Act; or

(b) the tenancy was vested in trustees and he, as a person beneficially interested (whether directly or derivatively) under the trusts, was entitled or permitted to occupy the house by reason of that interest.

References in this section to trustees include persons holding on the statutory trusts arising by virtue of sections 34 to 36 of the Law of Property Act 1925 in cases of joint ownership or ownership in common.

(2) Where a tenancy of a house is settled land for purposes of the Settled Land Act 1925, a sole tenant for life within the meaning of that Act shall have the same rights under this Part of this Act in respect of his occupation of the house as if the tenancy of it belonged to him absolutely, but without prejudice to his position under the settlement as a trustee for all parties entitled under the settlement; and:

(a) the powers under that Act of a tenant for life shall include power to accept an extended lease under this Part of this Act; and

(b) an extended lease granted under this Part of this Act to a tenant for life or statutory owner shall be treated as a subsidiary vesting deed in accordance with section 53 (2) of that Act.

(3) Where a tenancy of a house is vested in trustees (other than a sole tenant for life within the meaning of the Settled Land Act 1925), and a person beneficially interested (whether directly or derivatively) under the trusts is entitled or permitted by reason of his interest to occupy the house, then the trustees shall have the like rights under this Part of this Act in respect of his occupation as he would have if he were the tenant occupying in right of the tenancy.

(4) Without prejudice to any powers exercisable under the Settled Land Act 1925 by tenants for life or statutory owners within the meaning of that Act, where a tenancy of a house is vested in trustees, then unless the instrument regulating the trusts (being made after the passing of this Act) contains an explicit direction to the contrary, the powers of the trustees under that instrument shall include power, with the like consent or on the like direction (if any) as may be required for the exercise of their powers (or ordinary powers) of investment, to acquire and retain the freehold or an extended lease under this Part of this Act.

(5) The purposes authorised for the application of capital money by section 73 of the Settled Land Act 1925, or by that section as applied by section 28 of the Law of Property Act 1925 in relation to trusts for sale, and the purposes authorised by section 71 of the Settled Land Act 1925 or by that section as applied as aforesaid as purposes for which moneys may be raised by mortgage, shall include the payment of any expenses incurred by a tenant for life or statutory owners or by trustees for sale, as the case may be, in or in connection with proceedings taken by him or them by virtue of subsection (2) or (3) above.

8. Obligation to enfranchise. [459]

(1) Where a tenant of a house has under this Part of this Act a right to acquire the freehold, and gives to the landlord written notice of his desire to have the freehold, then except as provided by this Part of this Act the landlord shall be bound to make to the tenant, and the tenant to accept, (at the price and on the conditions so provided) a grant of the house and premises for an estate in fee simple absolute, subject to the tenancy and to tenant's incumbrances, but otherwise free of incumbrances.

(2) For purposes of this Part of this Act "incumbrances" includes rent-charges and, subject to subsection (3) below, personal liabilities attaching in respect of the ownership of land or an interest in land though not charged on that land or interest; and "tenant's incumbrances" includes any interest directly or indirectly derived out of the tenancy, and any incumbrance on the tenancy or any such interest (whether or not the same matter is an incumbrance also on any interest reversionary on the tenancy).

(3) Burdens originating in tenure, and burdens in respect of the upkeep or regulation for the benefit of any locality of any land, building, structure, works, ways or watercourse shall not be treated as incumbrances for purposes of this Part of this Act, but any conveyance executed to give effect to this section shall be made subject thereto except as otherwise provided by section 11 below.

(4) A conveyance executed to give effect to this section:

(a) shall have effect under section 2 (1) of the Law of Property Act 1925 to overreach any incumbrance capable of being overreached under that section as if, where the interest conveyed is settled land, the conveyance were made under the powers of the Settled Land Act 1925 and as if the requirements of section 2 (1) as to payment of the capital money allowed any part of the purchase price paid or applied in accordance with sections 11 to 13 below to be so paid or applied;

(b) shall not be made subject to any incumbrance capable of being overreached by the conveyance, but shall be made subject (where they are not capable of being overreached) to rentcharges and other rents falling within section 191 of the Law of Property Act 1925, except as otherwise provided by section 11 below.

(5) Notwithstanding that on a grant to a tenant of a house and premises under this section no payment or a nominal payment only is required from the tenant for the price of the house and premises, the tenant shall nevertheless be deemed for all purposes to be a purchaser for a valuable consideration in money or money's worth.

MATRIMONIAL HOMES ACT 1967
(1967 c.75)

1. Protection against eviction, etc., from matrimonial home   **[460]**
of spouse not entitled by virtue of estate, etc., to occupy it.

(1) Where one spouse is entitled to occupy a dwelling house by virtue of any estate or interest or contract or by virtue of any enactment giving him or her the right to remain in occupation, and the other spouse is not so entitled, then, subject to the provisions of this Act, the spouse not so entitled shall have the following rights (in this Act referred to as "rights of occupation"):

(a) if in occupation, a right not to be evicted or excluded from the dwelling house or any part thereof by the other spouse except with the leave of the court given by an order under this section;

(b) if not in occupation, a right with the leave of the court so given to enter into and occupy the dwelling house.

(2) So long as one spouse has rights of occupation, either of the spouses may apply to the court for an order declaring, enforcing, restricting or terminating those rights or regulating the exercise by either spouse of the right to occupy the dwelling house.

2. Effect of statutory rights of occupation as charge on   **[461]**
dwelling house.

(1) Where, at any time during the subsistence of a marriage, one spouse is entitled to occupy a dwelling house by virtue of an estate or interest, then the other spouse's rights of occupation shall be a charge on that estate or interest, having the like priority as if it were an equitable interest created at whichever is the latest of the following dates, that is to say—

(a) the date when the spouse so entitled acquires the estate or interest;

(b) the date of the marriage; and

(c) the commencement of this Act.

(2) Notwithstanding that a spouse's rights of occupation are a charge on an estate or interest in the dwelling house, those rights shall be brought to an end by—

(a) the death of the other spouse, or

(b) the termination (otherwise than by death) of the marriage,

unless in the event of a matrimonial dispute or estrangement the court sees fit to direct otherwise by an order made under section 1 above during the subsistence of the marriage.

(3) Where a spouse's rights of occupation are a charge on the estate or interest of the other spouse—

(a) any order under section 1 above against the other spouse shall, except in so far as the contrary intention appears, have the like effect against persons deriving title under the other spouse and affected by the charge; and

(b) subsections (2) to (5) of section 1 above shall apply in relation to any person deriving title under the other spouse and affected by the charge as they apply in relation to the other spouse.

(4) Where a spouse's rights of occupation are a charge on an estate or interest in the dwelling house, and that estate or interest is surrendered so as to merge in some other estate or interest expectant thereon in such circumstances that, but for the merger, the person taking the estate or interest of the other spouse would be bound by the charge, then the surrender shall have effect subject to the charge and the persons thereafter entitled to the other estate or interest shall, for so long as the estate or interest surrendered would have endured if not so surrendered be treated for all purposes of this Act as deriving title to the other estate or interest under the other spouse by virtue of the surrender.

(5) Where a spouse's rights of occupation are a charge on the estate or interest of the other spouse, and the other spouse—

(a) is adjudged bankrupt or makes a conveyance or assignment of his or her property (including that estate or interest) to trustees for the benefit of his or her creditors generally; or

(*b*) dies and his or her estate is insolvent;

then, notwithstanding that it is registered in accordance with the following provisions of this section, the charge shall be void against the trustee in bankruptcy, the trustees under the conveyance or assignment or the personal representatives of the deceased spouse, as the case may be.

(6) At the end of section 10 (1) of the Land Charges Act 1925 (which lists the classes of charges on, or obligations affecting, land which may be registered as land charges) there shall be added the following paragraph:

"Class F: A charge affecting any land by virtue of the Matrimonial Homes Act 1967";

and in the enactments mentioned in the Schedule to this Act there shall be made the consequential amendments provided for by that Schedule.

(7) Where the title to the legal estate by virtue of which a spouse is entitled to occupy a dwelling house is registered under the Land Registration Act 1925 or any enactment replaced by that Act, registration of a land charge affecting the dwelling house by virtue of this Act shall be effected by registering a notice or caution under that Act, and a spouse's rights of occupation shall not be an over-riding interest within the meaning of that Act affecting the dwelling house notwithstanding that the spouse is in actual occupation of the dwelling house.

(8) Where a spouse's rights of occupation are a charge on the estate or interest of the other spouse, and that estate or interest is the subject of a mortgage within the meaning of the Law of Property Act 1925, then if, after the date of creation of the mortgage, the charge is registered by virtue of subsection (6) above, the charge shall, for the purposes of section 94 of that Act (which regulates the rights of mortgagees to make further advances ranking in priority to subsequent mortgages), be deemed to be a mortgage subsequent in date to the first-mentioned mortgage.

4. Contract for sale of house affected by registered charge to [462] include term requiring cancellation of registration before completion.

(1) Where one spouse is entitled by virtue of section 2 above to a charge on an estate or interest in a dwelling house and the charge is registered in accordance with subsection (6) or (7) of that section, it shall be a term of any contract for the sale of that estate or interest whereby the vendor agrees to give vacant possession of the dwelling house on completion of the contract that the vendor will before such completion procure the cancellation of the registration of the charge at his expense:

Provided that the foregoing provision shall not apply to any such contract made by a vendor who is entitled to sell the estate or interest in the dwelling house freed from any such charge.

(2) If, on the completion of such a contract as is referred to in subsection (1) above, there is delivered to the purchaser or his solicitor an application by the spouse entitled to the charge for the cancellation of the registration of that charge, the term of the contract for which subsection (1) above provides shall be deemed to have been performed.

(3) This section applies only if and so far as a contrary intention is not expressed in the contract.

(4) This section shall apply to a contract for exchange as it applies to a contract for sale.

(5) This section shall, with the necessary modifications, apply to a contract for the grant of a lease or underlease of a dwelling house as it applies to a contract for the sale of an estate or interest in a dwelling house.

141

MISREPRESENTATION ACT 1967
(1967 c.7)

1. Removal of certain bars to rescission for innocent misrepresentation. [463]

Where a person has entered into a contract after a misrepresentation has been made to him, and—
(a) the misrepresentation has become a term of the contract; or
(b) the contract has been performed;
or both, then, if otherwise he would be entitled to rescind the contract without alleging fraud, he shall be so entitled, subject to the provisions of this Act, notwithstanding the matters mentioned in paragraphs (a) and (b) of this section.

2. Damages for misrepresentation. [464]

(1) Where a person has entered into a contract after a misrepresentation has been made to him by another party thereto and as a result thereof he has suffered loss, then, if the person making the misrepresentation would be liable to damages in respect thereof had the misrepresentation been made fraudulently, that person shall be so liable notwithstanding that the misrepresentation was not made fraudulently, unless he proves that he had reasonable ground to believe and did believe up to the time the contract was made that the facts represented were true.

(2) Where a person has entered into a contract after a misrepresentation has been made to him otherwise than fraudulently, and he would be entitled, by reason of the misrepresentation, to rescind the contract, then, if it is claimed, in any proceedings arising out of the contract, that the contract ought to be or has been rescinded the court or arbitrator may declare the contract subsisting and award damages in lieu of rescission, if of opinion that it would be equitable to do so, having regard to the nature of the misrepresentation and the loss that would be caused by it if the contract were upheld, as well as to the loss that rescission would cause to the other party.

(3) Damages may be awarded against a person under subsection (2) of this section whether or not he is liable to damages under subsection (1) thereof, but where he is so liable any award under the said subsection (2) shall be taken into account in assessing his liability under the said subsection (1).

3. Avoidance of certain provisions excluding liability for misrepresentation. [465]

If any agreement (whether made before or after the commencement of this Act) contains a provision which would exclude or restrict:
(a) any liability to which a party to a contract may be subject by reason of any misrepresentation made by him before the contract was made; or
(b) any remedy available to another party to the contract by reason of such a misrepresentation;
that provision shall be of no effect except to the extent (if any) that, in any proceedings arising out of the contract, the court or arbitrator may allow reliance on it as being fair and reasonable in the circumstances of the case.

RACE RELATIONS ACT 1968
(1968 c.71)

5. Housing accommodation, and business and other premises. [466]

It shall be unlawful for any person having power to dispose, or being otherwise concerned with the disposal, of housing accommodation, business premises or other land to discriminate:
(a) against any person seeking to acquire any such accommodation, premises or other land by refusing or deliberately omitting to dispose of it to him, or to dispose of it to him on the like terms and in the like circumstances as in the case of other persons;

(b) against any person occupying any such accommodation, premises or other land, by deliberately treating him differently from other such occupiers in the like circumstances; or

(c) against any person in need of any such accommodation, premises or other land by deliberately treating that other person differently from others in respect of any list of persons in need of it.

7. Exception in the case of residential accommodation. [467]

(1) It shall not be unlawful by virtue of section 2 or 5 of this Act to discriminate against any person with respect to the provision or disposal of any residential accommodation in any premises if at the time of the disposal:

(a) the premises are treated for the purposes of this subsection as small premises; and

(b) the person having power to provide or dispose of the accommodation (in this subsection and subsection (2) below referred to as "the landlord") resides and intends to continue to reside on the premises; and

(c) there is on the premises, in addition to the accommodation occupied by the landlord, relevant accommodation shared by him with other persons residing on the premises who are not members of his household.

RENT ACT 1968
(1968 c.23)

1. Protected tenancies. [468]

(1) A tenancy under which a dwelling-house (which may be a house or part of a house) is let as a separate dwelling is a protected tenancy for the purposes of this Act unless:

(a) the dwelling-house has or had on the appropriate day a rateable value exceeding, if it is in Greater London, £400 or, if it is elsewhere, £200; or

(b) the tenancy is one with respect to which section 2 below otherwise provides; or

(c) by virtue of section 4 or 5 below, the tenancy is for the time being precluded from being a protected tenancy by reason of the body in whom the landlord's interest is vested;

and any reference to a protected tenant shall be construed accordingly.

(2) For the purposes of this Act, any land or premises let together with a dwelling-house shall, unless it consists of agricultural land exceeding two acres in extent, be treated as part of the dwelling-house; and for this purpose "agricultural land" has the meaning set out in paragraph (a) of section 26 (3) of the General Rate Act 1967 (which relates to the exclusion of agricultural land and premises from liability for rating).

(3) If any question arises in any proceedings whether a dwelling-house is within the limits of rateable value in subsection (1) (a) above, it shall be deemed to be within those limits unless the contrary is shown.

2. Tenancies excepted from definition of "protected tenancy" [469]

(1) A tenancy is not a protected tenancy if:

(a) under the tenancy either no rent is payable or, subject to section 7 (3) below, the rent payable is less than two-thirds of the rateable value which is or was the rateable value of the dwelling-house on the appropriate day; or

(b) under the tenancy the dwelling-house is bona fide let at a rent which includes payments in respect of board, attendance or use of furniture; or

(c) subject to section 1 (2) above, the dwelling-house which is subject to the tenancy is let together with land other than the site of the dwelling-house; or

(d) the dwelling-house is comprised in an agricultural holding (within the

143

meaning of the Agricultural Holdings Act 1948) and is occupied by the person responsible for the control (whether as tenant or as servant or agent of the tenant) of the farming of the holding.

(2) In the following provisions of this Act, a tenancy falling within paragraph (*a*) of subsection (1) above is referred to as a "tenancy at a low rent".

(3) For the purposes of paragraph (*b*) of subsection (1) above, a dwelling-house shall not be taken to be bona fide let at a rent which includes payments in respect of attendance or the use of furniture unless the amount of rent which is fairly attributable to attendance or use of furniture, having regard to the value of the attendance or the use to the tenant, forms a substantial part of the whole rent.

3. Statutory tenants and tenancies. [470]

(1) Subject to sections 4 and 5 below—

(*a*) after the termination of a protected tenancy of a dwelling-house the person who, immediately before that termination, was the protected tenant of the dwelling-house shall, if so long as he occupies the dwelling-house as his residence, be the statutory tenant of it; and

(*b*) the provisions of Schedule 1 to this Act shall have effect for determining what person (if any) is the statutory tenant of a dwelling-house at any time after the death of a person who, immediately before his death, was either a protected tenant of the dwelling-house or the statutory tenant of it by virtue of paragraph (*a*) above;

and a dwelling-house is referred to as subject to a statutory tenancy when there is a statutory tenant of it.

4. No protected or statutory tenancy where landlord's [471] interest belongs to Crown.

(1) A tenancy shall not be a protected tenancy at any time when the interest of the landlord under that tenancy belongs to Her Majesty in right of the Crown or of the Duchy of Lancaster, or to the Duchy of Cornwall, or to a Government department, or is held in trust for Her Majesty for the purposes of a Government department.

(2) A person shall not at any time be a statutory tenant of a dwelling-house if the interest of his immediate landlord would at that time, belong or be held as mentioned in subsection (1) above.

5. No protected or statutory tenancy where landlord's [472] interest belongs to local authority, etc.

(1) A tenancy shall not be a protected tenancy at any time when the interest of the landlord under that tenancy belongs to any of the bodies specified in sub-section (2) below, nor shall a person at any time be a statutory tenant of a dwell-ing-house if the interest of his immediate landlord would belong at that time to any of those bodies.

(2) The bodies referred to in subsection (1) above are:

(*a*) the council of a county or county borough;

(*b*) the council of a county district or, in the application of this Act to the Isles of Scilly, the Council of the Isles of Scilly;

(*c*) the Greater London Council, the council of a London borough or the Common Council of the City of London;

(*d*) the Commission for the New Towns;

(*e*) the Housing Corporation;

(*f*) a development corporation established by an order made, or having effect as if made, under the New Towns Act 1965; and

(*g*) a housing trust (as defined in subsection (3) below) which is a charity within the meaning of the Charities Act 1960.

(3) In subsection (2) (*g*) above, "housing trust" means a corporation or body of persons which—

(a) is required by the terms of its constituent instrument to devote the whole of its funds, including any surplus which may arise from its operations, to the following purposes, that is to say, the provision of houses for persons the majority of whom are in fact members of the working classes, and other purposes incidental thereto; or

(b) is required by the terms of its constituent instrument to devote the whole or substantially the whole of its funds to the purposes set out in paragraph (a) above.

10. Grounds for possession of certain dwelling-houses. [473]

(1) Subject to the following provisions of this Part of this Act, a court shall not make an order for possession of a dwelling-house which is for the time being let on a protected tenancy or subject to a statutory tenancy unless the court considers it reasonable to make such an order and either:

(a) the court is satisfied that suitable alternative accommodation is available for the tenant or will be available for him when the order in question takes effect, or

(b) the circumstances are as specified in any of the Cases in Part I of Schedule 3 to this Act.

Schedule 3. [474]

Case 1

Where any rent lawfully due from the tenant has not been paid, or any obligation of the protected or statutory tenancy which arises under this Act, or:

(a) in the case of a protected tenancy, any other obligation of the tenancy, in so far as it is consistent with the provisions of Part II of this Act, or

(b) in the case of a statutory tenancy, any other obligation of the previous protected tenancy which is applicable to the statutory tenancy,

has been broken or not performed.

Case 2

Where the tenant or any person residing or lodging with him or any sub-tenant of his has been guilty of conduct which is a nuisance or annoyance to adjoining occupiers, or has been convicted of using the dwelling-house or allowing the dwelling-house to be used for immoral or illegal purposes.

Case 3

Where the condition of the dwelling-house has, in the opinion of the court, deteriorated owing to acts of waste by, or the neglect or default of, the tenant or any person residing or lodging with him or any sub-tenant of his and, in the case of any act of waste by, or the neglect or default of, a person lodging with the tenant or a sub-tenant of his, where the court is satisfied that the tenant has not, before the making of the order in question, taken such steps as he ought reasonably to have taken for the removal of the lodger or sub-tenant, as the case may be.

Case 4

Where the tenant has given notice to quit and, in consequence of that notice, the landlord has contracted to sell or let the dwelling-house or has taken any other steps as the result of which he would, in the opinion of the court, be seriously prejudiced if he could not obtain possession.

Case 5

Where, without the consent of the landlord, the tenant has, at any time after December 8th, 1965 or, in the case of a controlled tenancy, after September 1st, 1939, assigned or sub-let the whole of the dwelling-house or sub-let part of the dwelling-house, the remainder being already sub-let.

Case 6

Where the protected or statutory tenancy is a controlled tenancy and the

145

dwelling-house consists of or includes premises licensed for the sale of intoxicating liquor for consumption off the premises only, and:

(a) the tenant has committed an offence as holder of the licence, or

(b) the tenant has not conducted the business to the satisfaction of the licensing justices or the police authority, or

(c) the tenant has carried on the business in a manner detrimental to the public interest, or

(d) the renewal of the licence has for any reason been refused.

Case 7

Where the dwelling-house is reasonably required by the landlord for occupation as a residence for some person engaged in his whole-time employment, or in the whole-time employment of some tenant from him or with whom, conditional on housing being provided, a contract for such employment has been entered into, and the tenant was in the employment of the landlord or a former landlord, and the dwelling-house was let to him in consequence of that employment and he has ceased to be in that employment.

Case 8

Where the dwelling-house is reasonably required by the landlord for occupation as a residence for:

(a) himself, or

(b) any son or daughter of his over eighteen years of age, or

(c) his father or mother, or

(d) if the dwelling-house is let on or subject to a regulated tenancy, the father or mother of his wife or husband,

and the landlord did not become landlord by purchasing the dwelling-house or any interest therein after March 23rd, 1965 or, if the dwelling-house is let on or subject to a controlled tenancy, after November 7th, 1956.

Case 9

Where the court is satisfied that the rent charged by the tenant for any sub-let part of the dwelling-house which is also a dwelling-house let on a protected tenancy or subject to a statutory tenancy is or was in excess of the maximum rent for the time being recoverable for that part, having regard to the provisions of Part III or as the case may be, Part V of this Act.

TOWN AND COUNTRY PLANNING ACT 1968
(1968 c.72)
15. New provision as to enforcement notices. [475]

(1) Where it appears to the local planning authority that there has been a breach of planning control after the end of 1963, then, subject to any directions given by the Minister and to the following provisions of this section, the authority, if they consider it expedient to do so having regard to the provisions of the development plan and to any other material considerations, may serve a notice under this section (in this Act and the principal Act referred to as an "enforcement notice") requiring the breach to be remedied.

(2) There is a breach of planning control if development has been carried out, whether before or after the commencement of this Part of this Act, without the grant of planning permission required in that behalf in accordance with Part III of the principal Act, or if any conditions or limitations subject to which planning permission was granted have not been complied with.

(4) An enforcement notice shall be served on the owner and on the occupier of the land to which it relates and on any other person having an interest in that land, being an interest which in the opinion of the authority is materially affected by the notice.

16. Appeal against enforcement notice.   [476]

(1) A person on whom an enforcement notice is served or any other person having an interest in the land may, at any time within the period specified in the notice as the period at the end of which it is to take effect, appeal to the Minister against the notice on any of the following grounds:

(a) that planning permission ought to be granted for the development to which the notice relates or, as the case may be, that a condition or limitation alleged in the enforcement notice not to have been complied with ought to be discharged;

(b) that the matters alleged in the notice do not constitute a breach of planning control;

(c) in the case of a notice which, by virtue of section 15 (3) above, may be served only within the period of four years from the date of the breach of planning control to which the notice relates, that that period has elapsed at the date of service;

(d) in the case of a notice not falling within paragraph (c) above, that the breach of planning control alleged by the notice occurred before the beginning of 1964;

(e) that the enforcement notice was not served as required by section 15 (4) of this Act;

(f) that the steps required by the notice to be taken exceed what is necessary to remedy any breach of planning control;

(g) that the specified period for compliance with the notice falls short of what should reasonably be allowed.

(2) An appeal under this section shall be made by notice in writing to the Minister, which shall indicate the grounds of the appeal and state the facts on which it is based; and on any such appeal the Minister shall, if either the appellant or the local planning authority so desire, afford to each of them an opportunity of appearing before and being heard by a person appointed by the Minister for the purpose.

17. Certification of established use.   [477]

(1) For the purposes of this Part of this Act, a use of land is established if:

(a) it was begun before the beginning of 1964 without planning permission in that behalf and has continued since the end of 1963; or

(b) it was begun before the beginning of 1964 under a planning permission in that behalf granted subject to conditions or limitations, which either have never been complied with or have not been complied with since the end of 1963; or

(c) it was begun after the end of 1963 as the result of a change of use not requiring planning permission and there has been, since the end of 1963, no change of use requiring planning permission.

(2) Where a person having an interest in land claims that a particular use of it has become established, he may apply to the local planning authority for a certificate (in this Act referred to as an "established use certificate") to that effect:

Provided that no such application may be made in respect of the use of land as a single dwelling-house, or of any use not subsisting at the time of the application.

(8) If any person, for the purpose of procuring a particular decision on an application (whether by himself or another) for an established use certificate or on an appeal arising out of such an application—

(a) knowingly or recklessly makes a statement which is false in a material particular; or

(b) with intent to deceive, produces, furnishes, sends or otherwise makes use of any document which is false in a material particular; or

(c) with intent to deceive, withholds any material information,

he shall be guilty of an offence and liable on summary conviction to a fine not exceeding £400 or, on conviction on indictment, to imprisonment for a term not exceeding two years or a fine, or both.

21. Determination of planning and similar appeals by persons appointed by the Minister.   [478]

(1) An appeal to which this section applies, being an appeal of a prescribed class, shall, except in such classes of case as may for the time being be prescribed or as may be specified in directions given by the Minister, be determined by a person appointed by the Minister for the purpose instead of by the Minister.

(2) This section applies to:

    (a) appeals under section 23 of the principal Act (planning decisions), as originally enacted or as applied by or under any other provision of that Act;

    (b) appeals under section 14 of the Civic Amenities Act 1967 (default powers and appeals in connection with tree preservation orders);

40. New provisions restricting demolition etc., of listed buildings.   [479]

(1) In this Part of this Act the expression "listed building" means a building which is for the time being included in a list compiled or approved by the Minister under section 32 of the principal Act (buildings of special architectural or historic interest).

(2) Subject to this Part of this Act, if a person executes or causes to be executed any works for the demolition of a listed building or for its alteration or extension in any manner which would affect its character as a building of special architectural or historic interest, and the works are not authorised under this Part of this Act, he shall be guilty of an offence.

65. Limit of duration of planning permissions past and future   [480]

(1) Subject to the provisions of this section, every planning permission granted or deemed to have been granted before the commencement of this section shall, if the development to which it relates has not been begun before the beginning of 1968, be deemed to have been granted subject to a condition that the development must be begun not later than the expiration of five years beginning with the said commencement.

LAW OF PROPERTY ACT 1969
(1969 c. 59)

23. Reduction of statutory period of title.   [481]

Section 44 (1) of the Law of Property Act 1925 (under which the period of commencement of title which may be required under a contract expressing no contrary intention is thirty years except in certain cases) shall have effect, in its application to contracts made after the commencement of this Act, as if it specified fifteen years instead of thirty years as the period of commencement of title which may be so required.

24. Contracts for purchase of land affected by land charge, etc.   [482]

(1) Where under a contract for the sale or other disposition of any estate or interest in land the title to which is not registered under the Land Registration Act 1925 or any enactment replaced by it any question arises whether the purchaser had knowledge, at the time of entering into the contract, of a registered land charge, that question shall be determined by reference to his actual knowledge and without regard to the provisions of section 198 of the Law of Property Act 1925 (under which registration under the Land Charges Act 1925 or any enactment replaced by it is deemed to constitute actual notice).

(2) Where any estate or interest with which such a contract is concerned is affected by a registered land charge and the purchaser, at the time of entering

148

into the contract, had not received notice and did not otherwise actually know that the estate or interest was affected by the charge, any provision of the contract shall be void so far as it purports to exclude the operation of subsection (1) above or to exclude or restrict any right or remedy that might otherwise be exercisable by the purchaser on the ground that the estate or interest is affected by the charge.

(3) In this section:

"purchaser" includes a lessee, mortgagee or other person acquiring or intending to acquire an estate or interest in land; and

"registered land charge" means any instrument or matter registered, otherwise than in a register of local land charges, under the Land Charges Act 1925 or any Act replaced by it.

(4) For the purposes of this section any knowledge acquired in the course of a transaction by a person who is acting therein as counsel, or as solicitor or other agent, for another shall be treated as the knowledge of that other.

(5) This section does not apply to contracts made before the commencement of this Act.

25. Compensation in certain cases for loss due to undisclosed land charges. **[483]**

(1) Where a purchaser of any estate or interest in land under a disposition to which this section applies has suffered loss by reason that the estate or interest is affected by a registered land charge, then if:

(a) the date of completion was after the commencement of this Act; and

(b) on that date the purchaser had no actual knowledge of the charge; and

(c) the charge was registered against the name of an owner of an estate in the land who was not as owner of any such estate a party to any transaction, or concerned in any event, comprised in the relevant title;

the purchaser shall be entitled to compensation for the loss.

MATRIMONIAL PROCEEDINGS AND PROPERTY ACT 1970
(1970 c. 45)
37. Contributions by spouse in money or money's worth to the improvement of property. **[484]**

It is hereby declared that where a husband or wife contributes in money or money's worth to the improvement of real or personal property in which or in the proceeds of sale of which either or both of them has or have a beneficial interest, the husband or wife so contributing shall, if the contribution is of a substantial nature and subject to any agreement between them to the contrary express or implied, be treated as having then acquired by virtue of his or her contribution a share or an enlarged share, as the case may be, in that beneficial interest of such an extent as may have been then agreed or, in default of such agreement, as may seem in all the circumstances just to any court before which the question of the existence or extent of the beneficial interest of the husband or wife arises (whether in proceedings between them or in any other proceedings).

38. Rights of occupation under Matrimonial Homes Act 1967 of spouse with equitable interest in home, etc. **[485]**

There shall be inserted in section 1 of the Matrimonial Homes Act 1967 (which protects against eviction from the home the spouse not entitled by virtue of any estate or interest, etc., to occupy it) a new sub-section—

(9) It is hereby declared that a spouse who has an equitable interest in a dwelling house or in the proceeds of sale thereof, not being a spouse in whom is vested (whether solely or as a joint tenant) a legal estate in fee simple or a legal term of years absolute in the dwelling house, is to be treated for the purpose only of determining whether he or she has rights of occupation under this section as not being entitled to occupy the dwelling house by virtue of that interest.

GLOSSARY

OF LATIN AND OTHER WORDS
AND PHRASES

Absolute. An estate which is not conditional nor determinable nor defeasible, but will continue for ever.

Abstract of title. A document containing a chronological list of the documents and events through which a vendor traces his title from the root of title the contents of the documents being set out in shortened form supplied by the vendor to enable a purchaser to check the validity of the vendor's title.

Active trust (use). A trust or use which imposes upon the trustee or feoffee the performance of some activities, *e.g.* to collect the rents and profits and pay them to a beneficiary or to sell the land, as opposed to merely holding the land.

Ad hoc. Arranged for this purpose; special; a settlement or trust for sale created specially so as to overreach certain equitable rights under S.L.A. 1925 s. 21 or L.P.A. 1925 s. 2.

Ad medium filum. *See* Usque.

Ad valorem. Calculated in proportion to the value or price of the property.

Advancement. (1) When property is purchased by a husband and transferred or given to his wife or child, it is presumed to be a gift, and not to be held on resulting trust for the donor; (2) a payment of capital made by trustees from a trust fund to an infant beneficiary contingently entitled to establish him in life or in a career.

Advowson. The right to nominate a clergyman as rector or vicar of a church when the living becomes vacant.

Alienation. The transferring of property to the ownership of another person.

Alienatio rei praefeetur juri accrescendi. The law prefers that a joint tenant should be able to transfer his interest during his lifetime to a third party than that it should go to augment the interest(s) of the surviving joint tenant(s) on his death.

Argumentum ab indonvenienti. An argument which asserts that a proposed construction of a document or a theory must be wrong because it would give rise to awkward results in practice.

Assent. A document by which personal representatives having completed the administration of the estate transfer part of the estate to the beneficiary entitled to it.

Assignment. A document by which property (esp. a lease) is transferred by one party to another.

Assurance. A document by which property is transferred by one party to another; insurance against death.

Attorney. Solicitor. **(Power of.)** Document under seal given to an agent authorizing him (1) to execute deeds on behalf of his principal, or (2) to carry out the transactions specified therein, *e.g,* to sell or buy property on his principal's behalf.

Bare trustee. One who holds property in trust for the absolute benefit of beneficiaries who are all of full age and capacity and has no duties to perform except to transfer the property to them or as they may direct.

Base fee. The estate created when a tenant in tail in remainder barred the entail without the consent of the protector; it lasted only as long as the entail would have lasted, and therefore ended on the failure of the issue of the tenant in tail.

Beneficial owner. A person entitled to enjoy property for his own benefit who does not hold it as trustee for the benefit of someone else. In a

150

conveyance for valuable consideration by a beneficial owner who is expressed to convey as such there are implied covenants for (1) right to convey, (2) quiet enjoyment, (3) freedom from incumbrances, and (4) further assurance. L.P.A. 1925 s. 76.

Beneficiary. Person entitled to benefit under a will or trust.

Bona fide. In good faith; honest.

Bona vacantia. Property of which no one claims the ownership.

Caution. An entry made in the register at the request of a person interested in registered land requiring the Land Registry to notify him of any proposed dealings with the land.

Cestui(s) que trust (use). Person(s) for whose benefit property is held in trust; beneficiary(-ies).

Cestui que vie. Person for the duration of whose life an estate is granted to another person.

Chargee. The person entitled to the benefit of a charge.

Clam. Secretly; by stealth.

Collateral. Blood relations descended from a common ancestor.

Commorientes. Persons who die at the same time.

Consensus ad idem. Agreement as to the same terms.

Consolidation. The right of a mortgagee who holds two mortgages made by the same mortgagor to refuse to allow him to redeem the one without also redeeming the other.

Contingent interest. An interest or right which a person cannot enjoy unless or until an event which may not happen has occurred.

Contra proferentem. *See* VERBA.

Conveyance. Deed or document other than a will whereby one party transfers property to another.

Coparceners. The nearest surviving relatives of an intestate (normally females all of the same degree) who took his land in equal shares as his heir.

Copyhold. Land forming part of a manor title to which was proved by copies of the entries in the manorial court rolls in which all dealings with the land had to be registered.

Counterpart. A deed prepared in two identical forms, *e.g.* a lease and its counterpart. The lease is executed by the lessor and the counterpart by the lessee and then the two documents are exchanged. *See* INDENTURE.

Covenant. An agreement contained in a deed.

Covenants for title. Covenants entered into by the vendor in a conveyance on sale of land, which give the purchaser a right to an action for damages in respect of the title. They are implied by Law of Property Act 1925 section 76.

Covenantee. A person in whose favour another person agrees by deed to do or refrain from doing something.

Covenantor. A person who binds himself by deed to do or refrain from doing something.

Coverture. Marriage; the status of a married woman; the period during which her husband is alive.

Cuicunque aliquid conceditur, conceditur et id sine quo res ipsa non esse potuit. Where property is granted to someone, the grant is deemed to include anything without which the property could not exist as such.

Cujus est solum ejus est usque ad coelum et ad inferos. He who owns the soil also owns everything above it as far as the heavens and everything below it as far as the nether regions.

Curtesy. A husband enjoyed a life estate in the land of his deceased wife, provided that she had borne him a child who was alive at birth and capable of inheriting the land.

De donis conditionalibus. "Concerning conditional gifts"—the opening words of the statute which established the estate in fee tail.

Deed. A document which has been signed sealed and delivered.

Deed poll. A deed made by one party only.

Defeasible. An estate or interest which has vested in someone but is liable to be "defeated" or terminated if or when a specified event (which may not happen) occurs.

Demise. Transfer or devolution of a right; the grant of a lease.

Development. (1) Carrying out building, engineering, mining and other operations in or over or under land, or (2) making any material change in use of buildings or land.

Devise. Gift of real property in a will.

Discretionary trust. A trust under which the trustees have a complete discretion as to the amount of income (if any) which they decide to pay to any member of a class of beneficiaries, and the beneficiary has no right to claim any part of the income.

Disentailing assurance. A document by which a tenant in tail barred his estate tail so as to convert it (1) into a fee simple if the protector consented or there was no protector, or (2) without the protectors' consent into a base fee.

Distrain. To seize goods by distress.

Distress. The right to seize chattels belonging to a wrongdoer to compel the performance of an obligation; to seize and sell the goods of a tenant to pay the arrears of rent.

Dominant tenement. Land the ownership of which confers rights over land of another person.

Dominium. Ownership.

Donatio mortis causa. Gift made in contemplation of death but conditional on its occurrence.

Donee. He who receives a gift.

Donor. He who gives a gift.

Dower. The right of a widow to a life interest in one-third of any realty owned by her deceased husband during the marriage, unless it was disposed of by a deed or will containing a declaration barring dower.

Dum casta (et sola) fuerit (vixerit). For as long as she remains chaste (and unmarried).

Easement. A right enjoyed by the owner of land over the lands of another, e.g. rights of way, rights of light.

Ejusdem generis. Of the same type; a rule of construction which implies that where a list of specific things which are of the same type or have a common characteristic is followed by general words which would normally have a wide meaning, the general words are construed as describing only things "of the same type" as the specific things.

Emblements. Growing crops which could be taken by a tenant

whose tenancy ended unexpectedly, or by the personal representative of a deceased tenant for life.

Entail. Estate or interest which descends only to the issue of the grantee ascertained under the pre-1926 rules; since 1925 entails cannot exist as legal estates, only as equitable interests.

Entireties. The inseparable joint ownership by husband and wife of their joint property.

En ventre sa mère. Conceived but not yet born.

Equity. An equitable right enforcible by equitable remedies only in a court of equity; the right of a deserted wife to continue to live in the matrimonial home.

Equity of redemption. The equitable right of a mortgagor to redeem the mortgaged property on payment of the loan with interest and costs even after the legal or contractual right to redeem has been lost by failure to repay the loan with interest on the date when repayment was due under the terms of the mortgage. Also the interest held by the mortgagor in his mortgaged property while a right to redeem exists.

Escheat. The right of a feudal lord to claim the land of a tenant who (1) died intestate and without heirs, or (2) was convicted of felony.

Escrow. Document delivered subject to a condition which must be fulfilled before it can become a deed.

Estate. (1) The extent of a man's interest in land; (2) all the property of a deceased person.

Estate clause. The clause formerly inserted after the general words in a conveyance to pass "all the estate", etc., of the grantor; now implied by Law of Property Act 1925 s. 63.

Estate contract. A contract by the owner of a legal estate to convey or create a legal estate; also an option or right of pre-emption.

Estoppel. A rule of evidence which stops a man from denying the truth of (1) a statement previously made by him to and relied on by another person who is induced to change his position on the faith of it, or (2) an issue decided by the court in previous litigation between the same parties.

Estovers. The right of a tenant for

life or holder of a common to cut trees for fuel or repairing his house fences or implements.

Exception. An exclusion clause in a grant of land of something already existing which otherwise pass on the grant, *e.g.* minerals retained by a vendor.

Executor(s). Person(s) appointed by a testator in his will to administer or wind up his estate. *See also* DE SON TORT.

Executory interest. A future interest in land or personalty which does not comply with the rules relating to legal remainders (*i.e.* does not depend upon the determination of a prior particular estate); examples are shifting and springing uses, which are to take effect at some future time.

Ex gratia. Out of kindness; voluntary; without accepting legal liability.

Factum. That which has been done; a deed.

Falsa demonstratio non nocet cum de corpore constat. Where the substance of the property in question is clearly identified, the addition of an incorrect description of the property does no harm.

Fee simple. Freehold; the most extensive interest which can be held in land.

Fee tail. *See* ENTAIL.

Feme covert. Married woman.

Feme sole. Unmarried woman.

Feoffe to uses. Person to whom property has been transferred which is to be held to the use of another; trustee.

Feudum. Fee; land held by a tenant under a lord.

Fine. (1) A fictitious action used as a means of conveying land, and of converting an estate tail into a base fee; (2) a premium paid for the grant or renewal of a lease.

Foreclosure. Proceedings by a mortgagee which put an end to the mortgagor's right to redeem the property.

Fructus industriales. Crops or fruit produced annually requiring periodic cultivation.

Fructus naturales. Vegetation or fruit which grows naturally without cultivation.

General power of appointment. A power given by deed or will which empowers the donee of the power to appoint any person (including himself) to take an interest in property.

General words. Words formerly added to the parcels clause in a conveyance to pass all the grantor's rights in the property; now implied by Law of Property Act 1925 Section 62.

Grant. The transfer of the ownership of an estate or interest (by deed in the case of legal estates).

Grantor. He who transfers.

Grantee. The person to whom the ownership of a right of estate is transferred by another.

Habendum. Part of a deed which describes the interest granted, *e.g.* "To hold the same unto the purchaser in fee simple".

Hereditament. A right, estate or interest in or over land or buildings which before 1926 passed to the heir on intestacy; real property.

Heritable issue. Issue capable of inheriting the land.

Hotchpot. A clause in a will or settlement which requires a beneficiary who has received prior benefits or payments from the testator or settlor to add those benefits to a fund (so as to enable each beneficiary to receive an equal share) before he can receive any part of the fund.

In aequali jure melior est conditio possidentis. Where the legal rights of the parties are equally matched, the party with possession is in the better position.

In alieno solo. On another person's land.

In capite. In chief: holding as tenant directly under the Crown.

Incorporeal. Intangible; a right which is enjoyed without taking physical possession, *e.g.* a right of light, way, etc.

Incumbrance. A burden affecting land, *e.g.* a mortgage, easement, profit, etc.

Indenture. A deed made between two or more parties. Originally it was a document written in duplicate on one piece of parchment and then severed by cutting on an indented line so that the parts could be fitted together as evidence of their being genuine. The two parts were called counterparts. A deed takes effect as an indenture, though not expressed to be one, and, whether or not an indenture may be described as a deed. Law of Property Act 1925 s. 56(2). and 57. *See* COUNTERPART.

In gross. A thing which exists "as an entity in its own right" not as an appurtenance or appendage of another thing; a right the existence of which does not depend upon ownership of land to which the right is ancillary.

Inhibition. An order of the Court or Land Registrar forbidding dealings with registered land.

Injunction. An order of a court requiring a person to do or refrain from doing a particular thing.

In personam. Against the person of the defendant; *see also* JUS IN PERSONAM.

In posse. In a state of possibility; something which may come into existence in the future.

Interesse termini. The interest of the term; the right to enter the land acquired by the lessee on the granting of a demise.

Inter vivos. Between people who are alive.

Intestacy. Where a man dies having failed to dispose of all or part of his property by will.

Issue. Descendants (including children grandchildren and remoter generations).

Jointure. Provision made by a husband for his widow in a settlement.

Jus. A right which is recognised in law.

Jus accrescendi. The right of survivorship; the right of joint tenants to have their interests in the joint property increased by inheriting the interests of deceased joint tenants until the last survivor inherits the entire property (**inter mercatores locum non habet pro beneficio commercii** —does not apply as between partners in a business, so that the growth of commerce may be fostered).

Jus accrescendi praefertur ultimae voluntati. On the death of a joint tenant the right of survivorship overrides any disposition of his interest contained in his last will: a joint tenancy cannot be severed by will.

Jus in personam. A right which can be enforced against a particular person or a limited number of persons only.

Jus in re aliena. A right exercise over the property of another person.

Jus in rem. A right which can be enforced over the property in question against all other persons.

Jus quaesitum tertio. A right vested in a third party (who is not one of the parties of the contract or deed).

Jus spatiandi in alieno solo. A right to wander over another's land.

Jus tertii. The title of a third party; a plea that the property in question was owned by a third party and not by the plaintiff.

Laches. Delay in taking action which is sufficient to disqualify a party from obtaining a remedy in equity.

Lapse. When a person to whom property is given by will dies before the testator the gift if of specific property lapses and falls into residue and if of a share of residue lapses and devolves as on intestacy.

Letters of administration. The document which is evidence of the appointment of **administrators** by the Court, and of their authority to administer the deceased's estate.

Levant et couchant. The number of cattle which can be supported by (*i.e.* lying down and rising on) the dominant tenement through the winter.

Licence. Permission to do what would otherwise be unlawful, *e.g.* to enter on land when the licensee would otherwise be a trespasser.

Lien. The right to retain possession of goods, deeds or other property belonging to another, or to charge the property, as security for payment of money owing.

Limitation. Words in a document which limit or declare the nature of the estate given to a person and the period during which it is to continue *e.g.* to the purchaser "and his heirs", or "in fee simple".

Limitation Acts. Statutes which prescribe time limits within which actions must be commenced failing which the right of action is barred, *e.g.* actions for the recovery of land must be commenced within 12 years.

Lis pendens. A pending action.

Lites pendentes. Pending actions.

Locatio conductio. Leasing or hiring.

Mala fide(s). (In) bad faith.

Mesne. Intermediate; middle; dividing.

Mesne profits. Profits of income of land lost by the plaintiff while the defendant remained wrongfully in possession.

Minority. The period during which a person is under 18 years old.

Mitter l'estate. Transferring the estate.

Mortgage. A document in which a debtor transfers or creates a legal or equitable estate or interest in land in favour of his creditor in order to secure the repayment of a debt.

Mortgagee. The lender to whom property is mortgaged to secure repayment of the loan.

Mortgagor. The borrower who mortgages his property to secure repayment of the money which he borrowed.

Mortmain. A grant of land to the "dead hand" of a corporation which never died (*e.g.* to a monastery).

Nec vi (per vim) nec clam nec precario. Neither by force, nor by stealth, nor by permission.

Nemo dat quod non habet. No one can transfer the ownership of something which he does not own.

Nemo est haeres (heres) viventis. No one can be the "heir" of a person who is still living (since the identity of a man's heir is not ascertained until the man dies).

Next of kin. The closest blood relations.

Nihil commune habet proprietas cum possessione. Ownership and possession have no features in common.

Nisi. Unless (used of a decree or order which will later be made absolute "unless" good cause be shown to the contrary); provisional.

Non est factum. *See* SCRIPTUM.

Nudum pactum. A bare agreement (not supported by consideration).

Operative part. That part of an instrument which carries out its main object. *See* RECITALS.

Operative words. Words of grant in an assurance of land, e.g. "convey", "assign", "release"; "surrender".

Option. An agreement which gives a person the right to buy property or renew a lease within a period (which must not exceed the duration of the lease or 21 years) if he so wishes.

Ousterlemain. The right of a lord at the end of the wardship to half a year's profits "for removing his hand" from the land.

Overreach. To free land from rights which are thereafter exercised over the capital moneys representing the proceeds of sale of the land.

Overriding interests. Interests held by third parties in or over registered land which bind a purchaser although they are not referred to in the register, *e.g.* easements, rights of persons in actual occupation, squatters rights, leases not exceeding 21 years.

Parcels. Portions of land. The part of a conveyance following the operative words and defining the land being granted.

Parol. By word of mouth, or unsealed document.

Particular estate. An estate which is only a part of (*i.e.* less than) the fee simple; an estate which is followed by a reversion or remainder.

Per my et per tout. By nothing and by the whole; a joint tenant holds the entire property in conjunction with his fellow joint tenant(s) yet cannot claim exclusive possession of any part of the property against them. Sometimes translated "by the half and by the whole" as a joint tenant can only transfer half of the property by severance.

Perpetuity. A disposition of property under which an interest does not or cannot vest until after the expiry of a life or lives in being and a further period of 21 years thereafter, or after a specified period not exceeding 80 years, is void as being a perpetuity.

Per se. By itself; in itself; considered alone.

Persona(e) designata(e). A person(s) specified as an individual(s), not identified as a member(s) of a class nor as fulfilling a particular qualification.

Personal representative. The person who winds up the deceased's estate, *i.e.* his executor or administrator.

Personalty. Movable property,

goods, money, choses in action and leaseholds.

Per stirpes. According to the stocks of descent; one share for each line of descendants; where the descendants of a deceased person (however many they may be) take between them only the one share which the deceased would have taken if alive.

Portions. Provisions for establishing children in life, especially lump sums provided for the younger children under a will or settlement.

Possessory title. The title obtained by someone who by 12 years' adverse possession has destroyed the title of the former owner of the land and vested it in himself.

Possibility of reverter. The right of the grantor or his successors to recover the land if or when a determinable fee determines.

Post-nuptial. Made after marriage.

Power of appointment. *See* GENERAL POWER *or* SPECIAL POWER.

Praedium dominans. Dominant tenement (*q.v.*).

Praedium serviens. Servient tenement (*q.v.*).

Precario. By permission.

Pre-emption. An agreement which gives a person the right to be offered the chance to buy property before the property is offered for sale to anyone else.

Prescription. The acquisition of easements or profits by long use without the consent of the owner of the servient tenement.

Probate. An official copy of a will which has been proved in the Probate Division. It is sealed by the Court and is confirmation of the appointment of an executor in the will, and evidence of his authority to administer the deceased's estate.

Profit à prendre. The right to enter the land of another and take part of its produce.

Protective trust. A trust under which the principal beneficiary has a life interest which is determined in the event of his bankruptcy or attempting to sell or charge his interest, and thereupon the trust income is to be applied by the trustees at their discretion for the maintenance of the beneficiary and his family or any of them.

Protector. The person whose consent was required by a tenant in tail who wished to completely bar the entail: normally he was the tenant for life in possession, unless the settlement named one or more persons as Special Protectors.

Puisne. Inferior; legal mortgage not secured by deposit of title deeds; junior; High Court judge.

Punctum temporis. Point of time; moment.

Pur autre vie. During the life of another person.

Pur cause de vicinage. By reason of contiguity; because two commons adjoin.

Purchase. Words which confer an interest upon the person to whom they refer.

Purchaser. A person who takes an estate in land by act of parties (*e.g.* by gift or sale), and not by operation of law (*e.g.* on intestacy).

Q.v. Which should be referred to.

Qua. As; in the capacity of.

Quaere. Consider whether the statement is correct.

Quantum. How much; extent; amount (of damages).

Quare clausum fregit. Because he broke into the plaintiff's enclosure.

Quasi. As if; seemingly; pseudo.

Quasi-catallum. Semi-chattel.

Que estate. Dominant tenement.

Quia emptores. Opening words "Because purchasers" of the statute which forbade subinfeudation.

Quicquid plantatur solo solo cedit. Whatever is planted in the soil belongs to the soil.

Qui prior est tempore potior est jure. He who is earlier in point of time is in the stronger position in law.

Qui sentit commodum sentire debet et onus. He who enjoys the benefit ought also to bear the burden.

Rack rent. The rent for which the property could be let together with the buildings thereon on the open market if the tenant were bound to pay the rates and the landlord to do the repairs.

Ratione soli. By reason of occupying the land.

Realty. Land.

Recitals. Statements in an instrument leading to the operative part. Narrative recitals state the facts on which the instrument is based. Introductory recitals explain the immediate purpose of the deed. Recitals in deeds at least twenty years old are prima facie evidence of the truth of the matters stated.

Recovery. A fictitious action used as a means of converting an estate tail into a fee simple.

Remainder. An estate granted to a person other than the settlor which vests in possession on the determination of a prior particular estate (*e.g.* after the death of a tenant for life).

Reservation. A clause in a grant of land reserving to the grantor a right which did not previously exist, *e.g.* a right of way in a conveyance or a rent in a lease. *See* EXCEPTION.

Rentcharge. Rent payable in respect of land to a person other than a reversioner or landlord which is secured by a right of distress.

Requisitions on title. A written list of questions and objections sent by a purchaser (or his solicitor) to the vendor (or his solicitor) regarding any apparent defects or doubts which he finds in the abstract of title and which the vendor is required to answer in order to prove that he has as good a title to the property as was stipulated in the contract for the sale.

Residue. The balance of a deceased person's estate which remains after payment of debts, funeral expenses, specific gifts, and legacies.

Res sua. Something which a man mistakenly believes to belong to another, when in fact it was "his own property" all the time.

Restitutio in integrum. Restoration of a party to his original position.

Restraint on anticipation. A clause in a settlement to protect a woman from the influence of her husband by preventing her from disposing of or charging the capital or future payments of income.

Restriction. An entry made on the application of the proprietor of registered land in the register which prevents any dealing with the land unless or until some condition is complied with, *e.g.* that proceeds of sale should be paid to two trustees or a trust corporation.

Restrictive covenant. An agreement contained in a deed which restricts or prohibits the use of land for certain purposes.

Resulting trusts. A trust implied by equity whereby the beneficial interest in property which is transferred into the name of a person other than a purchaser "results" or comes back to the person who provided the purchase price or transferred the property.

Reversion. Where the owner of an estate in land grants an estate or interest which is less than his own estate but retains the residue of his own estate, he has a reversion, as the land will revert into his possession on the determination of the particular estate which he has granted. The owner of the fee simple who grants a term of years by a lease retains a reversion expectant on the expiry of the lease.

Reverter. *See* POSSIBILITY.

Root of title. The document stipulated in the contract for sale as being the commencement of the vendor's title.

Scintilla juris. Vestige of title.

Scintilla temporis. Moment of time.

Scriptum praedictum non est factum suum. A plea that "the aforesaid document is not his deed".

Search. Examination by a purchaser (normally by submitting a printed form of enquiry) of official records and registers in order to find details of any incumbrances affecting the title to the property, *e.g.* bankruptcy of the vendor, estate contracts, puisne mortgages, demolition orders, etc. The purchaser is not bound by any incumbrances which are not so registered.

Servient tenement. Land over which rights are exercisable by the owner of other land.

Settlement. A document (deed or will) by which property is limited upon trust for persons who take successive interest, *e.g.* to A. for life with remainder to B. in fee simple.

Severance. (1) The conversion of a joint tenancy into a tenancy in common effected by the act of one joint tenant; (2) words of severance show that grantees are to take as tenants in common, not as joint tenants, *e.g.* in equal shares.

157

Shifting use. An executory use which shifts from one person to another on the happening of some event.

Sic utere tuo ut alienum non laedas. Use your own property in such a way as not to injure your neighbour's property.

Simpliciter. Simply; standing alone; by itself; without any qualification; in the absence of any additional factors.

Special power of appointment. A power given by deed or will which empowers the donee of the power to appoint any member of a specified class of persons to take an interest in property.

Special protector. *See* PROTECTOR.

Special tail. An estate which descended only to the issue of the grantee descended from a specified spouse.

Spes successionis. The hope of inheriting property on the death of another person.

Springing use. An executory use which is to come into existence on the happening of some future event.

Squatter's title. *See* POSSESSORY TITLE.

Statutory owners. The persons who under a settlement within the Settled Land Act have the powers of a tenant for life while there is no tenant for life, or the tenant for life is an infant—*i.e.* usually the trustees of the settlement.

Statutory tenant. A tenant who is entitled to remain in possession of a rent controlled house by the Rent Restriction Acts after his contractual tenancy has ended.

Statutory trusts. Trusts which are imposed by statute, *e.g.* the trusts for sale which are imposed where (1) land is conveyed to persons as joint tenants or tenants in common, or (2) the property of an intestate is administered by his administrators.

Subinfeudation. The grant by one feudal tenant of the whole or part of his land to another person to hold of him as his tenant subject to the incidents of tenure.

Sui juris. Of his own right; of full age and legal capacity.

Survivorship. *See* JUS ACCRESCENDI.

Tabula in naufragio. Tacking was for a mortgagee like "a plank in a shipwreck" for a drowning man, as it gave his mortgage priority over earlier equitable mortgages.

Tacking. The adding of a later mortgage to an earlier mortgage or a further advance by the earlier mortgagee to his mortgage in order that the later loan might share the priority of the earlier mortgage, provided the lender had no notice of intervening mortgages.

Tail male. An entail or estate which descended only to male descendants of the grantee who claimed through males.

Tenement. Land which is held by tenure.

Tenet terram in dominico suo. Holds the land in his own occupation.

Terre tenant. He who is in the actual possession of land.

Testator. The maker of a will.

Testatum. Beginning of the operative part of a deed: "Now This Deed Witnesseth".

Testimonium. Final clause in a deed: "In Witness whereof".

Title. The evidence of a person's right to the ownership of property consisting of the documents and events in the law through which the property has passed into his ownership.

Totum tenet et nihil tenet. He holds the entirety and yet holds no specific part of the property.

Trust for sale. A trust which imposes on the trustees a duty to sell the property and convert it into money, but allows them to postpone the sale in their discretion for as long as they all agree.

Ultra vires. Outside the powers recognised by law as belonging to the person or body in question; without authority; unauthorised.

Undivided share. The interest of a tenant in common or coparcener in the land which was not subject to JUS ACCRESCENDI but formed part of his estate on his death.

Usque ad medium filum (aquae) (viae). As far as the line of the middle (of the water) (of the road).

Usucapio. The acquisition of ownership by long use or possession; prescription.

Usus fructus. The right to use or reap the fruits of something belonging to another person without altering the substance of the thing enjoyed.

Ut res magis valeat quam pereat. Words must be construed so as to make the meaning of a document more effective rather than to destroy its sense.

Verba fortius accipiuntur contra proferentem. Ambigious wording is construed more strongly against the party who introduced it into the document and who seeks to rely on the words in question, and in favour of the other party.

Vest. Clothe with possession; confer an unconditional legally enforcible right; fall into the absolute ownership of someone.

Vested in interest. Where the owner has an existing absolute right to possess the property in the future.

Vested in possession. Where the owner has an absolute right to possess the property at present.

Vesting assent. Where settled land remains subject to the trusts of the settlement after the death of a tenant for life or statutory owner, the special personal representatives of the deceased vest the settled land in the person entitled as tenant for life or statutory owner by an assent containing the same particulars as in a vesting deed.

Vesting deed. A deed by which the legal estate in settled land is transferred to the person(s) who is/are the tenant for life (or statutory owners) for the time being. It must contain: (1) a description of the settled land, (2) a statement that it is vested in the transferee on the trusts of the settlement, (3) the names of the settlement trustees, (4) any additional powers given to the tenant for life by the settlement, (5) the name of the person entitled to appoint new trustees.

Vi. By force.

Vice versa. The other way round; in turn.

INDEX

BOUNDARIES,
  agreement as to, 280
  disputes concerning, 236
  error in, 39
  highway, of, 7
  river bed, 188
BREACH. *See* CONTRACT.
BUILDER,
  breach of agreement by, 234
  negligence by, 179, 234
  plan and specification, work in accordance with, 253
  warranty, breach of, 321
    implied, 270
BUILDINGS,
  alteration or removal of, orders for, 452
  habitation, fitness for, 216
  listed, 479
  meaning, 78
BUILDING SCHEMES,
  restrictions imposed, 396

CAUTIONS,
  charges protected by, 398
  effective, 294
  registration of, 316
  undisclosed, 294
  vacation of, 316
CHARGES. *See also* LAND CHARGES.
  companies, created by, 432–434
  discharge of, 17
  equitable, 68
  legal, 68, 70, 102
  notice of, 398
  registration of, 288
  void, 395
CHATTELS,
  conveyance of real property does not include, 275
  passing of, 114
  real estate law, 424
COMMISSION,
  agency, 158, 342
  claim for, 342
  entitlement to, 402
  sale incomplete, 33
  uncertainty, refused for, 212
COMPANIES,
  charges, registration of, 432–434
COMPENSATION,
  agricultural holdings. *See* AGRICULTURAL HOLDINGS.
  business carried on at loss, 163
  caution not disclosed, 294
  choice of method avoiding, 394
  compulsory purchase, 29
  derequisitioning, 178
  description, error in, 238
  development value, loss of, 347
  drainage, 440
  error, for, 293, 311, 380
  improvements, 437
  land, payable in respect of, 360
  misrepresentation, 221
  notice, registration of, 360

COMPENSATION—*cont*
  planning permission, 360
    mistake in, 347
    refusal of, 111, 245, 273, 394
  precarious tenancy, 290
  rectification of register, 39
  undisclosed land charges, 483
COMPLETION. *See* CONTRACT.
COMPULSORY PURCHASE,
  compensation, 29
  reinstatement, 29
  specific performance in cases of, 194
CONDITIONS,
  construction against person framing, 168
  omission of words, 96
  planning permission. *See* PLANNING PERMISSION.
  right to waive, 243
CONSIDERATION. *See* CONTRACT.
CONTRA PROFERENTES,
  principle of, 100
CONTRACT,
  acceptance, 183, 258
    postal, 200
  agreement subject to, 79
  anticipatory breach, 217
  authority, 24
  bankruptcy, act of, 217
  breach of, 12, 60, 85, 95, 103, 113, 140, 154, 157, 197, 211, 250, 295
  collateral, 355
  completion, 37, 102, 140, 157, 163, 170, 196, 211, 254, 299, 307, 308, 316, 343, 350, 352, 361, 377
  conditions, 2, 196, 243, 249, 309, 338, 389
  consideration, 115
  damages, 11
  debentures, sale of, 117
  defect, latent, 311
  deposit,
    forfeiture of, 264, 277, 350, 361, 377
    return of, 251, 254, 259, 345, 388
  disclosure, 132, 175, 343, 344, 361
  document not binding, 400
  draft, 197
  enforceability, 352
  enquiries, 166
  equity, enforceability in, 48
  errors, 169, 238, 389
    compensation for, 311
    innocent, 380
  evidence of, 9, 184
  exchange of, 126, 345, 352
    withdrawal before, 228
  existence or non-existence of, 130, 191
  frustration, 194
  future, 37
  identification, 165
  implied terms of, 85
  indemnity, of, 71
  insufficiency, 137
  interest in land, sale of, 92
  land affected by land charge, 482
  land, sale of, 117

All references are to paragraph numbers

All references are to paragragh numbers

All references are to paragraph numbers

RIGHT OF WAY—*cont*
  acquiescence, 209
  dedication, proof of, 362
  defect, as, 411
  identification of, 220
  limit of, 7
  loading and unloading, 255
  non-disclosure of, 379
  passing of, 83
  planning permission, condition of, 176
  private or public, 411
  reservation of, 59, 148
  swing space, 384
  trespass, 209
  use, excessive, 214
  user, permissive, 186
ROAD,
  boundary of, 7
  costs of making up, 355
  dedication of, 10, 225
  promise of construction of, 211
  tolls and, 10

SALE,
  power to postpone, 328
  trusts for, 233, 308, 317, 328, 354
SETTLED LAND,
  dispositions, restrictions on, 415
    time of taking effect, 414
  invalid transactions, 395
  jointure rent charge, 336
  purchasers, protection of, 418
  tenant for life, limited owners having
    powers of, 416
  transactions, completion by conveyance,
    417
  trustees not discharged, 415
  vesting instrument made, 414
SETTLEMENT,
  bankruptcy, 69
  constitution of, 413
  post-nuptial, 90
  title, transfer of, 45
  trustees not discharged, 415
  voluntary, 69
SPECIFIC PERFORMANCE,
  agreement not binding on purchaser,
    348
    to sell, 170
  assignment, 240
    in favour of specified nominee, 104
  completion, failure in, 307
  compulsory purchase, where, 194
  consent, refusal of, 240
  contract, 352
    non-existent, 357
  documents of doubtful meaning, 218
  exercise of option, 390
  jurisdiction, outside, 393
  mistake, fundamental, 171
  notice to quit, 106
  omission of term, 98
  option, exercise of, 366
  oral promise, 257
  refusal of, 338

SPECIFIC PERFORMANCE—*cont*
  sale of property, 128
  useless, 91
  vacant possession, 184
  vendor, fraud of, 223
    non-disclosure by, 132

TENANCY. *See also* RENT.
  agricultural holdings. *See* AGRICUL-
    TURAL HOLDINGS.
  assign, covenants not to, 431
  bankrupt tenant, 237
  covenants not to assign, 431
  determination of, 4
  distinct, 406
  double, 406
  enfranchise, obligation to, 459
  enfranchisement, entitlement to, 457
  equitable tenancy in common, 58
  exclusive occupation, 252
  extension, entitlement to, 457
  freehold, right to acquire, 181
  furnished, 162
  furnished or unfurnished, 230
  holding, part of, 139
  joint, 207, 266, 336, 405
    bankruptcy of tenants, 453
    sale of land by survivor of, 453
  misrepresentation, 351
  option to renew, 121
  precarious, 290
  protected, 327
  removable fixtures, sale to landlord, 237
  room as extension of flat, 267
  security of tenure, 252
  separate dwellings, 406
  squatters, 35, 374
  statutory, 171, 263
  sub-tenancy, 81, 383
  tenant for life, assignment of powers of,
    262
    dealings with, 395
    powers of, 262, 335
    trustees as, 149
  tenant, licensee, contrasted with, 1
    property vested in, 325
  tenants in common, 336
  trustees, rights of, 458
  underlease, 118
TITLE,
  adverse, 125
  adverse possession, by, 80, 146, 407
  assent, vestment by, 358
  assignees, in, 338
  chattels, 275
  completion, proof before, 308
  covenant for, 379
  debts not paid, notice of, 354
  deeds, retention of, 276
  defect in, 11, 160, 224, 292, 387
  document of, 241, 272
  doubtful, 218, 283
  encumbrance on, 102
  evidence of, 284
  foreshore, 146